THE
AMERICAN
ECONOMY

THE
AMERICAN
ECONOMY

AN *HISTORICAL INTRODUCTION TO THE PROBLEMS OF THE 1970'S*

EDITED AND WITH INTRODUCTORY ESSAYS BY

Arthur M. Johnson

THE FREE PRESS
A Division of Macmillan Publishing Co., Inc.
NEW YORK

Collier Macmillan Publishers
LONDON

The Free Press
A Division of Macmillan Publishing Co., Inc.
866 Third Avenue, New York, N.Y. 10022

Collier-Macmillan Canada Ltd.

Library of Congress Catalog Card Number: 74–2652

Printed in the United States of America

printing number
1 2 3 4 5 6 7 8 9 10

Library of Congress Cataloging in Publication Data

Johnson, Arthur Menzies, date   comp.
    The American economy; an historical introduction to the problems of the 1970's.

    (Urgent issues in American society)
    Bibliography: p.
    1. United States--Economic conditions--Addresses, essays, lectures. 2. United States--Economic policy--Addresses, essays, lectures. I. Title.
HC106.J59   330.9'73'0924   74-2652
ISBN 0-02-916580-6
ISBN 0-02-916590-2 (pbk.)

ACKNOWLEDGMENTS

From an address by President Theodore Roosevelt at the State Fair, Syracuse, New York, September 7, 1903; reprinted from William Griffith, ed., *The Roosevelt Policy* (New York: The Current Literature Publishing Co., 1919), Vol. 1, pp. 149–158. See p. 14.

Reprinted from *The World's Work*, Vol. 1 (January 1901), pp. 286–292. See p. 21.

From *Goals for Americans: The Report of the President's Commission on National Goals* © 1960 by The American Assembly, Columbia University, pp. 7–14. Reprinted by permission of Prentice-Hall, Inc. Englewood Cliffs, New Jersey. See p. 27.

From a statement of the Counsellor to the President, Daniel P. Moynihan, in Report of the National Goals Research Staff, *Toward Balanced Growth: Quantity with Quality* (Washington, 1970), pp. 11–15. See p. 35.

From *Population and the American Future,* The Report of The Commission on Population Growth and the American Future (Washington, 1972), pp. 118–122. See p. 41.

From *Resources,* No. 42, January 1973, Resources for the Future, Inc., Washington, D.C., pp. 1–2. See p. 46.

From President Franklin D. Roosevelt's Budget Message to the Seventy-fifth Congress, First Session, January 7, 1937. *Congressional Record,* Vol. 81, Pt. I, pp. 116–119. See p. 68.

From the *Economic Report of the President,* Washington, U.S. Government Printing Office, February 1971, pp. 19–22. See p. 72.

From *Proceedings of a Symposium on Public Policy and Economic Understanding, November 17, 1969* (New York: The American Bankers Association, 1970), pp. 10–19. See p. 79. Extracted with permission of The American Bankers Association.

From Gardner Ackley, "International Inflation," in *Economic Policies of the 1970s,* edited by Alfred K. Ho (Ann Arbor: Bureau of Business Research, Graduate School of Business Administration, The University of Michigan, 1971), pp. 48–50, 63–69. Copyright © by The University of Michigan and reprinted by permission. See p. 89.

From *The New York Times,* January 28, 1973, Sec. 3, pp. 1–2. Copyright © 1973 by The New York Times Company. Reprinted by permission. See p. 97.

From *The New York Times,* June 17, 1973, Section E, p. 1. Copyright © 1973 by The New York Times Company. Reprinted by permission. See p. 101.

From "The Invisible Poor" by Dwight Macdonald. Reprinted by permission; Copyright © 1963 The New Yorker Magazine, Inc. See p. 116.

From *The State of Welfare* by Gilbert Y. Steiner pp. 6–11; Copyright © 1971 by Brookings Institution, Washington, D.C. See p. 120.

From President Lyndon B. Johnson's Message to the Eighty-eighth Congress of the United States on the Economic Opportunity Act of 1964, March 16, 1964. *Congressional Record,* Vol. 110, Pt. 4, pp. 5352–5362. See p. 126.

Acknowledgments vii

From *Economic Report of the President,* Washington, U.S. Government Printing Office, January 1963, pp. 92–96. See p. 243.

From a statement by Gottfried Haberler, Galen L. Stone Professor of International Trade, Harvard University, before Subcommittee on Foreign Economic Policy, Joint Economic Committee, 91 Cong 2 Sess.; *Hearings* on "A Foreign Economic Policy for the 1970's," Sept. 30, 1970, pp. 999–1001. See p. 248.

From remarks of Arthur F. Burns, Chairman, Board of Governors of the Federal Reserve System, before the International Banking Conference, Montreal, Canada, May 12, 1972, reprinted in *Federal Reserve Bulletin* (June 1972), pp. 545–549. See p. 252.

From *Business in Brief* (April 1973), a publication of the Economics Group, Chase Manhattan Bank, N.A. See p. 258.

Contents

CONTRIBUTORS

GARDNER ACKLEY is an economist who, in addition to long service at the University of Michigan, has served the federal government in varied capacities. A member of the President's Council of Economic Advisers under Presidents Kennedy and Johnson and its Chairman from 1964 to 1968, he was Ambassador to Italy in 1968–1969.

GEORGE L. BACH, a leading American economist, headed the Economics Department at Carnegie Institute of Technology from 1946 to 1962 when he moved to Stanford University. He has worked with numerous federal agencies, particularly the Federal Reserve System. He has written extensively in the field of economics, with *Making Monetary and Fiscal Policy* (1971) the work most closely related to the selection in this book.

DANIEL BELL, educator and sociologist, was an editor and writer until 1952 when he joined the faculty of Columbia University. Since 1969 he has been a member of the Harvard University faculty. His numerous books, which include *Towards the Year 2000* (1968) and *Capitalism Today* (1971), have addressed problems of contemporary American society and its future.

ARTHUR F. BURNS, Chairman of the Board of Governors of the Federal Reserve System, has had an outstanding career as a scholar and public official. Chairman of President Eisenhower's Council of Economic Advisers, he became a personal economic adviser to President Nixon in 1969 before assuming his present post.

EDWIN L. DALE, JR., is the chief business writer of *The New York Times*.

MITCHELL I. GINSBERG is Dean of the School of Social Work at Columbia University and a former Commissioner of the New York City Department of Welfare.

GOTTFRIED HABERLER, educator and economist who was trained abroad, taught at the University of Vienna and worked with the Financial Section of the League of Nations before he was appointed Professor of International Trade at Harvard University in the mid-1930's. He has served as Chairman of the Board of the National Bureau of Economic Research (1956) and as President of the American Economic Association (1963).

ROBERT L. HEILBRONER is an economist trained at Harvard University and the New School for Social Research. His literate style and gift for presenting complex economic problems in terms that the layman can understand have won a wide audience for his works, one of the most popular being *The Wordly Philosophers* (1967).

LYNDON B. JOHNSON, thirty-sixth President of the United States, served as Senate Majority Leader before becoming President Kennedy's Vice-President. Succeeding to the Presidency after Kennedy's assassination and elected to a new term in 1964, he pushed a broad program of social reforms before the Vietnam War overshadowed domestic issues and finally drove him from office.

A. D. H. KAPLAN, an economist, served with the Office of Price Administration and as Economic Adviser to the House Committee on Postwar Economic Policy and Planning during World War II. He joined the staff of the Brookings Institution in 1945; in that capacity he wrote *Big Enterprise in a Competitive System,* from which the selection included in this volume is reprinted.

DEXTER S. KIMBALL, a mechanical engineer and Dean of the Cornell University College of Engineering 1920–1936, wrote extensively on industrial design and plant management, and during World War II served on the War Production Board.

BISHOP WILLIAM LAWRENCE was a member of a famous Massachusetts textile family and served as Episcopal Bishop of that state from 1893 to 1926.

SAR A. LEVITAN, an economist, served as a member of the Review and Appeals Committee of the Wage Stabilization Board and in the Legislative Reference Service of the Library of Congress before becoming a research Professor of Economics at George Washington University in 1967. He has written extensively in the fields of labor economics and particularly on federal policy with respect to depressed areas.

DWIGHT MACDONALD is a distinguished editor, author and critic.

GEORGE MARSHALL was a career soldier who served as U.S. Army Chief of Staff during World War II and then as U.S. Ambassador to China (1945–1947). President Truman then appointed him Secretary of State, and in that capacity he outlined the broad program of relief and rehabilitation known as the Marshall Plan. It proved a brilliant success in reviving the war-devastated economies of America's European allies.

DANIEL P. MOYNIHAN served as Assistant Secretary of Labor in the Kennedy and Johnson administrations before becoming Director of the Joint MIT-Harvard Center for Urban Studies in 1966. He served from 1969 to 1971 as President Nixon's Assistant for Urban Affairs, in which capacity he wrote the selection contained in this book.

JAMES M. ROCHE is retired Chairman of General Motors Corporation. From 1927 when he joined the GM organization as a statistician, Mr. Roche moved steadily up the ladder of corporate leadership until he became Chairman, a post from which he retired in 1972.

FRANKLIN D. ROOSEVELT was thirty-second President of the United States and the only president elected to three terms. His administrations (1933–1945) were characterized by pragmatic approaches to managing the economy in depression and then in World War II.

THEODORE ROOSEVELT, twenty-sixth President of the United States, had a varied career as author, public administrator, soldier, and Governor of New York State before he was elected Vice-President in 1900. Succeeding to the Presidency upon William McKinley's assassination in 1901, Roosevelt became one of America's most vigorous Presidents. Although famed for his antitrust activities, he was no enemy of big business but rather sought ways to bring a nation divided by rapid industrialization and urbanization to a sense of a "New Nationalism."

GILBERT Y. STEINER, political scientist, served on the faculty of the University of Illinois at Urbana from 1950 to 1966, when he became a Senior Fellow of the Brookings Institution. Since that time he has been particularly concerned with studies of governmental policies relating to social welfare.

MIRA WILKINS is a specialist in business history, particularly its international aspects. At Columbia University she did research on the history of Henry Ford and his company, as part of a project led by Allan Nevins. In 1964 she was co-author with Frank Hill of *American Business Abroad: Ford on Six Continents*. Since that time she has taught at various colleges and universities while writing *The Emergence of Multinational Enterprise*, from which the selection included in this volume is taken.

Preface

THIS BOOK is organized on the assumption that economic history, like other forms of history, is most relevant for the non-specialist when it has a demonstrable relationship to contemporary events or developments. In this form, history can make a potentially substantial contribution to understanding the present, at least in terms of how we got where we are. But understanding also involves the "why" as well as the "how" of past decisions as they affect us today. Therefore, starting with the present may help one to ask more meaningful questions of the past than is the case when starting with events remote from one's direct knowledge and personal interests.

The case for applying this fundamental proposition to economic history would seem especially strong. The American economy of the 1970's is clearly in transition, and the repercussions of its problems in terms of jobs, prices, and incomes—indeed the viability of its traditional goals and institutional arrangements—are being felt at every level of American society. Basic questions about whether and how the economy can be managed confront all of us in the 1970's, and on the answers will depend the quality of American life in the decades ahead.

This volume does not purport to be a complete economic history of the American economy in this century. Rather, it addresses selected contemporary economic issues in the hope that by defining them broadly and illuminating them historically, the reader may grasp the nature and significance of the transition through which the American economy is passing.

The complexity of the contemporary economy and the finite length of this book necessitated difficult choices in selecting the specific topics to be covered. The focus is on five selected problem areas of the economy in the 1970's. Each of the five areas is introduced by a brief essay, which attempts to sketch the overall parameters of the problem in historical perspective during this century. The terminal date of 1900 is arbitrary, in the sense that many of the problems discussed have roots that stretch much farther into the past. But by 1900 the outlines of modern industrial, urbanized America were already clearly outlined, and the country was already in transition in adjusting to them. It is from the results of that transition that the United States is now seeking the path to yet another, more difficult resolution of its economic problems.

Chapter I considers continuity and change in the definition of national goals and associated social values, since they in turn define the context and objectives of economic activity. Chapter 2 examines the development, use, and adequacy of economic tools for managing the national economy, with special emphasis on the period after 1933. Chapter 3 reviews the distribution of national income and the persistent problem of poverty in an affluent society. Chapter 4 discusses the nature and role of the enterprise system, the problems and the progress that it has created for society as well as for business itself. Chapter 5 addresses the problem of the United States' place in a changing world economy, where losing a position of dominance following World War II in recent years it has confronted an alarming adverse balance of trade and payments.

Following each overview essay on these topics is a series of selections intended to illuminate the central issue of the chapter. The alternatives proposed, analyzed, chosen, or rejected, are presented roughly chronologically. In each chapter, the time period covered by these selections differs, depending on the direct relevance of the past to contemporary problems. Where space forced choices to be made, material has been included from the more recent rather than the more distant past.

Despite the effort to keep the focus on a single issue in each chapter, the obvious overlaps between chapters suggest what is in fact the case. The American economy is a complex network of interrelationships in which changes in one sector significantly affect one or more of the others. As even this limited coverage of a relatively few areas of the economy shows, efforts to manage the economy are profoundly affected by this fact. Advocates of a return to the market-enterprise system see this phenomenon as an argument for their position of less government intervention in the economy; critics of that system see it reenforcing their demands for yet more centralized direction of the economy. History does not seem to be on the side of the former. But whether this conclusion is warranted because of, or in spite of, failures to manage the economy effectively is for the reader to decide.

Arthur M. Johnson

Castine, Maine

CHAPTER 1

National Goals
and the Economy

SEVENTY YEARS AGO, the national goal of continued economic growth was so widely accepted in the United States that there was little or no questioning of its validity. Reliance on private initiative and enterprise as the means to this end was in the American tradition, though even in 1900 there was some skepticism even in the middle class about its complete adequacy for distributing income and economic power. By the end of the 1960's the consensus on the desirability of economic growth as a primary national goal was breaking down. The social and economic costs of seeking this goal had become more obvious, and national affluence had taken the edge off acceptance of economic goals as ends in themselves.

In the 1970's national goals, values, and the means for managing the American economy in light of them are being reexamined for their adequacy in a world vastly changed from that of 1900. Private enterprise and private initiative in economic affairs today operate under direct and indirect governmental constraints and respond to governmental stimuli of bewildering variety. Under the pressure of war in the 1940's and continuing international responsibilities and crises thereafter, the economy has changed and expanded at an unprecedented rate. However, instead of opting for more babies as economic historian Walt W. Rostow had suggested in the late 1950's might be the solution, a growing number of Americans in the early 1970's were joining a movement for "zero population growth." From the national level to the smallest community, public concern has grown about the quality of American life.

1

Economic growth without regard to its social and ecological costs is no longer acceptable to many Americans. In 1900, however, with the frontier officially at an end for only a decade, Americans viewed the conquest of nature as a national challenge and triumph over it as proof of virtue. Bishop William Lawrence of Massachusetts could write with conviction in 1901: "Man, when he is strong, will conquer Nature, open up her resources, and harness them to his service. This is his play, his exercise, his divine mission."

Bishop Lawrence was reflecting nineteenth-century American values and goals. A vast, undeveloped continent had offered an alluring and specific challenge defined by the character of the land itself. Progress in the national undertaking to turn the land to man's service could be measured in miles of railroad built, homesteads occupied, and acreage cultivated. The onslaught on this great public domain was encouraged by a political and economic system that invited the individual to seek and play his role as he perceived it. A national goal of economic growth and acceptance of material wealth as evidence of individual contributions to it required no elaborate rationale. The national challenge offered its own social justification, bolstered by the ethic that riches acquired through diligence and thrift were evidence of personal virtue. As Bishop Lawrence put it, "Godliness is in league with riches."

But even in 1900 the self-justifying character of economic growth was being questioned by a growing number of Americans who had not shared fully in the nation's bounty. The scramble for wealth in a competitive, private enterprise system, where rewards went not only to the swift and able but also to the unscrupulous and undeserving, had produced wide disparities in the distribution of personal income and in political and economic power. The self-adjusting market mechanism, which for many Americans had reconciled the quest for private gain with promotion of the public interest, succumbed to concentrated economic power in important sectors of the economy. In industries like oil, steel, and sugar, vigorous but often destructive competition was replaced by the stabilizing dominance of one or a few very large firms.

President Theodore Roosevelt (1901–1909) sensed the problem that Bishop Lawrence failed to recognize. Dedication to economic growth and development in the nineteenth century had produced an increasingly urban, industrialized nation which required a restatement and reaffirmation of national goals and values to fit changed conditions. This perception and the policies that the Republican Roosevelt advocated to implement it helped the country early in this century to adjust to swift economic and technological change without discarding the traditional emphasis on private enterprise and continuing economic growth. Although the powers of the federal government were expanded during Roosevelt's administration, they were still used primarily to police a privately directed economic system that remained basically unchanged both in structure and in the location and use of private economic power. Nevertheless, the Rooseveltian rhetoric of change helped to forestall the need for more drastic action.

The inadequacy of material measures of progress, which had long held the allegiance of most Americans, was emphasized by Roosevelt in an address to the American Tract Society in March 1905. "If we permit the people of this Republic to get before their minds that material well-being carried to ever higher degree is the one and only thing to be striven for," he said, "we are laying up for ourselves not merely trouble but ruin."

Sixty-five years later, President Richard M. Nixon raised the same issue in a larger context. He suggested in his 1970 State of the Union message that American wealth would increase 50 percent in the coming decade, but he asked: "Does this mean we will be 50 percent richer in a real sense, 50 percent better off, 50 percent happier? Or does it mean that in 1980, the President standing in this place will look back on a decade in which 70 percent of our people lived in metropolitan areas choked by traffic, suffocated by smog, poisoned by water, deafened by noise and terrorized by crime?"

The unpleasant relevance of these questions to life in contemporary America was one testimony to the social costs of the economic growth that had taken place in the decades between the first Roosevelt and Nixon. By conventional economic measures the country was unquestionably "better off." Gross National Product, the output of goods and services measured in constant dollars, rose from $123.2 billion in 1911 to $720 billion in 1970. Disposable personal income per capita, or what each individual could spend if national income were distributed evenly throughout the population, rose from $994 to $2,595 in the same period, again using a constant dollar for purposes of meaningful comparison.

Quantitative measures of national affluence, however, have drawbacks. Income and wealth are not in fact evenly distributed, and more income, whether national or personal, is not necessarily synonymous with a "better" life. As the National Goals Research Staff reported in July 1970, "We have developed a new and acute awareness that the quality of life cannot be measured in quantitative terms." On the other hand, as the same report also pointed out, it is impossible to have quality without quantity. Therefore, it is necessary to consider both in setting national goals for America's future. In the words of the report, quantity alone is no longer "adequate either as a goal or as a standard of measurement."

A decade earlier a panel of distinguished Americans had reviewed national programs and policies in the light of goals that they considered appropriate to various spheres of national interest. Reporting their findings to President Dwight D. Eisenhower (1953–1961), this panel stressed the traditional overall national goals of safeguarding the rights of the individual, insuring his development and enlarging his opportunity. But they saw this goal threatened as never before by a world in "political, social, economic, and technological revolution." Nationally and internationally, subsequent events confirmed the justification for their concern.

In the decade of rapid change between the two reports on national goals, the strengths and weaknesses of attachment to quantitative measures of national progress were reflected most dramatically in the space program. The success of the pioneering Russian sputnik in 1957 caused Americans to reassess their educational system and their international position, with particular reference to the sciences. Soon after President John F. Kennedy entered office in 1961, he called for a landing on the moon by a manned American spacecraft within a decade. A massive concentration of private and public resources achieved this goal with the deadline set by Kennedy, though he did not live to see it. Prodded into action by international competition, the United States space program achieved the kind of triumph that the world and Americans had come to expect of American technology. The goal was specific; its achievement called for the application of technological and industrial resources that had brought the American economy to its high level of development; and progress towards the final objective could be measured quantitatively. In the last year of World War II, David E. Lilienthal, who had managed the development of another great American experiment, the Tennessee Valley Authority, stated without a qualm that "there is almost nothing, however fantastic, that . . . a team of engineers, scientists, and administrators cannot do today." The American space effort of the 1960's more than vindicated his optimistic prediction, but only as it related to a specific, technological challenge.

Ironically, the very success of the space program helped to undermine the popular acceptance of quantitative measures of national progress. Many taxpayers questioned the desirability of spending the nation's resources to reach the moon when mounting social and economic problems in the United States demanded attention and a share of the resources that were being funneled into the space effort. More significant, perhaps, was the fact that the space program permitted American astronauts to view their world from outer space and for millions of their countrymen to share this experience via television. From this new perspective it became obvious that the carefully engineered life-support systems of the spacecraft only mirrored what nature had provided earthbound Americans, who for so long had taken so much pride in their conquest of nature.

While the interdependence of man and his natural environment had been recognized for a long time by scientists, most Americans had dismissed this relationship as irrelevant to their daily routine. They had created a highly productive, interdependent economy, but they had ignored its ultimate dependence on a highly interdependent natural environment. Americans had understandably accepted their natural resources inheritance casually. The country's prodigal endowment of these resources had led to their prodigal exploitation from colonial days. In Theodore Roosevelt's time there was some recognition that America's resources might have finite limits. By the 1970's this perception had become unavoidable. Not only the miracle of televised views of planet earth from space made this fact obvious, but growing evidence, especially in crowded urban, industrial centers, showed that undiscriminating emphasis on economic growth and accompanying technological change could be destructive of human values, even of life itself. For the first time the self-justifying rationale for economic growth was brought into serious question for many Americans.

Environmental protection measures, almost unthinkable in the 1950's, were adopted in the 1960's at both federal and state levels. In the 1970's they promise to have a major impact on all types of economic activity, ranging from the availability of energy sources to the types of detergents used by housewives, to the kind of insecticides used by farmers, and to the range of factors considered relevant to the location of industrial plants. Evidence of a new environmental awareness was reflected in the 1971 Congressional decision to drop development of a supersonic transport, despite the threat that American prestige at the frontiers of technological development might suffer. And the space program, which for a decade had called forth a major national effort, suffered serious cutbacks as the President, Congress, and the nation reassessed national goals and priorities in the light of changing values.

While this reassessment was taking place, the nation was slowly and painfully trying to extricate itself from an undeclared and unpopular war in Southeast Asia, which had had a major impact on the economy. An unprecedented combination of inflation and unemployment, exacerbated by a defense cutback, plagued the economy. Existing means for managing the economy seemed inadequate to meet these new conditions; yet the need and the resolve to consciously manage it, to promote sound growth while improving the quality of life, had become pressing problems.

Unlike the situation in 1900, the federal government since 1946 has been charged with the ultimate responsibility for the performance of the American economy. Its choice of national priorities and the means employed to achieve them set the framework for private economic decisions. From policeman of a privately directed economy whose direction was set by thousands upon thousands of private business decisions, the government has emerged in less than seventy years, and more particularly since the advent of the New Deal in depression-ridden 1933, as both the director and the guarantor of the economy. Today, businessmen look as much to signals from Washington as to those from the marketplace. While interaction between the two is still important, the relative emphasis on each has shifted markedly away from Main Street and Wall Street to Pennsylvania Avenue.

To some extent this shift can be measured quantitatively. At the turn of the century, government at all levels—federal, state, and local—spent about $20 per capita, or about 8 percent of Gross National Product. In 1900 government at all levels employed only one out of every 30 workers. In 1960 government spent more than 25 percent of GNP, and one out of every ten workers was on a government payroll. On a per capita basis, the federal government was spending almost double the amount expended by state and local governments combined.

Until the 1930's, with the exception of the national emergency of World War I, massive governmental intervention in the economy would have defied both traditional American values and conventional economic wisdom. Competition in the marketplace, with excesses correcting themselves through price adjustments, or elimination of competitors, was accepted as an impersonal, self-adjusting mechanism for the domestic economy. Internationally, the gold standard was regarded as similarly self-adjusting. Domestically, government was supposed to act like a rational, conservative head of household and balance its income and outgo over the fiscal year. There was little need, and few means, to manage the economy— or so it was thought.

As the Great Depression of the 1930's settled over the country, dire necessity forced a departure from these traditional tenets of economic faith. Instead of the economy managing itself, it became increasingly evident that it would have to be managed—not only to recover from depression but for stable long-run economic growth. English economist John Maynard Keynes, and some of his American counterparts, pointed the way towards economic recovery in the 1930's by recommending deficit government spending to take up the slack left by the decline of private investment plus inadequate consumption expenditures. President Franklin D. Roosevelt embraced this remedy gingerly and only to meet specific problems. For him, as for his predecessors, the goal of a balanced budget was not lightly discarded. As Keynes pointed out, however, halfway measures in government spending would not (and they did not) suffice to restore prosperity. In fact, World War II, rather than peacetime economic measures, launched the American economy on a new and sustained upward movement.

World War II confirmed the government's newly assumed and

tentative leadership role in the economy. During the war the American people, against a background of ten years of depression, made it clear that full employment had to be a major postwar national goal. Both Republicans and Democrats subscribed to it, and the Employment Act of 1946 spelled out government's responsibility to foster and sustain full employment, though the importance of the private sector was also strongly reaffirmed. The President was instructed to provide the nation with an annual economic report, and he was to be aided by a Council of Economic Advisers of professional competence. Congress was to be represented in these economic assessments by a Joint Economic Committee. Through such means it was hoped that governmental policies and actions could be developed to smooth out the peaks and valleys of the business cycle, while steering the economy along the path of stable economic growth.

Contrary to the expectations of some reputable economists and leading businessmen that the postwar economy would slump, as it had after World War I, it moved ahead with few reverses. As a result, though there were periodic contractions, there was little need for—and under Eisenhower in the 1950's a positive aversion to—governmental use of its new economic powers, other than to counter excessive swings in the business cycle.[1]

When President John F. Kennedy (1961–1963) entered office in 1961, the nation was experiencing one of its more severe postwar recessions and its rate of economic growth was slackening. The new President early in his brief term saw the need and the potential for creating a sustained rise in the economy. The rapid growth of the Soviet economy relative to that of the United States, with all this implied in terms of international power relationships, was an important factor in his decision to utilize governmental powers to invigorate the economy. The tools for this job had been developed in the period between World War I and World War II. They ranged from advances in economic theory, such as Keynes's, to changes in the adequacy of statistical information about national income and its distribution. Whereas President Franklin D. Roosevelt (1933–1945) had little knowledge of, or interest in, formal

---

[1] The contractions of 1948–1949, 1953–54, 1957–58, and 1960–61 were shorter and milder than those of earlier cyclical swings.

economics, John F. Kennedy apparently grasped them at a relatively high level of sophistication.

Kennedy's basic approach, carried forward by his successor Lyndon B. Johnson (1963–1969), was linked to tax reduction and tax reform as a way to stimulate private investment and consumption. Thus, while the government might be forced to run a substantial deficit for a time, the theory was that the private sector would be infused with a new vigor that would generate more income and employment. As rising economic activity moved the nation towards full employment, more tax revenue would be generated and at full employment the federal budget could be balanced. The first phase, or tax reduction aspects of this program, could be counted on for popular and Congressional support. In the past fifty years there has been no case where Congress has failed eventually to enact tax reductions that a President has asked. Thus the tax cut of 1964, initiated before but enacted after President Kennedy's death, did not require an elaborate rationale for the public or Congress, though it was part of an economic program heavily influenced by Keynesian ideas. The government's program to stimulate the economy contributed to accelerated economic activity in the early 1960's, and it was reinforced by the growing demands of the Vietnam War. A sharp increase in spending for support of that conflict began in 1965 and placed heavy demands on an economy already "heated up" by the Kennedy-Johnson policies, to which business had responded with enthusiasm. But the success of these stimulative measures created new problems.

Painful political decisions are seldom based on economic theory. The theory that warrants increased government expenditure and reduced taxation in times of recession or depression also calls for reversing these policies as prosperity and inflation change the economic situation. By early 1966 the "new economists" of the Kennedy era were calling for just such action, but the Johnson administration and Congress were lukewarm with respect to this less pleasant aspect of responsible fiscal policy. It was easier, and politically less painful, to make monetary policy carry the burden of checking inflation. By taking steps to discourage borrowing and expansion of the money supply, the Federal Reserve System in theory should have been able to slow the escalating inflation. But, as experience in the 1930's had shown when the opposite attempt was made to encourage borrowing, the cost of borrowing does not necessarily determine the amount of borrowing. Expectations of the future and the rate of return to be obtained on borrowed money may, in a period of inflation, outweigh the high cost of credit as far as the borrower is concerned. And problems of applying the right degree of monetary restraint in terms of anticipated future response are formidable.

In any event, the task of combatting inflation was more than monetary policy alone could handle. Even when the Johnson administration acknowledged this fact by requesting a tax increase in 1967, Congress proved reluctant to act. When it finally did so in the summer of 1968, accompanied by insistence that government expenditures also be cut, inflation had a firm hold on the economy. The quagmire of the Vietnam War drove President Johnson from office, but the effort to restrain the government's contribution to inflation produced the first surplus of the decade when fiscal year 1969 ended.[2] The new occupant of the White House, Richard M. Nixon (1969–   ), still confronted an acute inflationary problem but hoped by deescalation of the Vietnam War and reduced government spending in nonmilitary areas to curb the inflationary fever. Instead, these steps to reduce the fever of inflation only added to it the sickness of increased unemployment.

The intricacies of dealing with these problems are illustrated in the making of the federal budget for fiscal 1971. The questions of national goals and priorities were very much involved. The administration gave increased emphasis to domestic needs such as health care and housing, pollution control, and the need for refurbishing the nation's faltering transportation system. By cutting back defense expenditures and by giving some existing programs lower priorities, the administration hoped that the budget would not be increased and that a modest surplus might be achieved.

Important forces affecting the budget were operating in opposite directions, however. The President had recommended and Congress had adopted a proposal to reduce by 50 percent the 1968 income tax surcharge (imposed to absorb excess purchasing power) effective January 1, 1970, and to allow it to expire as of June 30th of that year. This action meant a decline in government revenue; at

[2] The federal government ran a deficit in every fiscal year from 1961 to 1969, with the largest one occurring in 1968 when it rose to $25.2 billions.

the same time, Congress increased the President's recommended 10 percent increase in Social Security benefits to 15 percent, thus adding to government expenditures and their potential inflationary effect. In an effort to produce a budget surplus in the face of this development, the administration called for substantial cuts in the NASA budget, reduction of government aid to impacted school areas, reductions in the special milk program for school children, in agricultural conservation payments, and in some veterans' subsidies. But these trade-offs did not produce the desired results, and fiscal 1971 ended with a very substantial federal deficit.

The growth of real GNP (i.e. measured in terms of purchasing power rather than the number of inflated dollars) failed to respond to moderate measures. Unemployment climbed, and the balance of payments, which had posed a problem for over a decade, worsened. Like Kennedy, Nixon was forced, early in 1971, to accept the fact that management of a growing yet troubled economy would require deficit spending by government as a deliberate policy. Unlike Kennedy, Nixon had to make this hard choice in the knowledge that it might also contribute substantially to already unacceptable levels of inflation. In a matter of months, as it turned out, he had to take the unprecedented step of imposing direct peacetime economic controls. By 1973 the drain of the Vietnam War had been largely ended, controls had been relaxed, but inflation was escalating to such an extent that the President was refusing to spend money appropriated by Congress. New problems and doubts had arisen as to the government's ability to manage the economy. By 1974 most controls had been removed but inflation was rampant, aggravated by an acute energy shortage. Major changes seemed to lie ahead for the American economy.

In the seventy years between Bishop Lawrence's pronouncement that "godliness was in league with riches" and President Nixon's 1971 decision that government had to intervene directly in market decisions, many changes had occurred in the American economy and in Americans' ideas about how it should be managed. The emphasis on the value of private, decentralized decision making for the economy had been modified, though the business system remained the cornerstone of the economy. Businessmen, as well as wage workers, farmers, and most recently consumers, have for different reasons subscribed to the necessity for increased governmental intervention in, and management of, the economy.

A pragmatic, piecemeal adjustment of governmental policies to the values and goals of these groups, which were often in opposition to one another, has characterized the decades since 1900, but more particularly since 1930. New economic tools have been developed to assist in policy decisions, to mitigate excesses of the business cycle, and to promote economic growth and full employment. But in the early 1970's the adequacy of these tools, and the resolution to use them, have not been fully tested nor proven. To do so may require more emphasis on centralized planning and compulsory enforcement than has yet been accepted by the American people.

Aside from the commitment to full employment, the shifting character of national goals and values may well force resolution of this question in the 1970's. While quantitative economic progress will undoubtedly continue to be a major national goal, in fact one indispensable for the achievement of other goals, it probably will not be pursued so single-mindedly as in the past. While Americans want more economic goods and services, they have also awakened to the fact that material progress may come at too high a cost to the resources and natural environment on which all life ultimately depends. The challenge that confronts Americans in the 1970's is not to conquer nature but to combine stable economic growth with an improved quality of life, while minimizing the destructive consequences to their natural environment. How this challenge will be met depends on the generation born after World War II, on their understanding of the choices that confront them, and the means at their disposal.

INTRODUCTION:
AMERICAN GOALS AND VALUES,
1901–1972

The economic life of a nation reflects its underlying values and implicit or explicit goals of the society. In the following selections, which reflect these goals and values at the turn of the century and in the recent past, there is evidence of both continuity and significant change.

When President Theodore Roosevelt spoke in 1903 at Syracuse, New York, on "Class Government," memory of the Civil War was still fresh enough for him to incorporate specific reference to it in his speech. But in the intervening decades the industrial transformation of the economy had created a new society. Its problems did not dim Roosevelt's emphasis on traditional values: individualism, the ethic of hard work, and the importance of doing one's duty. He decried the divisions that had developed between rich and poor, invoked dedication to national goals, and stressed the worth and morality of each man's calling, whatever his class, so long as he dealt fairly and squarely with his fellow men. Women as wives and mothers deserved as much respect as lawyers or bankers.

Bishop William Lawrence, following many of the same themes, emphasized that America was the land of opportunity. Success, which he measured in material terms, was the reward of hard work and careful spending. It was a desirable, moral goal. The conquest of nature was a divine mission, and riches were evidence of godliness.

Some sixty years later the definition of national goals was assigned to a presidential commission. The emphasis on the importance of the individual was not diminished, but the context in which fulfillment of his potential must be achieved had changed significantly. The importance of economic growth as a contribution to achieving this goal is not renounced, but the role of government is accorded increased importance. The complexity of the economy, the importance of organization and planning in achieving national goals, and problems of underconsumption and oversupply suggest that the scope for individualism, as understood by Theodore Roosevelt and Bishop Lawrence, had been affected significantly by economic and technological change. In the wake of World War II and the commencement of the Cold War, national defense had gained major significance for the economic health of the nation. Women, treated as housewives and mothers by Theodore Roosevelt, were recognized by the President's Commission in 1960 as having an important place in the work-force.

In 1970 still another presidential task group examined national goals, this time in a new context that questioned an undiscriminating emphasis on economic growth. In his introduction to that report, Daniel P. Moynihan, Counsellor to the President, reviewed areas of progress towards earlier objectives, emphasized the way in which the statement of goals can arouse expectations of still more progress, and called for more social data to be used in assessing trade-offs between quantity and quality as the country moved towards the future.

The many changes of the 1960's are also reflected in the selection from the Report of the Commission on Population Growth and the American Future. The emphasis still remains on the individual, but the quality of his life has become a matter of major concern. Economic growth as an automatic path to a better life is brought into question. The market, while acknowledged as a useful way of allocating economic resources, is indicted as inadequate for answering questions of major social importance. To meet such problems as pollution, inequality of income, and urban blight, the Commission was prepared to recommend restraint on population growth and acceptance of a slower rate of economic growth than in the past.

The final selection in this section reports that in 1972, protection of environmental quality had become "a major national goal." While recording progress at both state and federal levels toward achieving this goal, the report indicates the complex and difficult nature of the necessary trade-offs with other goals, which are also supported by the American people.

CLASS GOVERNMENT, 1903

Theodore Roosevelt

In the history of mankind many republics have risen, have flourished for a less or greater time, and then have fallen because their citizens lost the power of governing themselves and thereby of governing their state; and in no way has this loss of power been so often and so clearly shown as in the tendency to turn the government primarily for the benefit of one class instead of a government for the benefit of the people as a whole.

Again and again in the republics of ancient Greece, in those of
mediaeval Italy and mediaeval Flanders, this tendency was shown,
and wherever the tendency became a habit it invariably and inevitably proved fatal to the state. In the final result it mattered not one
whit whether the movement was in favor of one class or of another.
The outcome was equally fatal, whether the country fell into the
hands of a wealthy oligarchy which exploited the poor or whether it
fell under the domination of a turbulent mob which plundered the
rich. In both cases there resulted violent alternations between tyranny
and disorder, and a final complete loss of liberty to all citizens—destruction in the end overtaking the class which had for the moment
been victorious as well as that which had momentarily been defeated.
The death knell of the Republic had rung as soon as the active
power became lodged in the hands of those who sought, not to do
justice to all citizens, rich and poor alike, but to stand for one
special class and for its interests as opposed to the interests of
others.

The reason why our future is assured lies in the fact that our
people are genuinely skilled in and fitted for self-government and
therefore will spurn the leadership of those who seek to excite this
ferocious and foolish class antagonism. The average American
knows not only that he himself intends to do about what is right,
but that his average fellow-countryman has the same intention and
the same power to make his intention effective. He knows, whether
he be business man, professional man, farmer, mechanic, employer,
or wage-worker, that the welfare of each of these men is bound up
with the welfare of all the others; that each is neighbor to the other,
is actuated by the same hopes and fears, has fundamentally the
same ideals, and that all alike have much the same virtues and the
same faults. Our average fellow-citizen is a sane and healthy man,
who believes in decency and has a wholesome mind. He therefore
feels an equal scorn alike for the man of wealth guilty of the mean
and base spirit of arrogance toward those who are less well off, and
for the man of small means who in his turn either feels, or seeks to
excite in others the feeling of mean and base envy for those who
are better off. The two feelings, envy and arrogance, are but opposite sides of the same shield, but different developments of the
same spirit. . . .

The line of cleavage between good and bad citizenship lies, not between the man of wealth who acts squarely by his fellows and the man who seeks each day's wage by that day's work, wronging no one and doing his duty by his neighbor; nor yet does this line of cleavage divide the unscrupulous wealthy man who exploits others in his own interest, from the demagogue, or from the sullen and envious being who wishes to attack all men of property, whether they do well or ill. On the contrary, the line of cleavage between good citizenship and bad citizenship separates the rich man who does well from the rich man who does ill, the poor man of good conduct from the poor man of bad conduct. This line of cleavage at right angles to any such arbitrary line of division as that separating one class from another, one locality from another, or men with a certain degree of property from those of a less degree of property.

The good citizen is the man who, whatever his wealth or his poverty, strives manfully to do his duty to himself, to his family, to his neighbor, to the State; who is incapable of the baseness which manifests itself either in arrogance or in envy, but who while demanding justice for himself is no less scrupulous to do justice to others. It is because the average American citizen, rich or poor, is of just this type that we have cause for our profound faith in the future of the Republic.

Ours is a government of liberty, by, through, and under the law. Lawlessness and connivance at law-breaking—whether the law-breaking take the form of a crime of greed and cunning or of a crime of violence—are destructive not only of order, but of the true liberties which can only come through order. If alive to their true interests rich and poor alike will set their faces like flint against the spirit which seeks personal advantage by overriding the laws, without regard to whether this spirit shows itself in the form of bodily violence by one set of men or in the form of vulpine cunning by another set of men.

Let the watchwords of all our people be the old familiar watchwords of honesty, decency, fair-dealing and common sense. The qualities denoted by these words are essential to all of us, as we deal with the complex industrial problems of to-day, the problems affecting not merely the accumulation but even more the wise distribution of wealth. We ask no man's permission when we require him to obey the law; neither the permission of the poor man nor yet of the rich man. Least of all can the man of great wealth afford to break the law, even for his own financial advantage; for the law is his prop and support, and it is both foolish and profoundly unpatriotic for him to fail in giving hearty support to those who show that there is in very fact one law, and one law only, alike for the rich and the poor, for the great and the small.

Men sincerely interested in the due protection of property, and men sincerely interested in seeing that the just rights of labor are guaranteed, should alike remember not only that in the long run neither the capitalist nor the wage-worker can be helped in healthy fashion save by helping the other; but also that to require either side to obey the law and do its full duty toward the community is emphatically to that side's real interest.

There is no worse enemy of the wage-worker than the man who condones mob violence in any shape or who preaches class hatred; and surely the slightest acquaintance with our industrial history should teach even the most short-sighted that the times of most suffering for our people as a whole, the times when business is stagnant, and capital suffers from shrinkage and gets no return from its investments, are exactly the times of hardship, and want, and grim disaster among the poor. If all the existing instrumentalities of wealth could be abolished, the first and severest suffering would come among those of us who are least well off at present. The wage-worker is well off only when the rest of the country is well off; and he can best contribute to this general well-being by showing sanity and a firm purpose to do justice to others.

In his turn the capitalist who is really a conservative, the man who has forethought as well as patriotism, should heartily welcome every effort, legislative or otherwise, which has for its object to secure fair dealing by capital, corporate or individual, toward the public and toward the employee. Such laws as the franchise-tax law in this State, which the Court of Appeals recently unanimously decided constitutional—such a law as that passed in Congress last year for the purpose of establishing a Department of Commerce and Labor, under which there should be a bureau to oversee and secure publicity from the great corporations which do an interstate business—such a law as that passed at the same time for the regulation of the great highways of commerce so as to keep these roads clear on fair terms to all producers in getting their goods to market—these laws are in the interest not merely of the people as a whole, but of the propertied classes. For in no way is the stability of property better assured than by making it patent to our people that property bears its proper share of the burdens of the State; that property is handled not only in the interest of the owner, but in the interest of the whole community.

In other words, legislation to be permanently good for any class must also be good for the Nation as a whole, and legislation which does injustice to any class is certain to work harm to the Nation. Take our currency system for example. This Nation is on a gold basis. The treasury of the public is in excellent condition. Never before has the per capita of circulation been as large as it is this day; and this circulation, moreover, is of money every dollar of which is at par with gold. Now, our having this sound currency system is of benefit to banks, of course, but it is of infinitely more benefit to the people as a whole, because of the healthy effect on business conditions.

In the same way, whatever is advisable in the way of remedial or corrective currency legislation—and nothing revolutionary is advisable under present conditions—must be undertaken only from the standpoint of the business community as a whole, that is, of the American body politic as a whole. Whatever is done, we can not afford to take any step backward or to cast any doubt upon the certain redemption in standard coin of every circulating note.

Among ourselves we differ in many qualities of body, head and heart; we are unequally developed, mentally as well as physically. But each of us has the right to ask that he shall be protected from wrongdoing as he does his work and carries his burden through life. No man needs sympathy because he has to work, because he has a burden to carry. Far and away the best prize that life offers is the chance to work hard at work worth doing; and this is a prize open to every man, for there can be no work better worth doing than that done to keep in health and comfort and with reasonable advantages those immediately dependent upon the husband, the father, or the son.

There is no room in our healthy American life for the mere idler, for the man or the woman whose object it is throughout life to shirk the duties which life ought to bring. Life can mean nothing worth meaning, unless its prime aim is the doing of duty, the achievement of results worth achieving. A recent writer has finely said: "After all, the saddest thing that can happen to a man is to carry no burdens. To be bent under too great a load is bad; to be crushed by it is lamentable; but even in that there are possibilities that are glorious. But to carry no load at all—there is nothing in that. No one seems to arrive at any goal really worth reaching in this world who does not come to it heavy laden."

Surely from our own experience each one of us knows that this is true. From the greatest to the smallest, happiness and usefulness are largely found in the same soul, and the joy of life is won in its deepest and truest sense only by those who have not shirked life's burdens. The men whom we most delight to honor in all this land are those who, in the iron years from '61 to '65, bore on their shoulders the burden of saving the Union. They did not choose the easy task. They did not shirk the difficult duty. Deliberately and of their own free will they strove for an ideal, upward and onward across the stony slopes of greatness. They did the hardest work that was then to be done; they bore the heaviest burden that any generation of Americans ever had to bear; and because they did this they have won such proud joy as it has fallen to the lot of no other men to win, and have written their names for evermore on the golden honor roll of the Nation. As it is with the soldier, so it is with the civilian. To win success in the business world, to become a first-class mechanic, a successful farmer, an able lawyer or doctor, means that the man has devoted his best energy and power through long years to the achievement of his ends. So it is in the life of the family, upon which in the last analysis the whole welfare of the Nation rests. The man or woman who as bread-winner and home-maker, or as wife and mother, has done all that he or she can do, patiently and uncomplainingly, is to be honored; and is to be envied by all those who have never had the good fortune to feel the need and duty of doing such work. The woman who has borne, and who has reared as they should be reared, a family of children, has in the most emphatic manner deserved well of the Republic. Her burden has been heavy, and she has been able to bear it worthily only by the possession of resolution, of good sense, of conscience, and of unselfishness. But if she has borne it well, then to her shall come the supreme blessing, for in the words of the oldest and greatest of books, "Her children shall rise up and call her blessed;" and among the benefactors of the land her place must be with those who have done the best and the hardest work, whether as law-givers or as soldiers, whether in public or private life.

This is not a soft and easy creed to preach. It is a creed willingly learned only by men and women who, together with the softer virtues, possess also the stronger; who can do, and dare, and die at need, but who while life lasts will never flinch from their allotted task. You farmers, and wage-workers, and business men of this great State, of this mighty and wonderful Nation, are gathered together to-day, proud of your State and still prouder of your Nation, because your forefathers and predecessors have lived up to just this creed. You have received from their hands a great inheritance, and you will leave an even greater inheritance to your children, and your children's children, provided only that you practice alike in your private and your public lives the strong virtues that have given us as a people greatness in the past. It is not enough to be well-meaning and kindly, but weak; neither is it enough to be strong, unless morality and decency go hand in hand with strength. We must possess the qualities which make us do our duty in our homes and among our neighbors, and in addition we must possess the qualities which are indispensable to the make-up of every great and masterful nation—the qualities of courage and hardihood, of individual initiative and yet of power to combine for a common end, and above all, the resolute determination to permit no man and no set of men to sunder us one from the other by lines of caste or creed or section. We must act upon the motto of all for each and each for all. There must be ever present in our minds the fundamental truth that in a republic such as ours the only safety is to stand neither for nor against any man because he is rich or because he is poor, because he is engaged in one occupation or another, because he works with his brains or because he works with his hands. We must treat each man on his worth and merits as a man. We must see that each is given a square deal, because he is entitled to no more and should receive no less. Finally we must keep ever in mind that a republic such as ours can exist only by virtue of the orderly liberty which comes through the equal domination of the law over all men alike, and through its administration in such resolute and fearless fashion as shall teach all that no man is above it and no man below it.

———————

THE RELATION OF WEALTH TO MORALS, 1901

Bishop William Lawrence

There is a certain distrust on the part of our people as to the effect of material prosperity on their morality. We shrink with some foreboding at the great increase of riches, and question whether in the long run material prosperity does not tend toward the disintegration of character.

History seems to support us in our distrust. Visions arise of their fall from splendor of Tyre and Sidon, Babylon, Rome, and Venice, and of great nations too. The question is started whether England is not to-day, in the pride of her wealth and power, sowing the wind from which in time she will reap the whirlwind.

Experience seems to add its support. Is it not from the ranks of the poor that leaders of the people have always risen? Recall Abraham Lincoln and patriots of every generation.

The Bible has sustained the same note. Were ever stronger words of warning uttered against the deceitfulness of riches than those spoken by the peasant Jesus, who Himself had no place to lay His head? And the Church has through the centuries upheld poverty as one of the surest paths to Heaven: it has been a mark of the saint.

To be sure, in spite of history, experience, and the Bible, men have gone on their way making money and hailing with joy each age of material prosperity. The answer is: "This only proves the case; men are of the world, riches are deceitful, and the Bible is true; the world is given over to Mammon. In the increase of material wealth and the accumulation of riches the man who seeks the higher life has no part."

In the face of this comes the statement of the chief statistician of our census—from one, therefore, who speaks with authority: "The present census, when completed, will unquestionably show that the visible material wealth in this country now has a value of ninety billion dollars. This is an addition since 1890 of twenty-five billion dollars. This is a saving greater than all the people of the Western Continent had been able to make from the discovery of Columbus to the breaking out of the Civil War."

If our reasoning from history, experience, and the Bible is correct, we, a Christian people, have rubbed a sponge over the pages of the Bible and are in for orgies and a downfall to which the fall of Rome is a very tame incident.

May it not be well, however, to revise our inferences from history, experience, and the Bible? History tells us that, while riches have been an item and an indirect cause of national decay, innumerable other conditions entered in. Therefore, while wealth has been a source of danger, it has not necessarily led to demoralization.

That leaders have sprung from the ranks of the poor is true and always will be true, so long as force of character exists in every class. But there are other conditions than a lack of wealth at the source of their uprising.

And as to the Bible:—while every word that can be quoted against the rich is as true as any other word, other words and deeds are as true; and the parables of our Lord on the stewardship of wealth, His association with the wealthy, strike another and complementary note. Both notes are essential to the harmony of His life and teachings. His thought was not of the conditions, rich or poor, but of a higher life, the character rising out of the conditions —fortunately, for we are released from that subtle hypocrisy which has beset the Christian through the ages, bemoaning the deceitfulness of riches and, at the same time, working with all his might to earn a competence, and a fortune if he can.

Man "Born to Be Rich"

Now we are in a position to affirm that neither history, experience, nor the Bible necessarily sustains the common distrust of the effect of material wealth on morality. Our path of study is made more clear. Two positive principles lead us out on our path.

The first is that man, when he is strong, will conquer Nature, open up her resources, and harness them to his service. This is his play, his exercise, his divine mission.

"Man," says Emerson, "is born to be rich. He is thoroughly related, and is tempted out by his appetites and fancies to the conquest of this and that piece of Nature, until he finds his well-being in the use of the planet, and of more planets than his own. Wealth requires, besides the crust of bread and the roof, the freedom of the city, the freedom of the earth." "The strong race is strong on these terms."

Man draws to himself material wealth as surely, as naturally, and as necessarily as the oak draws the elements into itself from the earth.

The other principle is that, in the long run, it is only to the man of morality that wealth comes. We believe in the harmony of God's Universe. We know that it is only by working along His laws natural and spiritual that we can work with efficiency. Only by working along the lines of right thinking and right living can the secrets and wealth of Nature be revealed. We, like the Psalmist, occasionally see the wicked prosper, but only occasionally.

Put two men in adjoining fields, one man strong and normal, the other weak and listless. One picks up his spade, turns over the earth, and works till sunset. The other turns over a few clods, gets a drink from the spring, takes a nap, and loafs back to his work. In a few years one will be rich for his needs, and the other a pauper dependent on the first, and growling at his prosperity.

Put ten thousand immoral men to live and work in one fertile valley and ten thousand moral men to live and work in the next valley, and the question is soon answered as to who wins the material wealth. Godliness is in league with riches.

Now we return with an easier mind and clearer conscience to the problem of our twenty-five billion dollars in a decade.

My question is: Is the material prosperity of this Nation favorable or unfavorable to the morality of the people?

The first thought is, Who has prospered? Who has got the money?

I take it that the loudest answer would be, "The millionaires, the capitalists, and the incompetent but luxurious rich;" and, as we think of that twenty-five billion, our thoughts run over the yachts, the palaces, and the luxuries that flaunt themselves before the public.

Who the Rich Are

As I was beginning to write this paper an Irishman with his horse and wagon drew up at my back door. Note that I say *his* horse and wagon. Twenty years ago that Irishman, then hardly twenty years old, landed in Boston, illiterate, uncouth, scarcely able to make himself understood in English. There was no symptom of brains, alertness, or ambition. He got a job to tend a few cows. Soon the American atmosphere began to take hold. He discovered that here every man has his chance. With his first earnings he bought a suit of clothes; he gained self-respect. Then he sent money home; then he got a job to drive a horse; he opened an account at the savings bank; then evening school; more money in the bank. He changed to a better job, married a thrifty wife, and to-day he owns his house, stable, horse, wagon, and bicycle; has a good sum at the bank, supports five children, and has half a dozen men working under him. He is a capitalist, and his yearly earnings represent the income of $30,000. He had no "pull;" he has made his own way by grit, physical strength, and increasing intelligence. He has had material prosperity. His older brother, who paid his passage over, has had material prosperity, and his younger brother, whose passage my friend paid, has had material prosperity.

Now we are beginning to get an idea as to where the savings are. They are in the hands of hundreds of thousands of just such men, and of scores of thousands of men whose incomes ten years ago were two and five thousand, and are now five and ten thousand; and of thousands of others whose incomes have risen from ten to thirty thousand. So that, when you get to the multi-millionaires, you have only a fraction to distribute among them. And of them the fact is that only a small fraction of their income can be spent upon their own pleasure and luxury; the bulk of what they get has to be reinvested, and becomes the means whereby thousands earn their wages. They are simply trustees of a fraction of the national property.

When, then, the question is asked, "Is the material prosperity of this nation favorable or unfavorable to the morality of the people?" I say with all emphasis, "In the long run, and by all means, favorable!"

In other words, to seek for and earn wealth is a sign of a natural, vigorous, and strong character. Wherever strong men are, there they will turn into the activities of life. In the ages of chivalry you will find them on the crusades or seeking the Golden Fleece; in college life you will find them high in rank, in the boat, or on the athletic field; in an industrial age you will find them eager, straining every nerve in the development of the great industries. The race is to the strong. The search for material wealth is therefore as natural and necessary to the man as is the pushing out of its roots for more moisture and food to the oak. This is man's play, his exercise, the expression of his powers, his personality. You can no more suppress it than you can suppress the tide of the ocean. For one man who seeks money for its own sake there are ten who seek it for the satisfaction of the seeking, the power there is in it, and the use they can make of it. There is the exhilaration of feeling one's self grow in one's surroundings; the man reaches out, lays hold of this, that, and the other interest, scheme, and problem. He is building up a fortune? Yes, but his joy is also that he is building up a stronger, abler, and more powerful man. There are two men that have none of this ambition: the gilded, listless youth and the ragged, listless pauper to whom he tosses a dime; they are in the same class.

We are now ready to take up the subject in a little more detail. How is it favorable? The parable of my Irish friend gives the answer.

In the first place, and as I have already suggested, the effort to make his living and add to his comforts and power gives free play to a man's activities and leads to a development of his faculties. In an age and country where the greater openings are in commercial lines, there the stronger men and the mass of them will move. It is not a question of worldliness or of love of money, but of the natural use and legitimate play of men's faculties. An effort to suppress this action is not a religious duty, but a disastrous error, sure to fail.

Self-Respect and Self-Mastery

Besides this natural play of the faculties comes the development of self-respect and ambition. In the uprise from a lower to a higher civilization, these are the basal elements. Watch the cart-loads of

Polish or Italian immigrants as they are hauled away from the dock. Study their lifeless expression, their hand-dog look, and their almost cowering posture. Follow them and study them five years later: note the gradual straightening of the body, the kindling of the eye, and the alertness of the whole person as the men, women, and children begin to realize their opportunities, bring in their wages, and move to better quarters. Petty temptations and deep degradations that might have overwhelmed them on their arrival cannot now touch them.

With this comes also the power of self-mastery. The savage eats what he kills and spends what he has. In the movement towards civilization through material wealth, questions come up for the decision every hour. Shall I spend? Shall I save? How shall I spend? How can I earn more? Shall I go into partnership with a capital of ten dollars, or shall I wait until I have fifty dollars?

Wage earners are not to-day, as they were in earlier days, hungering for the bare physical necessities of life. They are hungering now, and it marks an upward movement in civilization, for higher things, education, social life, relaxation, and the development of the higher faculties.

To be sure, a certain fraction wilt under the strain, take to drink, to lust, to laziness. There is always the thin line of stragglers behind every army, but the great body of the American people are marching upwards in prosperity through the mastery of their lower tastes and passions to the development of the higher. From rags to clothes, from filth to cleanliness, from disease to health; from bare walls to pictures; from ignorance to education; from narrow and petty talk to books and music and art; from superstition to a more rational religion; from crudity to refinement; from self-centralization to the conception of a social unity.

Here in this last phrase we strike the next step in development. In this increase of wealth, this rapid communication which goes with it, this shrinking of the earth's surface and unifying of peoples through commerce, men and women are realizing their relations to society.

That there are those who in the deepest poverty sustain the spirit of unselfishness and exhibit a self-sacrifice for others which puts their richer neighbors to the blush we know by experience. At the same time, the fact is that for the mass and in the long run grinding poverty does grind down the character: in the struggle for bare existence and for the very life of one's children there is developed an intense self-centralization and a hardness which is destructive of the social instinct and of the finer graces. When, however, through the increase of wealth man has extended his interests, his vision, and his opportunities, "he is thoroughly related." His lines run out in every direction; he lays his finger upon all the broader interests of life, the school, the church, and the college. He reaches through commerce to the ends of the earth. He discovers one bond which is essential to the social unity in this belief in others, our whole social and commercial fabric is built. And when a man has reached this point, he has indeed reached one of the high plateaus of character: from this rise the higher mountain peaks of Christian graces, but here he is on the standing-ground of the higher civilization.

As I write I can almost feel the silent protest of some critics. Are not these qualities, self-respect, self-mastery, a sense of social unity, and mutual confidence, the commonplaces of life? Is this the only response of material wealth in its relation to morality?

These are to us now the commonplaces of life: they are at the same time the fundamentals of character and of morality. If material prosperity has been one of the great instruments (and I believe it has) in bringing the great body of our people even to approach this plateau of character, it has more than justified itself.

One might, however, mention other and finer qualities that follow in these days the train of prosperity. I instance only one. We will strike up one mountain peak: it is that of joyful and grateful service. . . .

GOALS FOR AMERICANS, 1960
President's Commission on National Goals

The Arts and Sciences

Knowledge and innovation must be advanced on every front. In science we should allot a greater proportion of our total effort to basic research, first, to realize fully the rapidly unfolding opportunities to extend still further our understanding of the world, and second, to enrich applied science and technology so essential to the improvement of health, to economic growth, and to military power.

Today we must give high priority to those aspects of science and technology which will increase our military strength, but for the longer term we should recognize that our creative activities in science and all other fields will be more productive and meaningfull if undertaken, not merely to be ahead of some other nation, but to be worthy of ourselves.

These objectives should govern our civilian space programs and policies. We should be highly selective in our space objectives and unexcelled in their pursuit. Prestige arises from sound accomplishment, not from the merely spectacular, and we must not be driven by nationalistic competition into programs so extravagant as to divert funds and talents from programs of equal or greater importance.

We should ensure that every young person with the desire and capacity to become a scientist has access to the best science education our leading scholars can devise. Given the availability of such education, science will find its fair share of the pool of talent. But this pool of talent must itself be enlarged to the maximum, by seeing to it that those who have the capacity for the rigorous academic discipline required for all the professions start their course study early, are offered opportunities to develop their talents, and are urged to continue to do so.

We must use available manpower more efficiently. The practice of wasting highly trained people in jobs below their capacity, particularly in some defense-related industries, must be eliminated. On the other hand, we must recognize that many workers have potential for higher positions. We must intensify the practice of upgrading men and women who may not have had advanced training but who have demonstrated capacity.

As Dr. Weaver's chapter suggests, we should allot a larger proportion of federal research and development funds to basic research. The total program of basic research in industry and other insitutions should be increased.

The federal government supports more than half of the research and development in the United States. It is of urgent importance that the administration of its scientific and technical programs be strengthened, but without resort to bureaucratic overcentralization and planning.

The humanities, the social sciences, and the natural sciences all are essential for a rounded cultural life. Literature and history are vital to understanding, to capacity to feel and communicate, to a sense of values. Economics, psychology, all forms of study of human relationships, have become more urgent as the conditions of living have become more complex; our progress in dealing with national economic policy is an indication of what may be achieved by continuing to give these studies full weight. Our world-wide responsibilities require fresh emphasis on foreign languages and continued improvement in teaching them.

The arts are a vital part of human experience. In the eyes of posterity, the success of the United State as a civilized society will be largely judged by the creative activities of its citizens in art, architecture, literature, music, and the sciences. While an encouraging creative surge in the arts is already manifest, our society must, as Mr. Heckscher's chapter urges, stimulate and support richer cultural fulfillment. Our theater must be revitalized; it must have the kind of support in universities, colleges, and communities that will give it greater strength at the roots. Professional artists require rigorous discipline; provision should be made for the long years of training which are required. We should raise our critical standards and widen the area and depth of public appreciation. Thus far, television has failed to use its facilities adequately for educational and cultural purposes, and reform in its performance is urgent.

The Democratic Economy

The economic system must be compatible with the political system. The centers of economic power should be as diffused and as balanced as possible. Too great concentrations of economic power in corporations, unions, or other organizations can lead to abuses and loss of the productive results of fair competition. Individuals should have maximum freedom in their choice of jobs, goods, and services.

Government participation in the economy should be limited to those instances where it is essential to the national interest and where private individuals or organizations cannot adequately meet the need. Government, of course, must maintain its regulatory control in areas such as anti-trust laws, collusion, and protection of investors and consumers. We must take special precautions to prevent government officials from being influenced unduly by the sectors of the economy they regulate.

Collective bargaining between representatives of workers and employers should continue as the nation's chief method for determining wage and working conditions.

Conferences among management, union leaders, and representatives of the public can contribute to mutual understanding of problems that affect the welfare of the economy as a whole.

Corporations and labor unions must limit the influence they exert on the private lives of their members. Unions must continue to develop adequate grievance procedures and greater opportunities for legitimate opposition. Professional organizations and trade associations should conduct their affairs on a democratic basis.

Pension rights should vest more rapidly and fully, to improve the mobility of employees.

Barriers to the older workers must be removed. While women will maintain and enrich the home and the family, those whose children have left home for school, and those who are not married, are increasingly able to contribute their talents to jobs and voluntary organizations. They may well be the country's largest pool of inadequately used ability. Their enlarging opportunity will help significantly to meet the nation's needs.

Economic Growth

The economy should grow at the maximum rate consistent with primary dependence upon free enterprise and the avoidance of marked inflation. Increased investment in the public sector is compatible with this goal.

Such growth is essential to move toward our goal of full employment, to provide jobs for the approximately 13,500,000 net new additions to the work force during the next ten years; to improve the standard of living; and to assure United States competitive strength.

Public policies, particularly an overhaul of the tax system, including depreciation allowances, should seek to improve the climate for new investment and the balancing of investment with consumption. We should give attention to policies favoring completely new ventures which involve a high degree of risk and growth potential.

In practice, we must seek to keep unemployment consistently below 4 per cent of the labor force. Reduction in unemployment and operation of the economy closer to its capacity require steadily growing consumer demand, and proper management of interest rates, money supply, and government budget surpluses and deficits. If Congress were to raise or lower tax rates more readily, stabilization of the economy would be facilitated.

Increased reliance on research and improved technology will provide opportunity for American industry to expand its markets by producing new and authentically improved products rather than by too great a dependence on superficial changes in style. To these ends, universities, research institutes, governments, and industries should greatly increase basic research, the ultimate source of new ideas and new products.

Education at all levels should aim at a more capable and more flexible work force.

There is no consensus among the economists as to the growth rate those measures will produce. The chapter by Messrs. Stein and Denison presents carefully documented evidence indicating an annual increase in the gross national product of 3.4 per cent without extraordinary stimulating measures. Other estimates made with equal care indicate higher growth rates up to 5 per cent annually. The higher the growth rate, the fewer additional extraordinary measures will be necessary. If the growth rate is lower, it will impel consideration of higher taxes, increased quantity of labor, and the greater individual effort and sacrifice exemplified by forced savings and reduced consumption.

There is no merit in a statistical race with the Communist nations. The real test is capacity to achieve our own over-all goals.

Our economic decisions must be governed by ability to meet our needs for defense, for education, for a healthy private economy with rising standards of living, and for foreign aid.

Technological Change

Technological change should be promoted and encouraged as a powerful force for advancing our economy. It should be planned for and introduced with sensitive regard for any adverse impact upon individuals.

Education on a large scale is provided by many industrial firms for their personnel. Such activities combined with advance planning can minimize unemployment due to rapid technological change. Where re-employment within the industry is not possible, retraining must be carried out through vocational programs managed locally and financed through state and federal funds.

Private initiative can accelerate technological change in our non-military economy.

In our military economy, the federal government must strengthen the management of its programs in technology by improving its supervisory and contracting procedures. It must avoid undertaking impracticable and unnecessary projects and thereby wasting scientific and engineering manpower. Both government and industry need to encourage that combination of engineering and management talent which can master our increasingly complex technology.

We must continue to adapt the management and organization of the Department of Defense to changing military needs. We must encourage fundamental advances in military technology and their rapid introduction. Through bold and tough-minded management we should reduce lead-time in bringing new weapons to operational use. Civilian and military leaders, with the help and understanding of Congress, must make and make stick the difficult inter-service decisions required for the selection of major weapons systems from among available alternatives. The increasing complexity of these systems, the time required for their development, and their fabulous cost give these decisions overriding importance. Conservation of time is critical; it may be more important than the conservation of funds. Saving time is likely to save money.

Throughout the economy, collective bargaining between management and labor will have a marked influence on the process of technological change. It should anticipate needed adjustments, through retraining and transfer policies, and, if layoffs become necessary, by such means as severance pay. Problems of technological change will require farsighted planning by industry, labor, and government on a cooperative basis.

Public and private leadership are required where whole areas are economically distressed. As Mr. Watson's chapter suggests, measures to encourage industries to move to such communities and relocation programs for individuals are justified. Consideration should be given, where necessary, to state and federal government participation in loans and grants to aid community efforts and to underwrite support for programs of retraining.

Agriculture

The relative financial return to agriculture in the economy has deteriorated. The ultimate goal must be a supply-demand equilibrium to permit the market, with a fair return to farmers, to determine the manpower and capital committed to this sector of the economy. To avoid shock to the economy, this goal should be approached by gradual stages.

A separate problem concerns the 50 per cent of farmers who operate at subsistence levels and produce only 10 per cent of farm output. For them new opportunities must be found through training and through location of new industries in farm areas. During this decade non-farm jobs must be found—where possible locally—for about 1.5 million farm operators who now earn less than $1,500 a year.

Mr. Soth's chapter makes clear that farm industry is a notable example of rapid technological change and difficult adjustment. Productivity in agriculture rose in the last decade about three times as fast as in the economy as a whole. Therefore, more resources—more people, and more investment—are employed than are required to meet our domestic and foreign needs.

Farmers are leaving the industry. There are a million fewer

families operating farms than there were in 1950, a decline in the decade of about 20 per cent. This shift of occupation contributes to our economic growth, and ultimately to a healthy farm industry.

Major measures to reduce oversupply must include much increased retirement of farm land, with emphasis on whole farms. To increase demand we need energetic development of overseas markets. Agriculture could be competitive in world markets if there were reciprocal lowering of quotas and other trade barriers. In selected areas, our surpluses can meet human want without disrupting the markets of other nations. Improvement of nutritional levels for many Americans would not only increase the work efficiency of our population but also reduce farm surpluses.

Government programs of help for farmers, including price supports and other means to prevent collapse of incomes, will continue to be necessary for some time; they must be so managed that they cushion the shock of the transition, without unduly slowing the pace of necessary fundamental adjustments.

Living Conditions

We must remedy slum conditions, reverse the process of decay in the larger cities, and relieve the necessity for low-income and minority groups to concentrate there.

We should also seek solutions for haphazard suburban growth, and provide an equitable sharing of the cost of public services between central cities and suburbs. In many parts of the country, the goal should be a regional pattern which provides for a number of urban centers, each with its own industries, its own educational, cultural and recreational institutions, and a balanced population of various income levels and backgrounds. The needs of a growing population for parks and recreation must be met.

To these ends, we need dedicated private leadership, together with public and private action to provide improved services and facilities for residents of slum areas, stepped-up urban renewal programs, and an increased rate of construction of lower-priced homes and apartment units. Effective regional planning is essential, and there should be fresh emphasis on considerations of beauty. We should seek elimination of racial discrimination in housing.

Experience in the past decade has taught us some of the steps which must be taken. Further urban renewal programs, costing as much as $4 billion per year, are needed to purchase city land, clear it of delapidated buildings, and make it available for residential and business use. Roads and rapid transit facilities should be planned and financed as a unit, and effective regional planning should deal with all transportation, industrial location, and government-assisted housing plans. Services to residents of slum areas, including particularly education, need the same emphasis as slum clearance.

Because experimentation is needed and solutions to these problems may well vary from place to place, federal housing policies should permit local authorities much more discretion. Where local laws prohibit discrimination, federal officials should withhold assistance from housing projects that violate the local fair housing policies. Consideration should be given to federal support, for a limited period, of an intensive moderate-cost housing program, as Mrs. Wurster's chapter recommends, under which state and local governments could experiment with mortgage insurance, low-interest loans, non-profit corporations and other forms of industry-municipal cooperation.

Private and civic initiative are vital to such programs. The attainment of these goals will involve massive investment. In the long run this will pay handsome social and economic dividends. . . .

1818952

TOWARD BALANCED GROWTH

Daniel P. Moynihan

The perils of choosing national goals on the basis of inadequate or misinterpreted information are surely matched by the dangers that arise when progress toward national goals that have already been chosen is assessed on a similarly inadequate basis. The difficulty with the national goals is that they too quickly become standards by which to judge not the future but the present. In a sense, they institutionalize the creation of discontent. The setting of future goals, no matter how distant, drains legitimacy from present conditions. Once it is established and agreed upon that the future will have to be very different from the present, it becomes absurd to be content with the present. The past is annihilated. The most extraordinary progress counts for little if it has brought society only to a middling point in an uncompleted journey.

Yet the creation of discontent is in part the object of goal setting. Discontent is commonly a condition of creativity in an individual or a society: it is at all events an immensely useful spur to progress. The art of national goal setting, then, is to be realistic about what can be attained, and to use social data in such a way as to enable both the expert and lay publics to understand that progress toward any seriously difficult goal is going to take place by increments, and to measure that progress as it occurs (or fails to occur, which is often the case).

The most distinctive success in an effort of this kind has concerned the Employment Act of 1946 which set forth the national goal of promoting "maximum employment, production, and purchasing power." This undertaking was somewhat preceded and very much followed by an intensive and brilliantly successful effort to develop employment and income accounts which would make it possible to measure the Nation's approach to the somewhat attenuated goal set forth in the statute. Given the cyclical nature of much economic activity, periods of movement toward a high level of employment have alternated with periods of movement away from that condition, but *by and large* over the intervening quarter century the Nation has learned a good deal more about how actually to attain that goal, and has achieved a much stronger consensus than it ought to have attained.

The two areas of conspicuous failure have involved young workers and black workers, but even here changes are occurring in the direction of the Employment Act. Youth unemployment rates have risen sharply from those of the mid-1940's. The reasons for this are disputed, but certainly include declining rates of farm employment, and higher levels of youth wages, both of which represent improved income positions for those with jobs. The situation had nonetheless become intolerable by the 1960's, and a range of more or less permanent youth-employment programs were instituted. If they have not achieved the goals of the 1946 act, they certainly suggest that the Nation would be even worse off in this particular respect had not the existence of those goals added to the presumption of the necessity and normality of the responding programs. Similarly, in the period following the adoption of the Employment Act the position of black workers worsened with respect to that of white. A 2-to-1 ratio of unemployment rates was for 15 years a seemingly fixed feature of the economy. But this in turn hastened the adoption of programs in the 1960's heavily directed toward the problems of Negro employment. Moreover, at the very end of that decade the 2-to-1 ratio began to diminish. How permanent this change will be no one would yet want to predict, but again the fact is that accurate social data have made possible an increasingly informed and effective national debate on the achievement of the national goal of "maximum employment, production, and purchasing power."

In 1964, almost two decades after Congress adopted the national goals of the Employment Act, the Economic Opportunity Act went beyond the "maximizing" standards of the earlier legislation to proclaim the absolute goal "to eliminate the paradox of poverty in the midst of plenty in this Nation. . . ." The Economic Opportunity Act proclaimed this goal and a wide range of further legislative enactments set out to attain it. In statistical terms, there had been a remarkable success. During the first half of the 1960's there was very little decline in poverty, as measured by the subsequent Social Security Administration index. The number of Negro poor actually rose during 1960, 1961, 1962, and it was not until 1965 that it fell below the level of 1959. However, in the years that followed there was a near to precipitate decline in the number of persons living in poverty, while rates of exit reached 9 percent or better in 2 recent years.

Between 1964 and 1969, although the general population increased 25.3 million, the number of poor declined by 11.8 million persons, to a total of 24.3 million. Should that absolute level of decline persist, poverty will just about have been eliminated by the end of the present decade. This would mean an historic change in the economic position of black Americans. As late as 1962, 56 percent of blacks were living below the poverty level. By 1969 this proportion had dropped to 31 percent. This in itself is a change that might readily be recorded as a social transformation. During this period there has been a sharp increase in real family income for all recorded groups in the society. The overall ratio of Negro family income to that of white rose from 54 percent in 1965 to 61 percent in 1969, while for young married couples outside the South, parity, for the first time in history, was attained between black and white.

At the same time it would appear that profound changes took place during the 1960's—or first were recorded during that era—bearing on racial attitudes in the United States, and on the general role of the black citizen. After generations of massive disfranchisement in the South and a relative absence of significant political roles elsewhere in the Nation, the Negro electorate increased enormously in the aftermath of the Voting Rights Act of 1965, while Negro-elected officials became an increasingly familiar feature of urban government in all sections of the country. There were not less pronounced changes in racial attitudes, or at least attitudes that emerged from careful surveys were considerably different from those that had been assumed. Thus the study "Racial Attitudes in Fifteen American Cities" prepared for the National Advisory Commission on Civil Disorders presented a picture at once remarkably at odds with the view of the Commission's formal report, and with the general stereotype of rising racial hostility. American citizens black and white alike, emerged as notably accepting of one another, and fundamentally persuaded that it is individual effort and capacity that count in life, as against caste or class consignment.

Similarly, while the issue of school integration remained troubled and in ways increasingly disputatious during the 15 years following the Supreme Court decision in *Brown vs. Bd. of Education,* and white attitudes were thought either to have remained frozen or to have actually deteriorated, in May 1970 the Gallup Poll reported just the opposite. In 1963 six in ten Southern white parents had said they would object to sending their children to schools where Negroes are enrolled. By 1970 this proportion had dropped to only about one parent in six. The Gallup Poll remarked, "This finding represents one of the most dramatic shifts in the history of public opinion polling."

Yet this particular reality is counterbalanced by another. The 1960's not only saw immense changes in the objective situation of the black and the poor in America, it saw also an even greater escalation of the rhetoric of denunciation of the society for the failings that are, in a sense, implied by the very existence of such categories. This is not an inexplicable phenomenon. For well over a century observers of American society have been turning out elaborations of de Tocqueville's original perception that as conditions for a group improve, the gap that remains grows steadily less tolerable, with the rough result that the better things are the worse they are said to be. More recently social scientists have formulated this in terms of "goal gradients," with the hope that the phenomenon cannot only be described, but can be measured. But it remains part of the reality; part of the price a society pays when it consciously seeks to change things for the better.

A not dissimilar experience probably awaits the Nation as it moves—assuming it does—toward the conscious adoption of a national growth policy, as proposed by the President in his 1970 state of the Union message. There seems to be general agreement that under any circumstances the United States population will continue to grow for the next 30 or so years, and that this growth will result in adding 60 to 100 million persons to the population by the year 2000. (A fifth or more of this increase will come from immigration.) The extraordinary quality of elemental social data such as this is that, once it is known, all knowers are implicated in the knowledge.

The American population has been growing for three centuries. Somehow, however, it is not until now that this knowledge has forced itself on the national consciousness in a form suggesting that preparations ought to be made to accommodate the change which, in a sense, has already occurred because it is known that it will occur. It is abundantly clear that it is no longer sufficient to equate satisfactory national growth with a 4.2-percent increase in the gross national product. It is not clear, however, that those who manage this not especially remarkable perception are capable at the same time of seeing that it is only because growth in the GNP has come to be so large and so regular, that it is now open to the Nation to discuss which sectors of the GNP are to be encouraged, which discouraged. Similarly, as the American population accumulates in complex urban conurbations largely located on the coastal periphery of the Nation (including the Great Lakes area), it becomes possible to grow increasingly critical of the course of urban development, without recognizing that has been the wealth generated by this movement that makes possible the consideration of more elegant alternatives. Perhaps most significantly, as a growing proportion of the population becomes well educated and affluent, it becomes ever more likely that it will identify its own interests in redirected or even terminated national growth with that of the still much larger proportion of the population which still properly looks forward to a fairly straight-line increase in earnings and income. All in all, the decade of national growth policy is not likely to be an especially peaceable one.

More then will be the need for increasingly accurate and easy-to-follow social data that describes the past and present, and reasonably projects the future. A new role for social science emerges. If government is to be directed in terms of general policies, such as a national growth policy, it becomes increasingly important to be able to make some assessment in advance of the effects of particular interventions on the system as a whole. This is a form of evaluation that predicts results rather than simply measuring them. It is, in effect, evaluation in advance: a large, challenging, promising goal—a goal which if seriously and successfully pursued, holds out the prospect of a system of self-government that grows increasingly meaningful as citizens are asked to make choices among options that are not partially, or even deceptively, but fully described by governments which thereafter can be held just as fully accountable.

Do Americans wish this to happen? No one is in a position to say. Yet there exists at this moment a fact of very considerable significance. The Eighteenth Decennial Census has just been taken. It was not only the most comprehensive, detailed, informative census ever attempted, it also produced (at least by all early indications) far the most willing and universal response ever from the people themselves. This was not a routine event. A considerable effort had been mounted to restrict the scope of the census, and to present it as in some way an intrusion into the personal life of the citizenry. The citizenry thought otherwise. It is a good sign that in the decade ahead we shall considerably enhance our abilities not only to collect such data, but to put it to the good purpose of democracy.

THE QUALITY OF AMERICAN LIFE

The Commission on Population Growth and the American Future

We are concerned with population trends only as they impede or enhance the realization of those values and goals cherished in, by, and for American society.

What values? Whose goals? As a Commission, we do not set ourselves up as an arbiter of those fundamental questions. Over the decades ahead, the American people themselves will provide the answers, but we have had to judge proposals for action on population-related issues against their contribution to some version of the good life for this society and, for that matter, the world. What we have sought are measures that promise to move demographic trends in the right direction and, at the same time, have favorable direct effects on the quality of life.

We know that problems of quality exist from the variety of indicators that fall short of what is desirable and possible. There are inequalities in the opportunities for life itself evidenced by the high frequency of premature death and the lower life expectancy of the poor. There is a whole range of preventable illness such as the currently high and rising rate of venereal disease. There are a number of congenital deficiencies attributable to inadequate prenatal care and obstetrical services and, in some cases, to genetic origin. Not all such handicaps are preventable, but they occur at rates higher than if childbearing were confined to ages associated with low incidence and if genetic counseling were more widely available.

Innate human potential often has not been fully developed because of the inadequate quality of various educational, social, and environmental factors. Particularly with regard to our ethnic minorities and the female half of the population, there are large numbers of people occupying social roles that do not capitalize on their latent abilities and interest, or elicit a dedicated effort and commitment. There is hunger and malnutrition, particularly damaging to infants and young children, that should not be tolerated in the richest nation the world has ever known. Sensitive observers perceive in our population a certain frustration and alienation that appears to go beyond what is endemic in the human condition; the sources of these feelings should be explored and better understood.

And we can also identify and measure the limiting factors, the inequalities of opportunity, and the environmental hazards that give rise to such limitations in the quality of life—for example, inadequate distribution of and access to health, education, and welfare services; cultural and social constraints on human performance and development associated with race, ethnic origin, sex, and age; barriers to full economic and cultural participation; unequal access to environmental quality; and unequal exposure to environmental hazard.

There are many other problems of quality in American life. Thus, alongside the challenges of population growth and distribution is the challenge of population quality. The goal of all population policy must be to make better the life that is actually lived.

Opportunity and Choice

While slower population growth provides opportunities, it does not guarantee that they will be well used. It simply opens up a range of choices we would not have otherwise. Much depends on how wisely the choices are made and how well the opportunities are used. For example, slower population growth would enable us to provide a far better education for children at no increase in total costs. We want the opportunity presented by slower growth to be used this way, but we cannot guarantee that it will be. The wise use of opportunities such as this depends on public and private decisions yet to be made.

Slowing population growth can "buy time" for the solution of many problems; but, without the determined, long-range application of technical and political skills, the opportunity will be lost.

For example, our economic and political systems reward the exploitation of virgin resources and impose no costs on polluters. The technology exists for solving many of these problems. But proper application of this technology will require the recognition of public interests, the social inventiveness to discover institutional arrangements for channeling private interests without undue government regulation, and the political courage and skill needed to institute the necessary changes.

Slower population growth offers time in which to accomplish these things. But if all we do with breathing time is breathe, the value of the enterprise is lost.

Population change does not take place in a vacuum. Its consequences are produced through its joint action with technology, wealth, and the institutional structures of society. Hence, a study of the American future, insofar as it is influenced by population change, cannot ignore, indeed it must comment upon, the features of the society that make population growth troublesome or not.

Hence, while we are encouraged by the improvement in average income that will be yielded by slower population growth, we are concerned with the persistence of vast differences in the distribution of income, which has remained fixed now for a quarter of a century.

While we are encouraged by the relief that slower population growth offers in terms of pressure on resources and the environment, we are aware of the inadequacy of the nation's general approach to these problems.

We rely largely on private market forces for conducting the daily business of production and consumption. These work well in general and over the short run to reduce costs, husband resources, increase productivity, and provide a higher material standard of living for the individual. But the market mechanism has been ineffective in allocating the social and environmental costs of production and consumption, primarily because public policies and programs have not provided the proper signals nor required that such costs be borne by production and consumption activities. Nor has the market mechanism been able to provide socially acceptable incomes for people who, by virtue of age, incapacity, or injustice, are poorly equipped to participate in the market system for producing and distributing income.

Our economy's use of the earth's finite resources, and the accompanying pollution or deterioration of the quality of water, air, and natural beauty, has neglected some of the fundamental requirements for acceptable survival. Often the time horizon for both public and private decisions affecting the economy has been too short. It seems clear that market forces alone cannot be relied upon to achieve our social and environmental goals, for reasons that make exchange, though the main organizing principle, inadequate without appropriate institutional and legal underpinnings.

In short, even if we achieve the stabilization of population, our economic, environmental, governmental, and social problems will still be with us unless by will and intelligence we develop policies to deal with the other sources of these problems. The fact that such policies have shown little conspicuous success in the past gives rise to the skepticism we have expressed above in our discussion of the relations between government and population growth.

The problem is not so much the impact of population on government as the adequacy of government to respond to the challenge of population and the host of issues that surround it. Long-term planning is necessary to deal with environmental and resource problems, but there are only beginning signs that government is motivated or organized to undertake it. A major commitment is required to bring minorities into the mainstream of American life, but the effort so far is inadequate. It is clear that the "real city" that comprises the metropolis requires a real government to manage its affairs; but the nation is still trying to manage the affairs of complex, interconnected, metropolitan communities with fragmented institutional structures inherited from the 18th century.

Population, then, is clearly not the whole problem. But it is clearly part of the problem, and it is the part given us as the special responsibility of this Commission. How policy in this area should be shaped depends on how we define the objectives of policy in respect to population.

Policy Goals

Ideally, we wish to develop recommendations worthwhile in themselves, which at the same time, speak to population issues. These recommendations are consistent with American ethical values in that they aim to enhance individual freedom while simultaneously promoting the common good. It is important to reiterate that our policy recommendations embody goals either intrinsically desirable or worthwhile for reasons other than demographic objectives.

Moreover, some of the policies we recommend are irreversible in a democratic society, in the sense that freedoms once introduced cannot be rescinded lightly. This irreversibility characterizes several of the important policies recommended by this Commission. We are not really certain of the demographic impact of some of the changes implied by our recommendations. One or two could conceivably increase the birthrate by indirectly subsidizing the bearing of children. The rest may depress the birthrate below the level of replacement. We are not concerned with this latter contingency because, if sometime in the future the nation wishes to increase its population growth, there are many possible ways to try this; a nation's growth should not depend on the ignorance and misfortune of its citizenry. In any event, it is naive to expect that we can fine-tune such trends.

In the broadest sense, the goals of the population policies we recommend aim at creating social conditions wherein the desired values of individuals, families, and communities can be realized; equalizing social and economic opportunities for women and members of disadvantaged minorities; and enhancing the potential for improving the quality of life.

At the educational level, we wish to increase public awareness and understanding of the implications of population change and simultaneously further our knowledge of the causes and consequences of population change.

In regard to childbearing and child-rearing, the goals of our recommendations are to: (1) maximize information and knowledge about human reproduction and its implications for the family; (2) improve the quality of the setting in which children are raised; (3) neutralize insofar as it is practicable and consistent with other values those legal, social, and institutional pressures that historically have been mainly pronatalist in character; and (4) enable individuals to avoid unwanted childbearing, thereby enhancing their ability to realize their preferences. These particular policies are aimed at facilitating the social, economic, and legal conditions within our society which increase ethical responsibility and the opportunity for unbiased choice in human reproduction and child-rearing. At the same time, by enhancing the individual's opportunity to make a real choice between having few children and having many, between parenthood and childlessness, and between marriage and the single state, these policies together will undoubtedly slow our rate of population growth and accelerate the advent of population stabilization.

In connection with the geographic distribution of population, our objectives are to ease and guide the process of population movement, to facilitate planning for the accommodation of movements, and to increase the freedom of choice in residential locations.

To these ends, therefore, we offer our recommendations in the belief that the American people, collectively and individually, should confront the issues of population growth and reach deliberate informed decisions about the family's and society's size as they affect the achievement of personal and national values . . . .

ENVIRONMENTAL GROWING PAINS

Resources for the Future, Inc.

The volume of new legislation and other federal and state actions taken in 1972 make it clearer than ever that environmental quality, a minority concern less than a decade ago, has been accepted by most Americans as a major national goal. But some of the difficulties of realizing this aspiration also became more apparent during the year: conflicts with other goals such as economic growth, national security, or budget balancing; and practical problems of designing public programs that don't attempt too much or too little, and of administering and enforcing them.

Two of the most important developments—sweeping revision of the Federal Water Pollution Control Act, and efforts toward setting up new programs for air quality—are discussed in separate articles below. But other significant 1972 legislation at the federal level has not stood still.

The Noise Control Act characterizes noise as a serious polluter of the environment and for the first time recognizes a direct federal responsibility for doing something about it. The Environmental

Protection Agency (EPA) is directed to take the lead in establishing emission standards, with the notable exceptions that primary responsibility for aircraft standards is given to the Federal Aviation Administration and for railroads and motor carriers to the Department of Transportation.

The Environmental Pesticide Control Act gives the federal government much broader authority than it has had under the Insecticide, Fungicide, and Rodenticide Act of 1947. While that act required registration and correct labeling of pesticides, the procedures for banning dangerous products were cumbersome and there were no penalties for misuse of pesticides once they had been properly labeled. The new law provides penalties for misuse for different categories of application and for a permit system that will differentiate between general and restricted use. It also tightens and simplifies enforcement procedures. EPA will be the responsible agency; some measure of state participation is provided for, although few of the details are spelled out. One section of the new act provides for indemnities to cover losses sustained by persons holding supplies of a pesticide whose registration has been suspended "to prevent an imminent hazard." This provision has been severely criticized by many environmentalists. They feel that it runs counter to a recent trend in the courts toward shifting the burden of proof to polluters and, from this point of view, could be a dangerous precedent. Moreover, prospects of high indemnity cost might make regulators hesitate to exercise their authority. On the other hand, no indemnities are due a claimant who continues to produce a pesticide after having knowledge that the product does not meet the requirements.

An act to regulate dumping of wastes in ocean and coastal waters prohibits discharge of high-level radioactive wastes and certain products related to chemical and biological warfare, and makes disposal of other materials subject to permit from EPA.

A coastal zone management act provides federal funds to help coastal states develop land use plans that will balance needs for preservation against needs for industrial sites, power plants, port facilities, and recreation. In effect, this measure to protect ocean shorelines, estuaries, and wetlands is a segment of the broader national land use policy effort that failed of Congressional approval during the year.

In addition to cooperation called for in federally initiated programs, state activities reached a new high level in 1972. A *New York Times* survey last November reported that more than half of the 50 states had acted positively on a variety of environmental measures ranging from pollution control to limitation of population. In New York State, for example, voters approved a $1.15 billion bond issue for improving the environment. Florida adopted a constitutional amendment to permit buying more land for recreation, and voters there also approved a proposal to borrow $240 million to purchase land to be held against indiscriminate development. California voters approved creation of a public commission to control coastline development. In Colorado, voters turned down a proposal that the state spend $5 million to help prepare for the 1976 Winter Olympics, as an indication that they did not consider the expected economic benefits equal to the probable environmental damage. And several states established departments, commissions, or councils to deal with environmental problems.

Meanwhile there were difficulties and delays in administering the environmental programs. Some resulted from the large burden of fact finding for the determinations that EPA must make in establishing standards for air and water quality and for emissions of pollutants and in reviewing permits for waste discharges into streams. The Council on Environmental Quality (CEQ) also carried a heavy load in reviewing the impact statements prepared under the National Environmental Policy Act (NEPA)—statements required in connection with "major Federal actions significantly affecting the quality of the human environment."

Under NEPA, citizens may bring suit if they believe the act's purpose of preventing unnecessary environmental damage is not being carried out. Nearly 200 such suits were entered during the year, bringing to around 350 the total since the act went into effect at the start of 1970. Many of these cases, along with suits brought by or against EPA, have resulted in appeals to higher federal courts, so that a number of proposed government projects and EPA regulatory actions have been held up. It had been hoped that NEPA would be of assistance to the courts by providing guidelines in some complex and specialized areas. Thus far, CEQ and the Office of Management and Budget have done less than had been hoped toward policing administrative actions.

Some of the causes of delay may be reduced in the future as a larger body of judicial interpretations and precedents is established and all parties become more familiar with the comparatively new set of programs and procedures. The EPA workload, however, can be expected to increase, especially under the greatly expanded use of permits provided for in the new water quality act and the need for establishing an entirely new set of standards for noise.

CHAPTER 2

Managing the Economy

TODAY most Americans take it for granted that government has the capacity and the obligation to manage the economy in the national interest. Usually this means that governmental powers should be used to promote the kind of economic growth that will improve the national standard of living, prevent serious unemployment and unacceptable levels of inflation. Just how these goals are specifically defined over time and under different conditions is very important to the results produced. It is by no means clear that existing economic theories, governmental institutions and mechanisms can actually achieve specific goals; much still depends on the response of the private sector of the economy to government's economic goads and restraints, and the ways in which they are brought to bear.

In the early 1970's there was more public disillusionment with the possibilities for effective management of the economy than in the preceding decade. However, in the past seventy years, and more especially in the last thirty, government has been both pushed by politicians and pulled by events into a management role that once had been accepted as the responsibility of the private sector, aided but not guided by government.

Fiscal and monetary policies have emerged only in this century as important tools for managing the national economy. In the nineteenth century the federal government's largest asset was the public lands; by the liberal way in which it disposed of them to private interests, it was in effect engaging in a form of deficit financing. When it came to other forms of spending, however, fiscal conservatism and strong Presidential pressure restricted the role of the federal government. Numerous vetoes of government spending bills attest to the Executive's belief that the performance of the economy was a matter for private direction and that the role of government was to be a thrifty helpmate, not a co-director. The view that public debt had the same adverse effect on the nation's economic health as private debt had on private households acted as a spur to retire government debt when revenues were high and to cut expenditures when depression adversely affected revenues.

The tariff, revenue from land sales, and excise taxes were the major sources of revenue in the nineteenth century. Compared to other ways of raising revenue, the tariff was perhaps easiest to administer because it was applied directly where most money transactions in a money-short economy took place. But the tariff was political and sectional; tariffs were not levied simply on a revenue-raising basis, but on the basis of what sectional or political power could be brought to bear on specific tariff schedules. As a source of revenue, the tariff also had important drawbacks. In wartime, for example, when government needed increased revenue, tariff receipts fell. The levying of excise and income taxes during the Civil War was partly due to such decline. Although in 1872 the income tax along with many of the excises was dropped, the generally high level of tariff receipts at that time led to a problem of how to dispose of the surplus. One solution was to increase pension payments to veterans. With government's role in the economy limited, no effort was made to use fiscal policy consciously to manage the economy.

Monetary policies were equally unimportant a century ago. The National Banking Act of 1863 was passed as much to finance the Civil War as to provide a uniform national currency. Creation of money was tied to government bonds, not to the level of economic activity. However, the bond market tended to move in a direction opposite from the economy's; on the upswing, it discouraged the banks' acquisition of bonds at the very time the need for money was increasing. As a result, when a national financial crisis occurred in the mid-1890's and again in 1907, the government had to turn for rescue to private bankers like J. P. Morgan.

The Panic of 1907 started a study of a central banking system that resulted in the creation of the Federal Reserve System, in 1913. The resulting organization remains the cornerstone for the implementation of monetary policy today. Although it was recognized at the time that the System's activities might affect the economy significantly, this use of monetary power underwent a slow process of evolution and cautious experimentation.

World War I required a centrally directed mobilization of the nation's economic resources on a major scale for the first time. Under the pressure of wartime demands, it was impossible to rely on decentralized private decisionmaking to provide the resources or priority of allocations in their use that the market provided in more normal times. Planning to deal with this problem began in 1916 and by summer of 1917 had resulted in the creation of a War Industries Board (WIB). Staffed by civilians from various sectors of the private economy, the WIB had the power to determine how the Armed Forces' procurement needs would be met by American industry. Using a system of priorities and control over basic industrial commodities like steel, the WIB managed a significant part of the wartime economy.

The pressure of increased demand on limited resources had a major inflationary effect. Controlling prices became a major problem. Because the implications of direct government intervention in this area were regarded as serious in a predominantly private enterprise economy, the exercise of price-fixing powers was placed directly under President Woodrow Wilson (1913–1921).

In 1917–1918 government reached into the economic affairs of all Americans. Government support for collective bargaining was represented by the War Labor Board. The Fuel and Food Administrations exercised control over these areas so important to consumers. When privately owned and directed railroads had difficulty meeting the transportation needs of a war economy, they were taken over by the government. The Federal Reserve and Treasury cooperated in a major, successful undertaking to stimulate the public's purchase of Liberty Bonds in an effort unprecedented except during the Civil War.

The substantial federal deficit in 1918–1919, of course, had an expansionary effect on the economy. When war contracts were terminated and the country was returning to more normal conditions, however, there was a brief but severe depression. Wartime agencies had largely been dismantled, and the new Republican administration returned to the prewar philosophy that government's role was to encourage and aid business to operate the economy. Wartime collaboration of private and public sectors had paved the way. A new wave of prosperity seemed to confirm its wisdom.

Business and financial groups made strong claims on government in the 1920's to use its power and world position in their behalf. As a result of the war, the United States had become a mature creditor nation; American policy that insisted on repayment of war debts by our allies, and their insistence on reparations from the defeated, formed an important backdrop to overseas loans by American banks and foreign investments by other American firms. As a result, the export of American capital formed an important part of the underpinning for foreign purchases of American goods in the 1920's. A protective tariff policy closed or limited the domestic market for foreign goods that otherwise could have been used to pay for these purchases.

In some areas of the economy, especially agriculture, productive capacity outstripped demand. Caught between the cost of expanded facilities and acreage to meet wartime demand, and a revived foreign agriculture that erased that demand, the American farmer turned to government for assistance. However, proposals to deal with surplus production were defeated or vetoed until the enactment of the Agricultural Marketing Act of 1929. But its operation, in an economy moving rapidly into a tailspin, did little more than transfer the ownership of surplus farm products to the government.

Organized labor received little support from the federal government during the 1920's, except that the railway unions' position was buttressed by the Railway Labor Act of 1926. Even in prosperity, however, there was substantial unemployment. Today unemployment figures are watched closely as an indicator of the economy's condition, but in 1928 the Secretary of Labor did not know how many Americans were unemployed. In that decade of business prosperity, the level of unemployment was not regarded as a government responsibility.

Encouraged by the benevolent attitude of the federal government towards big business and by a rising stock market in the last half of the 1920's, a new merger movement took place. Assets of the 200 largest corporations not engaged in the financial business increased in the 1920's more than three and a half times as fast as national wealth. The performance of the economy came increasingly into the hands of business management, whose accountability to stockholders became tenuous as ownership of stock and, therefore, the power to control management, was increasingly dispersed.

But the popular theory that the economy was best directed by a self-adjusting market mechanism powered by business competition was not shaken by these developments. Although there was room in this theory for government to impose regulation to maintain equality of competitive opportunity or to prevent competitive abuses, government's role was still held to be basically that of protecting and promoting private enterprise. While consistent with traditional American faith in individualism and competition, this view ignored the fact that the rise of big business and the growth of a complex, interdependent society and world economy had undermined some of the basic assumptions that had encouraged relatively heavy reliance on free markets for managing the American economy.

If an individual lived by the traditional American philosophy of individual effort and responsibility and reaped its promised rewards, it was President Herbert Hoover (1929–1933). Although when the nation slipped from prosperity into depression, he had sufficient flexibility to support expanded government influence in the agricultural and financial sectors (as exemplified by creation of the Federal Farm Board and the Reconstruction Finance Corporation), he was not prepared to see the federal government intervene directly to manage the economy. While his position on governmental restraint had been unquestionably supported by the American people in the prosperous twenties, it was not tenable economically or politically in the depression-ridden thirties. Hoover's resounding defeat in 1932 by Franklin D. Roosevelt confirmed this beyond question. The businessman had been toppled from his throne by the severity of the depression. The new Congress was more than willing to cooperate with the new President.

From his first days in office, Roosevelt acted to increase the freedom of government to manage the economy. His first steps were to eliminate monetary restraints on the expansionist policies that his administration was preparing to take. For example, as long as the United States remained on the gold standard, gold imposed a major constraint on inflationary monetary policies. One of the first

New Deal measures, therefore, was to suspend the convertibility of dollars into gold. The export of gold was temporarily halted and later limited to transactions between the United States and foreign treasuries or central banks. Meanwhile, by legislative fiat, gold was devalued 40 percent in terms of dollars.

While thus insulating expansionary economic policies from the constraining effects of gold, the administration and Congress changed other aspects of banking and monetary policy. The Bank Holiday of 1933 was intended to restore public confidence in the nation's banks. Those that reopened, and they constituted most that had closed, did so under government guarantee of their liquidity. Meanwhile, in the Emergency Banking Act of 1933, the Federal Reserve System was authorized to lend to member banks with wide discretion on the security offered. A few months later the Banking Act of 1933 provided for federal insurance of bank deposits and separated commercial from investment banking. These actions were complemented by authority for the President to issue unsecured currency under the Thomas Amendment to the Agricultural Adjustment Act. A fund of some $2 billion, accruing from revaluation of gold, gave the government power to control the monetary consequences of expansionary policies. These were first steps in moving away from the presumably self-regulating mechanisms and decentralized decision making that had governed the economy towards limited but deliberate management for specified objectives. In fact, Roosevelt himself referred to these measures of 1933 as producing a "managed currency."

Like Hoover, however, Roosevelt initially accepted the desirability of a balanced federal budget. Unlike Hoover's, Roosevelt's approach to a balanced budget was a theoretical one, something that should be achieved and, if the economy returned to normal, would be achieved. In practice, this approach left considerable latitude for unbalanced budgets, and they characterized the Roosevelt years.

In keeping with the basic philosophy that government must keep its house in order, unbalanced budgets were treated as emergency departures from sound practice. But they involved government expenditures larger than government receipts. While Lord Keynes would later provide an elegant economic rationale for such an imbalance as a stimulant to the economy, the First New Deal was content to label them "relief." And relief was a pragmatic response to a practical problem. In terms of economic effects, however, it made no difference whether money spent by the Works Progress Administration (WPA) or its counterparts was called "pump priming," "relief," or "deficit spending," it put money into circulation and helped take up the slack left by the drying up of private investment. However, going into debt to seek a new prosperity made little sense to most Americans, and Roosevelt was very much aware of it. In December 1935, for example, a poll showed that 70 percent of the American people believed it was necessary to balance the budget and start reducing the public debt. Another poll just after the 1936 elections produced the same result. Apparently, deficit spending as a stimulant to the economy was neither understood nor condoned by the electorate. It was clearly unsettling to businessmen, many of whom had already parted company with Roosevelt.

Awareness of these deep-seated convictions undoubtedly strengthened Roosevelt's own belief that sound public finance called for reduced government expenditures as the private sector recovered. And this awareness contributed to his balanced budget proposal in 1937, accompanied by some reduction of relief expenditures. Budget balancing had the enthusiastic support of Secretary of the Treasury Henry Morgenthau, but it was opposed by Federal Reserve Chairman Marriner Eccles. Eccles had been influential in the adoption of the 1935 legislation that had expanded the Federal Reserve's powers, and it was his firm conviction that they should be used deliberately to influence the economy. Eccles protested that a balanced budget would undo much that had been accomplished for recovery, a fact not without significance in view of the continuing high rate of unemployment.

When the economy went into a sharp recession in the fall of 1937, criticism of New Deal recovery policies mounted. One view was that these policies had discouraged private investment and that tax reduction or other concessions to business were necessary. Another view was that the power of concentrated wealth and big business had caused the slump either deliberately to harass the administration or because excessive private power had been exercised to protect prices at the expense of employment and production. If so, vigorous antitrust action was in order. The Temporary

National Economic Committee was created in April 1938 to look into this question.

Substantial evidence was available to government economists, who in turn passed it on to Roosevelt, that the decline in government expenditures had caused a significant drop in national income. The mechanisms developed for government spending since 1933 had built up important political clienteles. These considerations contributed to Roosevelt's decision, announced in April 1938, to resume large-scale deficit spending. While some of these measures involved existing programs, which could be classified as relief, Roosevelt also called for $1.162 million for public works and $300 million for housing, making a total of over $3 billion, which he hoped would start pushing national income from its depressed level of $56 billion to the full-employment level of over $80 billion.

In this way, as a practical response to a pressing economic and political problem, the nation gradually came to associate deficit spending with a centrally directed effort to move the economy towards a goal of full employment. However, while he made this connection in his public speeches, Roosevelt, who was a politician, not a theoretician, did not attach to it the type of theory that Lord Keynes had worked out. From a variety of sources, Roosevelt took what he wanted to fit his needs, as he saw them. Deficit spending was only one part of wide-ranging measures that included efforts to stimulate competition, restructure parts of the economy, and redistribute income. Nevertheless, he saw that government could play a major role in stimulating the economy if business failed to do so. In his 1939 budget message he said: "We cannot by a simple legislative act raise the level of national income, but our experience in the last few years has amply demonstrated that through wise fiscal policies and other acts of government we can do much to stimulate it." What had started as necessary pragmatic experimentation to manage the economy for recovery was becoming accepted public policy on the eve of World War II.

Organizational changes marked the change. The Bureau of the Budget, which since 1920 had been a key office in managing federal fiscal matters, was transferred from the Treasury to the Executive Office of the President in 1939. At the same time, an economist was named to one of the newly created positions of administrative assistant to the President. These steps helped to lay the groundwork for systematic and informed executive direction of budget making for national economic objectives.

None of the measures adopted by the New Deal solved the basic problem of continuing unemployment, but defense expenditures and involvement in over four years of global war pressed the nation's economic resources, including manpower, to their limits. As in World War I, the economy had to be centrally managed. The rationing of civilian goods and resultant enforced savings constituted a backlog of postwar consumer demand while deficit financing to meet wartime demands put large amounts of government securities in private hands, offering the potential for major postwar investment. The expansionary possibilities of this situation suggested that government might have to use the monetary and fiscal powers with which it had been experimenting in the 1930's to keep the postwar economy on a stable course of economic growth.

During the thirties, economists had talked seriously of secular stagnation in the economy and the possibility that, as an economically mature nation, the United States had few prospects of economic growth. The war changed these views. A people who had suffered through a decade of prewar economic distress was determined that it should not be repeated when peace returned, and politicians in both major parties recognized the imperative of this demand. In the 1944 elections, both Republicans and Democrats called for recognition of government's responsibility to maintain a healthy economy.

The government's expanded role in the wartime economy helped refine the tools that could be used to exercise this responsibility. Attention was especially focused on taxation to affect consumption and investment. Accelerated depreciation for corporate income tax purposes was used to encourage business to provide new facilities for war production. As part of the wartime financing program, collection of taxes on income as it was earned was initiated. Since all wage-earning groups were included, changes in income taxation could be expected to affect a large segment of the population directly, in a relatively short time. Income taxation of this type has a stabilizing effect. A decline in pretax income is partially offset by a decline in tax liability. Therefore, the amount of income available for consumption does not drop as sharply as pretax income, with a resultant cushioning effect on the impact of recession or depression.

Conversely, increased income tax liability in a rising economy exercises a restraining influence on excessive demand. Social security taxation has a similar effect. Taxes paid in a booming economy reduce the amount of disposable consumer income, while the payment of benefits in a declining economy offsets some of the loss of private income. Since these mechanisms are actuated by the level of economic activity and have a countercyclical effect, they are called "built-in stabilizers."

Beardsley Ruml, who had suggested the wartime pay-as-you-go income tax, adapted the "automatic" concept to balancing the federal budget. Recognizing the hold that the balanced budget concept had among the American people, he suggested that the federal budget should be balanced at full employment. Using this approach, there would automatically be a budget deficit if the economy was not operating at full employment and a budget surplus if the economy was booming. In short, a full-employment budget would automatically exercise countercyclical pressures whether the economy's performance overshot or undershot the full-employment level.

Regardless of whether emphasis in managing the economy was placed on changes in government expenditures or revenue, these were but alternate routes to a postwar goal of high or full employment in a growing economy. Consensus on this objective led to adoption of the Employment Act of 1946. The language of this statute, reflecting compromises between those who feared that government might use its power too vigorously to insure full employment and those who feared that it would not act vigorously enough, called for "maximum" rather than "full" employment and required government to use all "its plans, functions and resources," to reach this objective. The Employment Act of 1946 represented a landmark in the transition from reliance on decentralized private decision making to centralized responsibility for planning the context in which such decisions would be made. Without minimizing the role of private enterprise, the Act clearly placed the final responsibility on government for maintaining employment and economic growth. Maintenance of stable prices, which later became a major problem, received little attention.

During most of the later 1940's and 1950's, unemployment was not a serious problem. Pent up consumer demand and numerous technological innovations ranging from television to computers, supplemented by an ambitious program of foreign economic and military aid and a substantial defense budget, kept the American economy moving upwards. Recessions occurred, but they were shorter lived and less severe than earlier ones. The fact that the economy's upward movement was accompanied by a moderate inflation did not displease the American people, since their incomes in real terms kept ahead of the rising prices.

Presidents Truman (1945–1953) and Eisenhower did not rely heavily on the "new economics" to guide the economy. The Eisenhower administration placed price stability ahead of growth and seemed reluctant to use the stimulative tools of modern fiscal policy despite the fact that from 1953 to 1960 the nation's economic growth rate was below long-term trends. In 1958 when private spending was declining at an annual rate of $20 billion, Eisenhower proposed only a $1 billion increase in government spending and refused to support a cut in taxes.

The Eisenhower administration's preference for monetary policy as the primary instrument in managing the economy had serious weaknesses. Restraints on the money supply probably checked realization of the nation's full economic potential and in effect discriminated against debtors and low-income groups in favor of corporations and high-income groups. "Tight money," while sometimes claimed to have a neutral effect as compared to selective controls, actually bears very heavily on housing, state and local government, and small business—sectors that depend heavily on borrowing. As a result of Federal Reserve tight-money policies and the Eisenhower approach, the total supply of money was stabilized from December 1954 to June 1957. When business activity picked up, monetary restraint did not prevent commercial banks from expanding loans by selling government securities and by transferring deposits to avoid reserve requirements. Also, financial institutions beyond control of the Federal Reserve speeded up their activities and thus increased the velocity of money transactions, which acted like an increase in money supply. Specific controls on consumer credit and increased taxes could have been used to offset the inflationary effects of this development, but they were not.

In managing the national economy, there must be a governmental decision about acceptable levels of inflation and unemployment—

that is, how much unemployment will be tolerated to keep prices from rising too rapidly. These are matters of judgment, politics and philosophy, fully as much as economics. But the limitations of monetary and fiscal policy also affect the outcome of any such decision. A tight-money policy, for example, can exercise a restraining influence on excess demand, but experience has shown that, if unaided, it is not likely to check major inflation. Reducing government spending without reducing taxation is another possible approach to inflation, but over two-thirds of the items in the federal budget are built-in and cannot be changed. Furthermore, reduced government spending hits Americans who work for, sell to, or receive benefits from government, and these Americans have votes. Increased taxation while holding government expenditures constant would, of course, reduce overall demand; but raising taxes is not a popular political step, and it runs the risk of increasing unemployment and starting the economy towards recession. The weight of government, by its very size and the nature of government commitments is, therefore, on the expansionary side.

The question of what constitutes an acceptable level of unemployment, or conversely what level represents full employment, is not easily answered. Generally, full employment is considered compatible with 4 percent unemployment in the work force. During World War II, unemployment approached 2 percent of the civilian labor force; during the Korean Conflict it was 3 percent. In the postwar period, aside from the Korean War, unemployment stayed below 4.5 percent for an appreciable period of time only from January 1947 to January 1949, May 1955 to September 1957, and from July 1965 to March 1970. Since the Eisenhower administration chose not to make unemployment its primary consideration, when the Kennedy administration took over in 1961, unemployment was running well over 6 percent. This level was not politically acceptable, and the emphasis of the new administration was placed on reducing it. The Kennedy economic advisers were quite willing to use deficit spending and selective tax cuts to stimulate the economy.

These measures produced accelerated economic growth without serious inflation in the first half of the 1960's. Real annual growth rates were forced up from less than 3 percent to over 6 percent; unemployment was forced down from over 6.5 percent to almost 4.5 percent; the money supply was expanded at a 3.2 percent annual rate yet wholesale prices from 1961–1965 changed very little, and consumer price rises were held to about 1.2 percent a year. Wage-price guidelines, geared to productivity increases, reduced the pressure for both wage and price increases. A 7 percent tax credit for new capital equipment and the 1964 income tax cut, plus depreciation allowances, spurred the economy, increasing national income as well as tax revenue.

When the pressure of added demand on the nation's resources resulted from the Vietnam War in the last half of the 1960's, inflation became a major issue. Popular tolerance of inflation was less than it had been previously for a number of reasons. A larger proportion of the population was living on fixed incomes. In service industries and government employment, leading areas of employment growth, wages did not keep up with the rising cost of living. The financial resources of a large element of the population were undermined. Inflation led to miscalculations by businessmen since it tended to make profits appear much larger than they actually were in terms of constant dollars.

Sound fiscal policy would have required an increase in taxes as the Vietnam War added excess pressure to demand, but the Johnson administration and the Congress were reluctant to apply this brake to the boom. Instead, primary reliance again was placed on monetary restraint, which in 1966 almost choked the economy without checking inflation. Thereafter the money growth rate began to climb as did prices. Not until 1968, however, were taxes increased, and the investment tax credit instituted under Kennedy to stimulate capital investment was allowed to remain in effect through the following year.

Meanwhile, on the theory that wage increases led to price increases that, in turn, led to further wage and price rises, President Johnson revived his predecessor's wage-price guidelines, urging labor not to seek wage increases that exceeded the long-term average productivity increase of 3.2 percent. Thus companies could be asked to restrain price increases because their increased wage bills would theoretically be offset by increased productivity. Although this program had some success, it relied on presidential persuasion and moral force and was a very generalized solution that could be inequitable in industries where productivity was significantly different from the 3.2 percent average. Another possibility would have been to break up concentrated private economic power, whether exercised by unions or business, that contributed to cost-push inflation. But, despite the rhetoric of antitrust, no administration has undertaken drastic industrial restructuring of this type. Certainly, Johnson's did not. Direct governmental control of prices and wages, as used in World Ward II, was still another alternative in coping with inflation, but controls are cumbersome to administer and restrict freedom, which American people are reluctant to accept unless a clearly perceived major national emergency is involved. The rapid rise in inflation in the early 1970's, accompanied by unemployment, was reaching an emergency stage. In mid-1971, the Nixon administration despite repeated previous refusals to consider controls reluctantly adopted them.

When President Nixon took office in January 1969, the 1957–1959 dollar had dropped in value to 81.1 cents. However, Nixon opposed use of the guidelines that had been used in Kennedy's administration, abandoned in 1966, but recommended late in 1968 by Johnson's Cabinet Committee on Price Stability. Instead, Nixon planned to hold down the money supply, which the Federal Reserve had loosened too freely after the 1966 clamp-down, and to create a federal surplus by fiscal measures. But the new President's first press conference was interpreted as indicating that he did not favor either jawboning persuasion of the Kennedy-Johnson type or a wage-and-price review; thus business considered Nixon as being on record for a laissez-faire price policy.

All of Nixon advisers, except Arthur Burns of the Federal Reserve, subscribed to the view that too drastic cuts in government expenditures in an effort to check inflation would start a major recession. Therefore, his first budget did not call for a major cutback. But Nixon and his advisers had clearly underestimated inflationary pressures. The February 1970 budget proposal called for a $1.3 billion surplus. But a new tight-money policy had slowed down the economy without curbing inflation. The recession was eating away at tax revenues and, therefore, the projected surplus turned into a major deficit.

Faced with the inadequacy of his original "game plan," Nixon had to reassess the acceptable limits of unemployment and inflation. In June 1970 the Bureau of the Budget became the Office of Management and Budget, and George Shultz was elevated from the Labor Department to the office. Shultz argued for the full-employment budget, increased money supply, and government efforts to affect wages and prices by removing props, such as import quotas.

The game plan was altered to fight recession, despite the inflationary consequences.

Meanwhile, the President gradually moved closer to the Kennedy-Johnson method of combatting price rises. In early 1971, he fought an impending domestic steel price rise by threatening to loosen restraints on steel imports. He temporarily suspended the Davis-Bacon Act, covering federal construction workers, in an effort to combat inflationary cost-push pressures in the construction industry. But in early summer of 1971, when the steel and railroad industries accepted new wage increases which further pushed up prices, the administration took no action against them. The nation was floundering in an unprecedented combination of escalating prices and unemployment, which had climbed to over 6 percent of the labor force. A Harris poll showed that 70 percent of those queried did not believe the President was doing well in handling the economy.

The wage-price structure of American industry is closely linked to the problem of inflation. Wages and prices move up in boom periods as labor's increased demands are met by industry, which passes the cost forward in prices charged to the consumer. Since wage agreements usually cover a period of several years, the effect on business costs of wage increases negotiated in a boom period can be extended into a period when recession has overtaken the economy. Thus, even in a major recession, higher prices can result from increased costs (wages, materials, etc.), which in turn justify demands for higher wages, that in turn lead to higher prices. This spiral can spread rapidly from one sector of the economy to another, even as unemployment is rising.

A variation on this sequence emerges in what is called "structural inflation." While there may not be excess aggregate demand in the economy, shifts of demand from one industry to another can have an inflationary effect. Costs and prices rise in an industry with excess demand, but those in industries with excess capacity do not fall. Indeed, with less output, unions in the latter industry may ask for higher wages following the example of those in the industry with excess demand. The result is rising costs and prices, even in industries that are experiencing recession. Productivity increases could offset some of this effect, but labor costs in many areas of the economy have outstripped increased productivity. In the early 1970's, labor costs rose 38 percent per manhour in American industry while productivity advanced only 8.2 percent. This relationship worked to the advantage of other industrialized nations, which flooded the American market with their products. To stem this competition the revised Nixon game plan of August 1971 imposed a 10 percent surcharge on imports.

From the 1930's to the 1970's, governmental efforts to manage the economy through monetary and fiscal policy have produced mixed results. It was demonstrated beyond question that these powers can be used to stimulate the economy, indeed even to overheat it. As long as the resulting trade-offs between the rate of inflation and the rate of unemployment proved acceptable, the results were impressive in terms of real gains in disposable income and economic growth. But when inflation began to gain the upper hand, it proved difficult to reverse the policies that had created such national euphoria. The size and momentum of the forces unleashed in the boom worked against any simple reversal of policies in order to contain inflation. Reliance on monetary policy alone proved a weak reed on which to lean, and political reluctance to increase taxes or severely cut government expenditures unduly delayed the application of countercyclical fiscal policy. The combination of reluctance, timidity, poor timing, and the perpetuation of wage and price structures that compounded the problem produced a confusing and dangerous situation by the early 1970's.

Unemployment and inflation, increasing at the same time, or so called "stagflation," was an unprecedented experience for Americans. It was clear to most that something had to be done. But for an agonizingly long time it did not seem equally clear to those who were responsible for such action that management of the economy requires governmental direction and sanctions that may be politically distasteful, but economically indispensable. While available tools may be inadequate, the extent of that inadequacy—whether political or economic—will not be know until they have been given a fair trial. On August 15, 1971, President Nixon instituted a major reversal of his previous laissez-faire policies and ordered a trial of virtually every weapon developed since the 1930's in an effort to simultaneously combat unemployment and inflation. It was an unprecedented peacetime exercise of governmental power to guide the economy in meeting an unprecedented situation. However, by mid-1974 these controls, most of which had been lifted after several years of modification, were thought by many Americans to have exacerbated rather than helped the problems to which they were addressed.

INTRODUCTION:
MANAGING THE ECONOMY,
1937–1973

Deliberate efforts to manage the total economy, with the exception of World War I, commenced in the 1930's. President Franklin D. Roosevelt, in his 1937 budget message, discussed the objectives of the fiscal policy of the federal government since his inauguration and outlined his fiscal program for the coming year. His emphasis on a balanced budget indicated that he had not yet abandoned classical economic theories; but his statement that, if an unbalanced budget were necessary to meet the needs of the American people, those needs would be met, suggests that balance was not the primary objective. The recovery from 1933 had spurred his hopes of reducing government expenditures, but, as he indicated, co-operation from an increasingly hostile private sector was essential. In fact, as this chapter has pointed out, a downturn in 1937 forced Roosevelt to return to large-scale deficit spending, but this selection indicates the tug-of-war that took place between earlier conventional economic wisdom and the new Keynesian economics.

The Employment Act of 1946, adopted by the Congress in that year, was a formal declaration of the government's responsibility for the overall performance of the economy. Twenty-five years later *The Economic Report of the President,* which was provided for in the legislation, reviewed the impact of the Act on government economic policy and the role of economic expertise at the highest levels.

In that same year, 1969, G. L. Bach, a distinguished economist, reviewed for a symposium sponsored by the American Bankers Association what economists had learned—or not learned—about the use of monetary and fiscal policy. The nation was then in the grip of an unprecedented combination of inflation and unemployment. Economists had no good solution to that problem, nor did the administration. In discussing the problem, Professor Bach emphasizes the complexity of the economy and the resulting difficulty of assessing how, when, and in what degree to apply the instruments of overall economic control.

In desperation, the Nixon administration resorted to direct peacetime controls on the American economy in August 1971. The problems of inflation, which they sought to solve had originated in the American effort to conduct a war in Southeast Asia, while domestic programs and economic life were continued as though no additional drain was being put on the nation's economic resources. In 1970, Gardner Ackley, chairman of President Lyndon Johnson's Council of Economic Advisers, reviewed these developments in the context of an inflation that had affected the entire Atlantic community. Ackley reviews the record of the inflation and his position as economic adviser to President Johnson regarding these problems; he states his belief that compulsory wage-and-price controls are undesirable and makes suggestions for alternative approaches.

In the selections on pp. 97–103, Edwin L. Dale, Jr., a perceptive analyst of the economy for *The New York Times,* records developments subsequent to the 1973 withdrawal of troops from South Vietnam. In the first selection he describes the relationship of the Vietnam War to domestic economic problems and the war's economic legacy. In the last selection he summarizes the steps taken after August 1971 to bring the economy under control. Unlike Ackley, Dale sees some positive benefits to the utilization of direct controls.

THE PRESIDENT'S ANNUAL BUDGET MESSAGE TO THE CONGRESS. JANUARY 7, 1937

Franklin D. Roosevelt

To the Congress of the United States:

Pursuant to provisions of law I transmit herewith the Budget of the United States Government for the fiscal year ending June 30, 1938, together with this message, which is a part thereof. The estimates have been developed after careful analysis of the revenues, obligations, and reasonable needs of the Government, and I recommend appropriations for the purposes specifically detailed herein.

Part 1

The programs inaugurated during the last four years to combat the depression and to initiate many needed reforms have cost large sums of money, but the benefits obtained from them are far outweighing all their costs. We shall soon be reaping the full benefits of those programs and shall have at the same time a balanced Budget that will also include provision for reduction of the public debt.

The fiscal plans of the Federal Government for these four years have been formulated with two objectives in mind. Our first was to restore a successful economic life to the country, by providing greater employment and purchasing power for the people, by stimulating a more balanced use of our productive capacity, and by increasing the national income and distributing it on a wider base of prosperity. Our second was to gain new advantages of permanent value for the American people. Both of these objectives can be accomplished under a sound financial policy.

Business conditions have shown each year since 1933 a marked improvement over the preceding year. Employment in private industry is increasing. Industrial production, factory payrolls, and farm prices have steadily risen.

These gains make it possible to reduce for the fiscal year 1938 many expenditures of the Federal Government which the general depression made necessary. Although we must continue to spend substantial sums to provide work for those whom industry has not yet absorbed, the 1938 Budget is in balance; and, except for debt reduction of $401,515,000, it will remain in balance even if later on there are included additional expenditures of as much as $1,537,123,000 for recovery and relief. We expect, moreover, if improvement in economic conditions continues at the present rate, to be able to attain in 1939 a completely balanced Budget, with full provision for meeting the statutory requirements for debt reduction.

In carrying out this policy the American people are obtaining lasting benefits. Economic protection of the aged and physically handicapped is being secured through the operations of the Social Security Act. Ability of the farmer to secure a more constant livelihood has been enhanced by the enactment of legislation especially designed for that purpose. The home owner has been benefited through the financing of mortgages at reasonable rates of interest. Investors in securities are being given a larger measure of protection by the Securities and Exchange Act. The market for corporate securities has been restored and industry has been able to finance its long-term requirements on a favorable basis. The rights of labor are being materially advanced through operation of the National Labor Relations Act.

I plan to submit at a later date an estimate of appropriation for additional relief for the fiscal year 1938, which I hope will not exceed the amount of $1,537,123,000, previously mentioned. This hope is based on the assumption that industry will cooperate in employing men and women from the relief rolls in larger numbers than during the past year. Many of those in charge of industrial management, recognizing their obligation to the Nation, have furnished a large measure of employment to the jobless. Today, while it is true that in some sections of the country certain types of skilled workers are still seeking employment, it is nevertheless a fact that the great majority of those now receiving relief belong to the unskilled group. It is my conviction that if every employer or potential employer will undertake during the next six months to give employment to persons now receiving Government help, the national Budget can thereafter be kept definitely in balance. Without such cooperation on the part of employers, the question of a balanced Budget for 1938 must of necessity remain an open one, for the very good reason that this Government does not propose next year, any more than during the past four years, to allow American families to starve.

To continue the gains we are making and to accomplish in the 1939 Budget a complete balance between receipts and expenditures including debt reduction, we must now lay the groundwork of our future fiscal policy.

While relief expenditures should decline with greater reemployment, the normal growth of the country naturally reflects itself in increased costs of Government. Many of the old functions and duties of Government naturally cost more as the industrial and agricultural activities to which they are related expand in volume. The cost of new functions and duties can be substantially reduced only by curtailing the function or the duty. I propose shortly to submit to the Congress a broad plan for placing the Executive branch of the Government on a sounder and more responsible basis of management. The carrying out of such a plan will undoubtedly result in some saving in expenditures; but it must be remembered that what is generally known as overhead represents only a small fraction of total expenditures in any large business, Government or private.

Expenditures must be planned with a view to the national needs; and no expansion of Government activities should be authorized unless the necessity for such expansion has been definitely determined and funds are available to defray the cost. In other words, if new legislation imposes any substantial increase in expenditures either in the expansion of existing or the creation of new activities, it becomes a matter of sound policy simultaneously to provide new revenue sufficient to meet the additional cost. The success of such a policy can be assured only through the full and friendly cooperation of the Congress and the Executive. Of this cooperation I am confident. . . .

Fiscal Program for 1938

The expected increase in revenue and decrease in expenditures for relief both reflect the general improvement which has taken place in the economic conditions of the country. The Revenue Act of 1936, which was designed for the purpose of replacing revenue lost through the invalidation of processing taxes, of providing sufficient revenue to amortize the cost of the adjusted compensation payments, and of equalizing tax burdens, gives every indication of satisfactorily accomplishing those purposes. I should like, at this point, to emphasize the importance of maintaining the productiveness of the present tax structure, so that we may properly provide for the fulfillment of our fiscal program.

In legislation enacted during the last session of Congress, which created authorizations for future appropriations aggregating more than $1,500,000,000, there is included about $130,000,000 in the estimates of appropriations contained in this Budget. Such authorizations are contained in the new Federal Highway Act, the Rivers and Harbors and the Flood Control Acts, and the Rural Electrification Act.

There is also included $812,225,000 for social security grants and for the Government's contribution to the old-age reserve account, more than double the expenditures for these purposes in 1937, and there will be for several years still further increases in these requirements. It should be pointed out that these expenditures will be offset to a large extent by the increasing revenues under the Social Security Act.

No estimate of appropriations is presented for the needs of the Civilian Conservation Corps, since its extension beyond March 31 of this year is dependent on the action of Congress. In furtherance of my recommendation for the enactment of legislation to continue it as a permanent agency of the Government, there is included in the "Supplemental Items" an amount sufficient to meet the expenditure requirements for the fiscal year 1938.

The following table shows the distribution, on a functional basis, of the expenditure figures contained in this Budget and compares them with similar figures for previous years.

A QUARTER CENTURY OF
THE EMPLOYMENT ACT
OF 1946

President's Council of Economic Advisers

"We meet to consider what I profoundly believe to be as important a proposal as any before the Congress within my memory." With these words Senator Wagner of New York, on July 30, 1945, convened the subcommittee of the Senate Banking and Currency Committee to begin hearings on S. 380, "The Full Employment Act of 1945." In February 1946, a quarter of a century ago this month,

Actual and estimated expenditures of the Government for the fiscal years 1932–1938
(Classifications include expenditures from both general and emergency funds)
[IN MILLIONS OF DOLLARS]

	ESTIMATED		ACTUAL				
	1938	1937	1936	1935	1934	1933	1932
Regular operating expenditures:							
Legislative, judicial, and civil establishments	771.8	859.0	781.1	597.7	572.5	697.5	978.8
National defense	991.6	964.9	911.6	709.9	540.3	667.8	707.6
Veterans' pensions and benefits	577.5	1,144.7	2,351.4	607.1	556.9	863.2	984.8
Interest on the public debt.	860.0	835.0	749.4	820.9	756.6	689.4	599.3
Total	3,200.9	3,803.6	4,793.5	2,735.6	2,426.3	2,917.9	3,270.5
Public works	908.3	1,146.7	868.7	704.3	551.9	427.7	439.5
Unemployment relief:							
Direct relief	13.0	106.7	591.7	1,914.1	715.8	350.7	—
Work relief (W.P.A. and C.W.A.)	a.2	1,400.5	1,264.4	11.3	805.1	—	—
Civilian Conservation Corps	(b)	368.0	486.3	435.5	331.9	—	—
Total	13.2	1,875.2	2,342.4	2,360.9	1,852.8	350.7	—
Loans (net)	c153.3	c419.9	c175.2	80.5	788.6	874.4	404.0
Subscriptions to stock	17.2	51.5	69.3	156.8	826.5	110.7	627.0
Agricultural adjustment program	482.4	467.6	542.6	743.0	290.3	—	—
Less revenues	—	—	76.6	521.4	353.0	—	—
Net	482.4	467.6	466.0	221.6	d62.7	—	—

Actual and estimated expenditures of the Government for the fiscal years 1932–38 (Continued)
(Classifications include expenditures from both general and emergency funds)

[IN MILLIONS OF DOLLARS]

	ESTIMATED		ACTUAL				
	1938	1937	1936	1935	1934	1933	1932
Social security	836.0	399.6	28.4	—	—	—	—
Debt retirement	401.5	404.5	403.2	573.6	359.9	461.6	412.6
Miscellaneous	1.8	2.0	6.8	21.1	8.7	—	—
Supplemental items	450.0	750.0	—	—	—	—	—
Grand total	a6,158.0	8,480.8	8,803.1	6,854.4	6,752.0	5,143.0	5,153.6

a To be increased by any amount appropriated by Congress for recovery and relief for the fiscal year 1938. As indicated in the message, it is hoped the amount will not exceed $1,537,123,000.
b Funds for continuation of the Civilian Conservation Corps are included under "Supplemental items."
c Excess of credits, deduct.
d Excess of revenues, deduct.

President Truman signed into law the "Employment Act of 1946." The 25th anniversary of that Act provides a useful opportunity to look at the road that we have been traveling and where we may be going.

The Employment Act of 1946 made two major contributions to the management of economic policy. Section 2 explicitly declares the objectives of national economic policy, the most familiar passage of that section being the last eight words: "to promote maximum employment, production, and purchasing power." More than a hundred other words in this one-sentence statement concern national economic objectives and they are all important. Economic programs and policies, for example, are to be consistent with "other essential considerations of national policy" and all are to be carried out by means "calculated to foster and promote free competitive enterprise and the general welfare. . ." While the closing words are the most widely quoted of Section 2, the framers of the Act did not ignore the complex nature of our economic objectives and the fact that we must strive for an optimum balance among competing objectives, since the single-minded pursuit of one would inevitably mean sacrifices elsewhere.

The Employment Act of 1946 also provided for some additions to the structure and activities of Government. It created the Joint Economic Committee of the Congress as well as the Council of Economic Advisers in the Executive Office of the President. During the quarter of a century that this structure has been in operation, 58 Members of the Senate and House (including the present Committee members) have served on the Joint Economic Committee. Mr. Patman of Texas, alternating Chairman of the Committee, played a major role and was floor manager for the bill in the House; and Senator Fulbright of Arkansas, a present member of the Joint Economic Committee, was a member of Senator Wagner's subcommittee that conducted the initial hearings. Two of the present members have served on the Joint Economic Committee since its inception. During this period 25 of the Nation's economists have served as Members of the Council of Economic Advisers under five Presidents. There have been eight Chairmen of the Council, five of whom had previously served as Members.

Have this structure and the operations that have evolved within it made any significant impact on policy? Considering their nature, this is a reasonable question. The Joint Economic Committee does not have legislative functions: proposed legislation that deals with the building blocks of economic policy is handled by other committees of the Congress. The Council of Economic Advisers is one of the smallest agencies in the Federal Government. It advises; it does not manage. On almost any issue of economic policy another senior official of the Administration will have immediate responsibilities—the Secretary of the Treasury for taxes, the Secretary of Agriculture for farm policy, the Director of the Office of Management and Budget for expenditure policy.

Even so the Joint Economic Committee and the Council of Economic Advisers have clearly influenced Government policy. To some extent this result was planned by those who framed the Act. They did not leave entirely to chance and the evolution of experience the responsibilities for implementing Section 2. They also added Sections 3, 4, and 5, which set up some quite explicit responsibilities. They call, for example, on the President to transmit each year an economic report that sets forth such matters as current and foreseeable trends in employment, production, and purchasing power and outlines a program for carrying out the policy declared in Section 2. They direct the Council, among other things, "to appraise the various programs and activities of the Federal Government in the light of the policy declared in Section 2 for the purpose of determining the extent to which such programs and activities are contributing, and the extent to which they are not contributing, to the achievement of such policy and to make recommendations to the President with respect thereto. . . ." They call on the Joint Economic Committee to make a continuing study of programs and their coordination and to report to the Congress. And the Act calls for cooperation among all groups in our society in attaining these objectives.

Within this general framework a substantial complex of activities has emerged. For one thing the Joint Economic Committee has come to be one of the major, ongoing, national seminars on economic policy. Witnesses at its hearings include Government officials, a wide range of scholars from the universities, leaders of unions and businesses, and students of economic policy from abroad. The membership of this Committee includes chairmen and senior members of major legislative committees; and the published

Proceedings of Hearings and other Committee publications have had a marked influence on national thinking about public policy and have increased the understanding in government and public circles of the problems and issues of economic policy and economic performance.

The Council of Economic Advisers has also had a pervasive influence in shaping policy. Through it the discipline of economic thinking has been introduced at a level where it directly affects decisions. While Government agencies have long had economists, the Council of Economic Advisers is an agency in which economists are the principals. Though small, it reports directly to the President. And having no particular constituency it can look at the broader public interest. The Council assists in the preparation of the President's *Economic Report,* which has become the major statement of national economic developments, programs, and policies. The requirement to submit an annual economic report subjects the Administration to the discipline of specifying its targets and appraising the adequacy of its policies for reaching the targets.

Have the results of efforts by these two bodies shown up in the performance of the economy during this quarter of a century? In employment the performance has been reasonably good. The unemployment rate during the past 25 years has averaged 4.6 percent, and the highest yearly rate was 6.8 percent in 1958. In the 25 years before the war, ending with 1940, the average unemployment rate was 10.9 percent, and its peak was 24.9 percent in 1933. This 25-year period includes the Great Depression, however, which dominates the record. If we look at the quarter of a century before the Great Depression, ending with 1929, the average was 4.7 percent, the highest unemployment rate was 11.7 percent in 1921, and in three other years (1908, 1914, and 1915) the 1958 rate was exceeded. This suggests that we have not appreciably reduced the incidence of small departures from maximum employment but that we have reduced the incidence of large departures, which is just what one would expect aggregate economic policy to be able to do.

During the quarter of a century since World War II, the goods and services made available to each consumer increased by 62 percent in real terms, and our stock of productive capital has increased by close to $800 billion (in 1970 prices). In the quarter of a century ending with 1929 the per capita output of goods and services produced grew about 50 percent, somewhat below our postwar performance.

A recurring question throughout these years has been whether the Employment Act of 1946 has caused an imbalance in our management of economic policy by lessening the attention paid to price stability. While Section 2 recognizes that "other essential considerations of national policy" must be weighed, there is no explicit recognition of a stable price level as an objective of economic policy. It is clear both from policies and statements about policies that all Administrations have considered a reasonably stable price level to be an important objective of policy, and such stability is one of the concerns implicitly expressed in the Employment Act of 1946. Indeed, it is clear from early comments that the Congress interpreted "maximum purchasing power" to involve concern about inflation.

During most of the first 20 years of the Act this question about the role of the price level in the objectives of national economic policy had a certain leisurely and academic quality. The basic trend of the price level was moderately upward. Between 1948, the time that prices established a new plateau, and 1965 the consumer price index rose 31 percent. Over one-half of this rise, however, is accounted for by two 2-year surges in the price level—one from 1950 to 1952, and a second from 1956 to 1958. And one of these surges could be attributed to the large rise in defense outlays incident to the Korean conflict. Apart from these, the price level was performing in a reasonably quiescent manner.

Concern about the price level as a consideration in the objectives and management of economic policy has come into sharper focus and taken on a new sense of urgency with the rise in prices since 1965. While the inflation was clearly set off by excessively expansive fiscal and monetary policies, its persistence as the overheating of the economy subsided has raised urgent questions. Can a free economy have a reasonably stable price level with its productive resources fully utilized? Has the concentration on "maximum employment, production, and purchasing power," as specified in the Employment Act, caused a bias in our policies that leaves us exposed to a sustained deterioration in the purchasing power of the dollar? Have new institutional structures and forces come into play that keep driving the price-cost level upwards regardless of the state of the economy?

This much seems clear: The Employment Act of 1946, and the concerns that gave rise to its passage, moved the quality of our economic performance to a higher place on the Nation's agenda. The Act provided a flexible and general statement of what our economic activity ought to do for us. The structures that it called for have evolved and adjusted to changing circumstances and problems. Our most urgent task, as we move into the second quarter century of the Employment Act of 1946, is twofold: to find ways of keeping the Nation consistently concerned about the problems raised by experience with inflation since 1965, and, with full regard for the requirements of a free economy and a free society, to develop new policies and programs needed to meet this national concern. We can be confident that this twofold task will be performed.

THE SEARCH FOR STABILITY— WHAT HAVE WE LEARNED?
G. L. Bach

One further parenthetical paragraph on the importance of recently developed data on the economy may be in order. It is easy to forget that in the 1920s and 1930s we had no figures on gross national product, on national income, on business investment and spending, and the like. Economists who wrote about economic behavior did so largely on *a priori* grounds and there was no way of checking up closely to see whether they were right or wrong. But the flood of economic statistics in the postwar period has made it possible now to study the economy in great detail and with greater confidence as to what we are seeing. Without this statistical revolution, the importance of which is easily overlooked, it is doubtful that the Keynesian revolution or the monetary counterrevolution of recent years would be more than economists' debating points. On the contrary, using these data and modern econometric techniques, economic scientists are making substantial headway toward a reliable understanding of hundreds of important economic relationships. We know a great deal more about the economy than we did 25 years ago.

But to return to the main analysis—that is, of the importance of the complexity of the modern economy. In such a complex economy any simplistic explanation of the impact of monetary or fiscal policy on aggregate spending seems implausible. It would be surprising indeed if *only* money or *only* fiscal policy turned out to influence aggregate spending in the economy, and careful research suggests that both are important. Neither monetary nor fiscal policy alone is likely to be enough to keep the economy on a stable growth path. While the monetary views of Professor Friedman have achieved great publicity and considerable acceptance among economists as well as with the general public—and I confess to a substantial sympathy for them myself—it is well to remember that the news media tend to pick up what is new, and therefore news, and that the number of newspaper words devoted to the monetarist viewpoint is not necessarily a good measure of the validity of those views. A similar popular consensus 10 years ago would have put equally strong stress on fiscal policy, with scarcely a mention of money. I suspect we shall need at least another decade before we are sure just how much weight to place on each policy instrument in controlling aggregate demand under different conditions.

A responsible reporter on the current state of economic analysis must say that there is a strong presumption that *both* monetary and fiscal policies can exert powerful effects on aggregate spending; that they work through different but related channels; that they operate with different time lags and have their primary impact on different sectors of the economy; and that poor Government policy on either front may create major problems for the other. The plight of the monetary policy makers at the Fed after 1965 is a good example of the last point. Highly expansionary fiscal policy in an already heated-up economy required strong monetary restraint to hold back the surging economy, with disruptive and widely protested impacts on housing and on state and local governments.

What does this complexity suggest for stabilization policy? To many, especially businessmen and bankers, it suggests primarily that we must use "judgment" in meshing together all the conflicting and interacting considerations. Clearly, such judgmental decisions are needed. But to many modern economists it points rather toward the need for more accurate analytical models of the economy to provide a surer basis for predicting alternative policy results. They do not question the search for simple, fundamental relationships that might directly serve policy makers, but they doubt that many have yet been isolated.

For still others this complexity points, as a practical matter, to the use of simple stabilization policy rules. In such a complex world, they argue, even well-meaning Government officials are likely to make mistakes that will worsen, not lessen, economic fluctuations. A simple policy rule—for example, stable growth in the money stock—will not give ideal results, but it will ensure that the Fed avoids major destabilizing mistakes and in all probability will produce better results than would judgmental policies that attempt to take everything into account in making each decision. This is essentially Professor Friedman's position on monetary policy. He does not claim that he can explain the complex interrelationships between changes in the money stock and the various components of aggregate demand. Rather, he argues that as a practical matter a simple policy of steadily increasing the money stock at about the growth rate of the economy would give a reasonably good result; it would certainly avoid serious destabilizing errors and it would probably do better than would elaborate judgmental decisions based on a large number of not very clearly measurable forces.

Which of these three inferences will lead to the best stabilization policy remains an unsettled issue.

The Political Economics of Stabilization Policy

If the new economists were naïve about their policies, it was not only because they oversimplified the economic process but also because they underrated the practical political difficulties of making the new economics work. Against massive depression or massive inflation fiscal policy can be a powerful weapon on which general consensus can be marshalled. But as a fine-tuning device its record has been considerably less than rosy; frequently the President and

Congress have rejected the policy mandates of the new economics.

Dr. Wilfred Lewis of The Brookings Institution has documented the record of fiscal policy during the 1950s and concludes that it played only a minor role as a stabilization instrument. During the 1960s the big fiscal policy moves were in the right direction, but in both cases two or three years late. President Kennedy's chief economic advisers began in 1960 to push for a tax cut to stimulate the lagging economy. It was not until 1962 that they convinced the President of the wisdom of this move, and then Congress took another year to accept the recommendation. The great tax cut of 1964, often hailed as a major symbol of the new economics, was thus good economics—three years late.

In 1966, President Johnson's economic advisers were urging privately that anti-inflationary taxes were needed as Vietnam war expenditures soared. Again, it took more than a year to persuade the President of the need for higher taxes, and even after he recommended the surtax Congress took another year and a half to finally pass it in mid-1968. During these extended periods fiscal policy was perverse. Government itself is part of the stabilization *problem* as well as part of its *solution.*

We have learned that flexible fiscal policy on the expenditure side is very hard to achieve. Federal spending decisions are dominated by some 30 appropriations subcommittees, many of which are ruled by committee chairmen who are virtually feudal lords in their fiefdoms. Thus particular program needs dominate expenditure decisions. Under present Congressional-Executive processes there seems to be little hope of using overall expenditure variations to help stabilize aggregate demand.

On the tax side there is only a little more hope for flexible action unless we can somehow disentangle stabilization policy from tax reform issues. If fiscal policy is to play the role allocated to it by the new economics, there must be significant changes in the tax and appropriation processes. Just avoiding destabilizing policies would be a significant step forward. Some concrete changes toward more flexible fiscal policy can be suggested—indeed, Dr. Stein has suggested some that I find very attractive—but this is not my assignment for today.

In substance, Congress, the executive branch, and the business-financial world have all bought the fundamental notion of the new economics: that we can indeed avoid major economic fluctuations by using fiscal and monetary policy to balance fluctuations in private spending. Few people now believe that another massive depression like the 1930s is possible. But, on the other hand, apparently neither Congress, nor the executive branch, nor the business and financial community has accepted the new economics firmly enough to accord first priority to stabilization when individual tax and expenditure issues are at stake. The new economics has not failed in the past few years; it has just been dominated by the old politics.

This somber evaluation of the probable political effectiveness of fiscal policy as a stabilization device turns the spotlight to monetary policy, the other main instrument for stabilizing the growth of aggregate demand.

Congress in its wisdom established a semi-independent Federal Reserve within the Government, a Federal Reserve System that looks a little like a Rube Goldberg device but, as may be true with some such devices, works much better than one might predict. On monetary policy, the critical decision-making powers are centralized in only a few men who are somewhat insulated from the day-to-day political pressures that confront the President and the Congress. As with fiscal policy, there is overwhelming consensus on the proper stance of monetary policy if a massive depression or a massive inflation should develop. In the former case the Fed's big job is to provide liquidity for the financial institutions of the nation and to help maintain aggregate demand by providing generous excess reserves to halt the decline in the nation's money stock. Against a big inflation, clearly the Fed's job is to dig in its heels and maintain as much monetary restraint as is feasible vis-à-vis the Congress and the executive branch, whose unbalanced budget is almost certain to be behind any major inflation.

But, as with fiscal policy, we have not yet learned to use monetary policy as an effective fine-tuning stabilization device. In retrospect, the Fed has done a good job in recognizing changes in the economic climate and reacting fairly promptly to undesirable swings upward or downward. But its policy reactions have often been too strong—a tendency to overshoot with stop-go monetary reactions to changes in the economy. It is hard to be critical of the Fed, because in large part these overshoots have been reactions to erratic fiscal policy—for example, the Fed's rapid tightening in mid-1966. But with unknown lags in the impact of monetary policy there is no assurance that such overreaction will not occur again.

Part of the problem has been the Fed's traditional focus on money market conditions (free reserves and short-term interest rates) as the primary indicator of the ease or tightness of its monetary policy. On this front I think it is fair to say that we have learned from the postwar experience and from our growing understanding of financial processes in the economy that more stress should be placed on a stably growing money stock or monetary base (not to get involved in the intricate economic arguments over exactly what measure of the money stock ought to be used). It is clear that in inflationary periods such as the recent past interest rates and money market conditions provide inadequate, indeed dangerous, signals to the monetary policy makers. Quoted interest rates reflect not only monetary policy and "real" forces in the economy but also to some unmeasurable extent the inflationary expectations of borrowers and lenders. Thus high interest rates may indicate an inflationary, easy money policy and not a restrictive, tight money policy.

This we have learned. But candor compels me to admit that we still don't know enough about the interactions between Federal Reserve actions, financial markets, and the real economy to be sure what is the best indicator for the Fed to watch or what is the best general rule for the Fed to follow in its day-to-day operations. Your committee could readily have found an economist who would have told you that the dispute is settled and that stable growth in the money stock (currency plus demand deposits) is the proper monetary policy for the future. I have confessed to considerable sympathy for this point of view myself, but there is no real consensus on this point now.

Since there is only limited hope that discretionary fiscal policy will help provide stable economic growth and there is a high probability of continuing inflationary pressures, we are probably fortunate to have a Fed that is somewhat independent from the day-to-day political pressure of our times. Although the Federal tax system will automatically tend to produce surpluses as the economy grows, the basic pressures are most likely to be toward persistent inflation in the economy. The Fed, partially insulated by the silken veil that cloaks money and the high temple of finance, can stand against inflation when neither the President nor the Congress feels politically able to do so.

In short, neither fiscal nor monetary policy alone is likely to be enough. Reasonably stable growth in the real economy will come only if there is both a reasonably stable growth rate in the money stock and a reasonably stable fiscal policy—a continually balanced "full employment budget" might approximate this fiscal stability. Even with such Federal monetary-fiscal stability there is no guarantee that private spending will not generate economic fluctuations. But at least such governmental policies would avoid destabilizing Federal sector actions and would sharply reduce the probability of serious recessions and inflations.

Even with Big Government the Private Economy Is Dominant

With the recent emphasis on big government and on fiscal policy, it is easy to forget that Federal, state, and local government spending is only about a quarter of total GNP. This is a very large amount, enough to make a critical difference between the impact of government spending now and its impact a half century ago. But in an economy approaching $1 trillion GNP private sector spending will total some $750 billion. Given this fact, small percentage changes in private spending may total billions of dollars. For example, the consumer saving rate out of disposable personal income is notoriously hard to predict within a range of 1 or 2 per cent. Yet a 2 per cent swing in that rate accounts for over $10 billion of final consumer spending—enough to generate a substantial effect on the rest of the economy. During the 1960s, big swings in government spending have provided powerful impetus to swings in the total economy. But it is still the private sector—a huge three-fourths of the total economy—that largely determines whether we have prosperity or recession, falling or rising prices. Thus it should not be surprising that governmental stabilization policy may have a hard time keeping the economy precisely on the track of stable growth.

The Importance of (Self-Fulfilling) Expectations

With widespread confidence that there need not be another great depression and with widespread expectation that at least creeping inflation is the American way of life, we are learning that these expectations tend to be self-fulfilling in the huge private sector of the economy. If, indeed, businessmen have come to believe that growth is the wave of the future, that costs will be higher next year than this, and that there is little danger of a serious drop in total spending, little wonder that they invest heavily in new plant and equipment and that they place high priority on getting capacity in place now as against waiting a year or two or three. Similarly, little wonder that trade unions push strongly for larger wage settlements calculated to offset past and expected rises in living costs *and* to provide increases in real income.

We have learned, too, that in a democratic political-economic system like ours, when total income claims exceed the total national output valued at present prices, the result is a steady upward pressure on costs and prices that must be validated by Government monetary-fiscal policy if it is not to produce unemployment as actual purchases fall short of full-employment levels at higher costs and prices. Nearly all economists recognize today that monopolistic business or labor groups can exert only limited inflationary pressure on the economy unless aggregate demand is growing to validate the higher wages and prices these monopolists set. But to say this misses the essence of the democratic process. For it is precisely these cost and price pressures that put Government monetary and fiscal authorities on the spot to increase aggregate demand so as to avoid the recession that rising costs and prices will produce without rising aggregate demand. And, given the strong commitment of our political system to high employment and prosperous times, it is predictable that monetary and fiscal policy will generally ratify higher wages and prices rather than permitting them to generate widespread unemployment.

This is not to say that the Government, including the Federal Reserve, will validate *all* wage and price increases through expanding aggregate demand. On the contrary, as inflation speeds up, popular complaints and resistance to higher prices spread. We have seen this reaction in the past two or three years as the rate of inflation has climbed to 5–6 per cent per year, with its predictable impact on those groups in society that lag behind in inflationary periods. The American public, and the American political process, clearly put first priority on avoiding mass unemployment and achieving general prosperity. But not far behind comes the fear of substantial inflation, with its pressures on the Government for anti-inflation measures. Thus the postwar period teaches us to expect persistently rising prices, that top priority will be given to maintaining prosperity and high-level employment but that counterpressures will grow rapidly if inflation goes beyond a modest rate.

This set of self-fulfilling expectations poses major problems for the monetary and fiscal authorities. The more strongly entrenched expectations of stable economic growth become and the more confident the private sector is that monetary policy will indeed provide enough purchasing power to bail out inflationary wage and price setters, the freer both unions and businesses will feel to push still harder for still bigger shares of income and profits. This phenomenon was clearly visible in 1968–69. It has meant that gentle monetary restraint is likely to have little effect on either unions or business investment—that a major disappointment of business and labor expectations may increasingly be required to level off the excess-income claims that underlie the inflation.

Professor Hyman Minsky has argued strongly that modern capitalism, with widespread reliance on expansionary monetary-fiscal policy, is inherently unstable upward—that the more successful we become in maintaining stable economic growth, the harder it will be to restrain inflation and the more we will have to face a serious recession to knock out overly optimistic, inflationary expectations and behavior. He seems to most economists to overstate the likelihood that very repressive monetary policy and serious recession is the only way to halt creeping inflation. But we have learned that there is some substance to the argument and to the role of self-fulfilling expectations in the modern economy—that there is an important problem here that we must learn to solve. Put more positively, we are learning that the nation needs a stable-money expectational base if the economy is to be maintained on a stable, noninflationary growth path.

Some Things We Have Not Learned

A brief note on the negative. Two things we have not learned were mentioned above, but they deserve reemphasis.

First, we have not learned how to deal with the high employment-inflation dilemma. Evidence mounts that this is fundamentally a problem of expectations although simple market mechanics alone will commonly produce inflation before full employment is reached if the rise in aggregate demand is rapid. Measures to improve labor market efficiency through better job information, retraining programs, and the like, can clearly help avoid the dilemma; but until stable-price expectations are more firmly established, monetary-fiscal policy makers can hardly hope to avoid this painful goal conflict in our big business-big labor-big government political economy.

One approach to solving this dilemma, tried by the United States and most European countries, is the use of "economic guideposts" or incomes policies. These range all the way from gentle governmental admonition to wage and price setters to legally binding, elaborately defined wage and price controls. The evidence is clear. Such "guideposts" may help moderate wage and price increases in an economy of mild inflationary pressure—for example, in the 1960–1965 period in the United States. Not least, their educational value on wage-price relationships can be substantial. But they are at most only a minor supplement to aggregate demand policy when there are large excess demand pressures. And elaborate wage-price control incomes policies have a short half-life in democratic nations when they place a major drag on market-determined wage-price levels.

Though we haven't learned how to handle the inflation-unemployment dilemma satisfactorily, modern theory and empirical data put us in a much better position to understand and deal with the issues than we were in a decade ago. Equally important, research over the past two decades has clarified the costs of accepting inflation as compared to unemployment. In this research some of the old clichés have come tumbling down. Though the comparison is a complex one, it seems clear that moderate inflation in a world increasingly used to it has much less disruptive effects than we had previously thought, basing our presumptions mainly on past big, war-period inflations. But the costs in inequities and potential disruption mount as inflation escalates. Research to clarify goals has contributed substantially toward effective policy, just as has research on the relationships stressed previously.

Second, we have not learned how to mesh satisfactorily our domestic and international economic policies, though the recent past has been highly encouraging: SDRs plus the two-tier gold system plus progress toward a more workable international monetary and trade stability while retaining reasonable national freedom to use inde-

pendent domestic stabilization policies. We have learned to understand the problems better and to cast aside some of the old pat
answers—but not well enough to justify putting the domestic-inter-
national goals dilemma into the "solved" category.

Conclusion

To end entirely on a somber note, listing all the difficulties we know
we face, would be unfortunate. We are, indeed, still a good way
from sure stable economic growth. But we have learned one lesson
of great importance: big depressions are the worst of all economic
disasters—and we now know, with a high degree of probability,
how to avoid them. Moreover, modern econometric research is
making good progress toward a thorough understanding of the dynamic complexities of the modern economy. We have learned much of
what we need to know to ensure stable economic growth. A decade
hence the successor to this paper will, I suspect, paint a still brighter
picture of success. But the road to success is one of *political* economy
in our society; economic knowledge alone will not be enough. . . .

INTERNATIONAL INFLATION

Gardner Ackley

During 1970, the average price level of consumer goods and services
rose by 5.7 per cent in the United States. During 1970—mainly, but
not entirely, by coincidence—the price level of consumer goods and
services also rose by an average of 5.7 per cent in the twenty-two
countries which make up the Organization for Economic Cooperation and Development—the OECD. Nineteen OECD members are
countries of western and southern Europe; the others are Canada,
the United States, and Japan. We often speak—a bit inaccurately—
of the OECD countries as constituting the "Atlantic Community."

In nine of these countries (including the United Kingdom, Japan,
and Sweden) the increase in consumer prices during 1970 exceeded

6.5 per cent. In only six countries (including Germany, Canada, and Belgium) was the rise in consumer prices 4.5 per cent or less. Moreover, the average advance of prices was only moderately faster during 1970 than in a number of other recent years. No wonder that some have referred to the present as an "age of inflation." That characterization—with a question mark at the end—might well serve as an alternative title for these remarks.

The existence and the extent of inflation can only be measured by an "index number," which purports to show the *average* increase of prices over time. Because of defects of concept or coverage— some of which are, even in principle, unavoidable—the accuracy of any price index is less than perfect, even in those countries which devote the most money and care to their preparation.

In particular, it is generally agreed that almost all price indexes have a built-in tendency to exaggerate the extent to which prices are increasing. Without going into detail, this "upward bias" arises from our inability fully to measure improvements in the "quality" of goods sold. Even more important is our inability to measure the improvement in the "quality" of the whole assortment of goods and services available to us in the market, or the improvement which arises from the introduction of completely new goods and services previously unavailable. Whether this bias in the price indexes is of the order of one-fourth of 1 per cent a year, or as much as 1.5 or 2 per cent a year is a matter of debate among economists. In any case, for this reason, as well as because a small upward creep in prices (as measured) is both extremely difficult to avoid and probably not seriously harmful, many authorities would reserve the term inflation for a persistent rise exceeding perhaps 1 or 2 per cent a year in the conventional price indexes.

However, even this minimal rate of price increase (1 or 2 per cent a year) has been exceeded much of the time in recent years in every country of the Atlantic Community. Over the past fifteen years, the twenty-one other countries recorded an average rate of increase of almost 4 per cent a year in consumer prices. The United States did much better—2.5 per cent a year—bringing the average for all twenty-two countries down to a little over 3 per cent a year. Between 1955 and 1965, the increase averaged a very creditable 1.7 per cent a year for the United States, 3.6 per cent a year for the other twenty-one countries, and 2.6 per cent for all twenty-two countries combined. During the past five years, 1965–70, however, the better performance of the United States has not been maintained. For the twenty-two countries combined, the average increase between 1965 and 1970 accelerated to 4.2 per cent, which happens also to be just the average rise in the United States. During the years since 1965 there has been a fairly steady, year-after-year, acceleration of price increases in many—though far from all—of the individual countries, reaching in 1970 the 5.7 per cent average rate that I referred to earlier. The only countries with price records about as good as ours over these fifteen years were Germany, Canada, Belgium, Switzerland, Greece, and Luxembourg.

There is *some* evidence, although it is not absolutely clear, that the trend toward larger price increases in the Atlantic countries in recent years has been accompanied by a trend toward greater uniformity of price increases among the countries. In the past there has always been at least one major country—often the United States or Germany that stood out as an island of stability in a sea of inflation. Recently there has been no such country.

Fears that the western world has now entered upon an age of inflation are supported by this record. To be sure, if we look to the immediate situation, there has recently been a clear slowing down in the rate of inflation. The trend of price increases *during the course of 1970* was clearly in the direction of progressively slower rates of increase in Germany, France, Italy, Belgium, and Canada. It probably was also toward smaller increases in the United States, the Netherlands, and Sweden. The trend in the United Kingdom and Japan is questionable; only in Switzerland was it clearly toward larger increases. Thus the rise in prices has slowed down, and further improvement is ahead of us in 1971.

Nevertheless, there is no possible basis for complacency about inflation in the Atlantic world. Even with its current slowing down, inflation remains at an uncomfortably high rate—certainly the highest since the period of immediate postwar reconstruction and the Korean War. Moreover, the experience of the last fifteen years and the analysis which I will summarize in the next few minutes strongly suggest that the problem of inflation is too deeply rooted in the economic conditions and institutional structures of the Atlantic countries to be readily overcome. . . .

Our current inflation was set off at the end of 1965, when the

Vietnam intervention moved from the provision of advisers to the deployment of regular forces. Federal defense spending—which had been declining in importance ever since the end of the Korean War—surged upward in an economy just reaching full employment. Damage would have been avoided if we had moved promptly to raise taxes at the beginning of 1966. The failure to do so allowed excessive demand to press against our productive capabilities. We exceeded full employment. We ran substantial federal budget deficits at full employment when we needed a surplus.

President Johnson understood the need for a tax increase. But he didn't recommend it in 1966 because his widespread consultations convinced him—quite correctly, I believe—that it would have been impossible to enact it. He hoped that either the need would go away, or the inflation and high interest rates that would result would soon convince the Congress and the public—among others, Wilbur Mills, the *New York Times,* and the *Washington Post*—to support a tax increase. Some of his political advisers may also have shrunk from asking the people to pay for a war that was already unpopular.

At the beginning of 1967, however, and again at the beginning of 1968, the President did recommend a tax increase, and he and his administration fought hard to get it. But it wasn't until mid-1968 that the surcharge finally was enacted. By that time, the annual rate of price increase was approaching 4 per cent. Thus, in January 1969, the Nixon administration inherited a booming economy and an inflation that was already nearly three years old.

The new administration decided—properly, I think—that the policy of fiscal restraint embodied in the tax surcharge should be continued a while longer. And in 1969 the Federal Reserve Board tightened even further its monetary restraint. The restrictive fiscal and monetary policies did the job. The economy stopped expanding. The unemployment rate bottomed out at about 3.5 per cent early in 1969; and at the beginning of 1970 it started to soar, exceeding 6 per cent at year-end. Yet even after the excess demand had disappeared, prices continued to rise. Instead of tapering off, inflation accelerated in 1969 and again in 1970. By mid-1970, the rate of price increase reached and exceeded 6 per cent, and is still not far from that.

In my book, the policy of fiscal and monetary restraint lasted too long, letting unemployment reach the excessive level where it now stands, and from which it will not be easily pushed back. To be sure, the Federal Reserve eased up progressively on monetary policy throughout 1970. The administration held on, however, to the rhetoric of restraint and, so far as it could, to the reality of fiscal restraint. Fiscal policy began to ease only as the tax surcharge expired at midyear and as Congress kept adding to the President's budget—despite his vetoes of several major appropriation bills. The reasoning was that if the previous big dose of restraint hadn't worked then even more was needed, and such restraint would do the job of stopping inflation.

Why hasn't it worked? Economists don't really know. Never before in this country has such a high *and rising* level of unemployment been accompanied by such a rapid *and accelerating* inflation.

One reason is undoubtedly that inflation got so much of a head start before effective restraint was applied. This might explain a slower than usual tapering off of inflation once restraint was imposed. But two and a half years of *accelerating* inflation? Certainly during this whole period, inflation has become deeply rooted in people's attitudes and expectations, and therefore resistant to change. But is it not more than that? Is it not that almost everyone, every group, has increasingly come to act on the conviction that the other guy—everyone else—is out to get what he can at our expense? It's not enough any more just to protect ourselves by keeping up with the inflation that everyone else is causing. Why shouldn't we try to get ahead of it, so that we get ours too—at the other guy's expense?

Of course, hardly any of us succeeds; we just cause the spiral to turn faster. Only a few really gain, and a few get badly hurt.

The President's political opponents—and that includes me—hold that the President made a crucial mistake when in taking office he said clearly and with evident conviction that he was putting an end to the efforts made by the Kennedy and Johnson administrations to persuade, shame, or browbeat labor and management into limiting their wage and price demands. Efforts by individual business men and unions to raise their incomes by hiking prices or demanding excessive wage increases are not, he said, properly a matter of government concern. They are none of the public's business. Both business and labor were thereby practically invited to abandon any self-restraint that they had been exercising, either through a sense of social responsibility or for fear of government criticism.

I was President Johnson's principal agent in wage-price policy for more than three years. In that post I was engaged in repeated and often nasty public and private confrontations with business men and labor groups, as well as in continuous softer selling on every possible occasion. I am convinced that our voluntary wage-price policy made some significant difference in restraining inflation. It could not possibly stop inflation when the failure to raise taxes put too much steam in the boiler. But even then, it helped not a lot, perhaps, but enough to make it well worth doing, especially since every time we can avoid, roll back, delay, or reduce one price increase the pressure for others is reduced.

I believe that one big element in our inflationary problem today is the development of a spreading attitude of truculence: "Everyone else is an S.O.B. We'll show them. We'll be bigger ones." If I am right in this belief, then the failure of the President to maintain even a posture of moral indignation about excessive selfishness in wage and price decisions, his failure to regard self-restraint as any appropriate concern of government, must be judged a tragic and costly error of leadership.

Now, belatedly and hesitantly, the President has started to use the jawbone. He recently threatened to loosen import restraints in steel; and he actually removed some restraints from both imports and production of petroleum when prices were raised. The President even threatened the construction industry with compulsory controls and has now suspended the Davis-Bacon Act. Some of my Democratic friends who were urging the President to do something about prices now say that it is unfair to pick on a single industry. I say, better late than never! And I hope that the President's efforts will develop in the direction of setting some systematic *standards* for responsible wage and price behavior—like our old "guideposts"—even though he knows and we know that they will often be violated. In fact, he will have to if he is to continue jawboning.

As some of you may know, I have strongly criticized the President's new budget as not yet being sufficiently expansionary, not doing much of anything to reduce unemployment. I believe that, even if the administration should now adopt a really expansionary fiscal policy that would start to reduce unemployment substantially, inflation would not accelerate but would gradually slow down. I hope that the President will use this period to start to build a reasonably viable incomes policy, one that will help to protect us from a renewal of inflation when we eventually get back to full employment again.

There is obviously no time for me to sketch the nature and causes of inflation in other Atlantic countries, even as impressionistically as I have done for the United States. Much of their inflation, like much of ours, has been due to an inability or unwillingness to place timely curbs on aggregate demand. But that cannot account for it all—certainly not for the wage explosions in France, Italy, and the United Kingdom that I mentioned earlier, which came when demand was clearly not excessive by any reasonable definition. And there are institutional factors peculiar to almost every country that need to be made a part of the full explanation for the inflation that each has suffered.

Over and above these domestic causes of inflation, some mention at least should be made of the international transmission of inflation—a far more plausible development for the countries of western Europe, especially the smaller ones, than for the United States. Not surprisingly, the United States has been blamed for much of Europe's inflation. This is largely nonsense: we were being blamed for exporting inflation to Europe in the early 1960s, when we really had none to export. There are, however, various ways in which one country can export inflation to another, and we may have exported some, once we had it. Instead of going into these questions, let me close with a few final comments on anti-inflation policy, in part merely repeating things I have already said.

1. I am opposed to compulsory wage-price controls as a basic solution to the long-run problem of endemic inflation that I fear we face in the United States and the Atlantic Community. Controls raise enough problems when they are used in wartime emergency. Those problems can be tolerated, however, precisely because the controls can reasonably be seen as temporary. But the same problems would be intolerable, in fact insuperable, if controls were intended to be permanent. I can imagine situations in which a quick, brief freeze might be useful if an inflationary situation got

temporarily out of hand. Indeed, if I had known that slowing down the present inflation would be anything like as tough a job as it turned out to be, I can even imagine favoring such a freeze at some point a year or two ago. But I would have done so only to break through the spiral and give a few months of stability while other defenses took hold.

2. Instead of compulsory controls, we are going to have to figure out some kind of a noncompulsory incomes policy as a significant part of our long-run anti-inflationary strategy. One or another kind of incomes policy has been tried in almost every Atlantic country over the past decade—including, of course, the U.S. guideposts and jawboning of 1962–68. Nowhere has such a policy been highly successful, at least for very long. But I believe that we have no alternative but to keep trying to design more effective and more viable policies.

3. I believe that there is a whole host of things we can do to help shift the terms of the present unacceptable trade-off between unemployment and inflation—to try to make 4 per cent unemployment consistent with a price increase averaging no more than, say, 2 or 2.5 per cent a year. Many of these things are forms of manpower policy, designed to make our labor supply more easily shiftable from one employer, one industry, one occupation, and one region to another. There is nothing more inflationary than to have a large number of unfilled jobs and at the same time a large number of unemployed workers, unable for all kinds of reasons to fill those jobs. Adequate manpower policies could permit us to get a lot closer to full employment without nearly as much strain as through wage and price policies.

There is also a host of private practices and government policies which grew up or were adopted at a time when we were more tolerant of high unemployment, but which today have no excuse for being. These give an upward bias to the price level at a time when we are determined to operate our economies with a continually low rate of unemployment, skirting always close to the edge of excessive demand. It is a thankless but necessary job to root out these practices and policies. Taken one at a time, none makes a great deal of difference; together their effect can be extremely telling.

4. Finally, we must pay primary attention to designing and

executing flexible and effective monetary and fiscal policies, so as to keep inflationary spirals from starting in the first place. This is partly a matter of continually improving our information and our technical economic analysis. But it is also a matter of improving the machinery—in the administration and especially in the Congress—by which policy is made. Most of all, perhaps, it is a matter of educating our political leaders and the public to recognize the overwhelming importance of avoiding future mistakes in fiscal policy of the kind we made in 1966–68, which must even today bear some significant share of the blame for our present inflationary problems.

WHAT VIETNAM DID TO THE AMERICAN ECONOMY

Edwin L. Dale, Jr.

WASHINGTON—The war in Vietnam produced what is widely recognized as the greatest blunder in Government economic policy since World War II—a blunder whose effects have still not been entirely eliminated.

Yet in economic terms the war leaves with a whisper, not a bang. The big money and the big strain are long since past. There is no present prospect of a massive postwar aid and reconstruction program in Indochina that will even equal the last, reduced cost of the war, even though there will be a significant program. On the other side of the ledger, there is almost no "peace dividend."

Finally, the war—or more precisely the aftermath of its poor economic handling—has left a major legacy: a new and probably lasting, though intermittent, willingness of the United States Government to use in essentially nonwar conditions direct controls over wages and prices. The war, and its economic handling, also played a part in the eventual collapse of the world monetary system established at Bretton Woods, N.H., a quarter of a century ago, though this might have happened anyway.

These points stand out in the process of reflecting on the economic aspects of the long agony. As in foreign and military policy, something has been learned.

First, a brief recall of the Great Botch of 1966. The blame was mainly that of President Johnson, and he finally realized it.

The war had "begun," in the sense of the introduction of American combat troops in force, in July, 1965. By coincidence, the economy at that time was approaching "full employment" after a long period of steady and non-inflationary expansion, with idle resources of men and machines gradually decreasing.

The beginning of the Botch came in December, 1965, with a gross underestimate of the cost of the war for the fiscal year 1967 (from mid-1966 to mid-1967) by the Defense Department under Robert S. McNamara. The new budget for fiscal 1967 included $10-billion for the war, though the final figure turned out to be $20-billion, an error of 100 per cent.

The President's economic advisers, then headed by Gardner Ackley, were increasingly suspicious of the Defense estimates. But, even before they knew the worst, they had recommended a tax increase. They knew that the economy was about to bump up against its full-employment ceiling, that inflation threatened and that a big budget deficit was the worst possible medicine. In December and January President Johnson declined their advice.

The President began to get a more accurate picture of the cost of the war by March. But, in polling people like key members of Congress and businessmen on whether they would support higher taxes, he never really told them how much the war was costing and would cost. And they, partly as a result, expressed no enthusiasm for a tax increase.

Besides, the President that year had a lot of Great Society legislation pending in Congress. If he had asked for taxes to pay for the war, the response in Congress might have been to scuttle the domestic legislation instead. In any case, that was the great blunder —the failure to recommend higher taxes in early 1966.

The President finally proposed a tax increase in January, 1967, asking that Congress not consider it until after mid-year. And Congress did not enact it until July, 1968.

The agonizing story is familiar. With the economy operating at full steam, the budget deficit began to zoom at exactly the wrong time, finally reaching $23-billion in fiscal 1968. Inflation followed as the night the day.

We shall never know for certain whether, had President Johnson proposed and Congress enacted a pay-for-the-war tax increase of some $10-billion in mid-1966, the ensuing distress of the American economy could have been largely avoided. Might-have-beens are the bane of history.

But insofar as economic analysis can judge and has judged, the answer is yes, the worst could have been easily avoided. The war was never big enough to clobber this nation's economy if properly financed. We could not have had zero inflation, but we need not have had anything like the 6 per cent inflation we finally got.

Enough of the Botch.

Next the whisper of the end of the war.

Everything is relative. Even the massive recent bombing of North Vietnam was costing "only"—about $2-billion at an annual rate. And the war as a whole at its end, measured by the Defense Department's definition of "incremental cost," was costing about $6-billion.

These numbers are small relative to the peak cost of the war, to the defense budget, to the total budget and above all to the total economy.

But they are very large relative to some of the recent domestic budget cuts—for example, about $200-million for rural electrification loans—which have caused great Congressional protest.

What can be said safely is that the end of the war will have very little direct dollar effect on the economy as a whole, now, but that it will make a bit easier the Administration's very serious effort to check the largely domestic-caused juggernaut of Federal spending.

As for the "peace dividend," as war spending has declined the dividend has almost entirely been spent within the military budget itself—but not mainly for expensive weapons. It has been spent on much larger pay for smaller total forces, partly to attain the goal of a volunteer army.

While the "peace dividend" concept has always been a little ambiguous, it is clear that total defense spending has remained remarkably stable in dollar terms for five years as the war wound down, to the range of $75-billion to $77-billion. Without the winding down of the war, it would have risen sharply, for reasons of inflation alone.

Then there is postwar aid in Indochina. The Government is silent pending consultation with other countries that may want to help. But officials continue to say that the "ball park" figure is $7.5-

billion, spread over five years, for all of Indochina including contributions by others than the United States. President Nixon first disclosed this figure in a message to Congress last February.

Depending still on details, the annual United States aid contribution—including our share of the roughly $2.5-billion five-year amount for North Vietnam contained within the over-all figure of $7.5-billion—is not likely to be a great deal larger than the amount of foreign aid that was being spent annually in South Vietnam anyway.

The best present estimate is that the relatively small military savings from the ending of the war will be greater than the even smaller incremental aid costs to follow the end of the war.

And, last, the legacy.

On the international side, the war had a direct role in creating the massive deficit in the United States balance of payments. This in turn ultimately led to the devaluation of the dollar and the end of the Bretton Woods system.

Just as important, inflation permitted to happen in the United States when the war was not paid for was important in eventually swinging the American trade balance—exports and imports—into massive deficit after years of regular surplus. This had an even worse impact on the balance of payments.

But, more than that, the war tended to sour the climate of international monetary negotiation, and it certainly did not help financial psychology. While it is probably too much to say that Vietnam wrecked the old monetary system, it was one of the wreckers. Of course, a better system may emerge from the wreckage.

But the main legacy is probably domestic.

In good part because of its failure to finance the war, the United States Government let the economy run away in the late nineteen-sixties. That has happened at other times and in other places. Still, a lasting lesson is likely to have been learned.

A Republican Administration took office in early 1969 at the peak of the inflationary boom. It began winding down the war rather soon. Independently of that, however, it put classic fiscal and monetary clamps on the economy. The winding down was simply an aid in fiscal restraint and was not the "cause" of the subsequent recession, as some Republican politicians (including President Nixon) occasionally implied.

The lesson, of course, is now commonplace. The classic restraint produced a recession and unemployment—a fairly mild recession but still deeper than anybody had planned—and yet inflation continued. The result was the experiment in controls: an experiment sufficiently successful, or certainly not unsuccessful, to give a similar venture a far higher probability in the future than would ever have seemed likely five or 10 or 15 years ago.

If the economy runs away again, for whatever reason, controls will be a lively possibility for any Government in power in the United States. It is to be hoped that, as in the current experiment, they would be imposed after and not before the more fundamental restraints have been applied.

But, whether applied at the wrong time or the right time, controls are now part of our heritage and are not automatically viewed as an ogre. Depending on one's philosophy, and the evolution of that philosophy over these trying years, it could even be a happy legacy from the long trauma of Vietnam.

PRICES GO BACK INTO THE FREEZER

Edwin L. Dale, Jr.

The sad irony of the present situation is that when President Nixon took office in early 1969 he found a booming economy but a then-distressing inflation rate of 6 per cent. Now, after more than four years of preoccupation with the problem and several policy changes, the inflation rate (consumer prices) is 9 per cent.

Mr. Nixon's first "game plan" was to use classic measures of budget restraints and a tighter Federal Reserve monetary policy (less availability of credit, higher interest rates, much slower growth of the nation's money supply). They achieved their purpose of sharply slowing the expansion of the economy. Indeed, they worked too well: by early 1970 the economy was slipping into a recession and unemployment was rising.

Yet the inflation was not stopped. The rate was reduced a little, but never dropped below about 4 per cent. By the summer of 1971 unemployment and inflation were both still high, and the President, acting against all of his original convictions, imposed the first freeze in August, at the same time acting to pump up the economy with tax reductions and a huge budget deficit. Again both policies worked for a while. The stimulus to the economy, in fact, is still working. Phase 1 during its three months cut the inflation rate to 2 per cent.

There was general support for the President's view that the freeze should be replaced by more flexible controls. Phase 2, adopted in November, allowed prices to rise to cover higher costs. Wage increases were limited to 5.5 per cent, with exceptions for those entitled to "catch-up" raises. Phase 2 worked fairly well.

The more voluntary, or "self-administering," Phase 3 was adopted last January for two main reasons. The first involved organized labor. The President was then having something of a honeymoon with George Meany, president of the A.F.L.-C.I.O. and Mr. Meany tacitly pledged moderation in labor demands so normal collective bargaining could be restored.

The second reason grew out of the fear that even Phase 2 controls were beginning to have bad effects: evasions, attempts to inflate costs in order to justify higher prices.

In any case Phase 3 was a disaster, as measured by results.

While economists are more than ordinarily humble these days, most of them are probably still convinced the best hope for reducing inflation from now on lies in a combination of increasing supplies in some things, above all farm products, and a general cooling of the boom. The new freeze may work for 60 days, but Phase 4 can succeed only in conditions of less feverish demand, not only by consumers but by business for inventories and for new plant and equipment.

According to early indications, Phase 4 is likely to resemble Phase 2. That would mean advance permission before the larger companies can raise prices, a fairly firm wage standard, a tight profit margin.

Mr. Shultz will undoubtedly be the main architect of the new program with assistance from Herbert Stein, the chairman of the Council of Economic Advisers, and John T. Dunlop, director of the Cost of Living Council. There is likely to be some input from Melvin R. Laird, the President's new domestic policy assistant, who is known to have helped swing the President's mind toward a freeze, which was sponsored at first by Mr. Schultz and Mr. Stein.

Ironically, the President repeated several times in his television message his basic abhorrence for controls. "We are not going to put the American economy in a straightjacket," he said, and "we must not let controls become a narcotic—and we must not become addicted."

Narcotics or not, there will be more controls. And despite the present understandable skepticism, they might work, particularly if the boom slows, as the Administration wants and expects.

CHAPTER 3

Poverty and
Income Distribution

THE FRUITS OF A GROWING ECONOMY are not spread evenly among those whom the economy serves. Deep poverty can exist along side great affluence; the more affluent the society the more striking the contrast becomes. In the United States, the most affluent nation in the world, poverty persists. It raises basic political, social, and moral—as well as economic—questions about income distribution. The real national product in the United States has almost doubled every twenty years since 1890, indicating an average annual compounded rate of growth of about 3 percent. Rising national income has improved the national standard of living, established the nation's relationship with other countries, and created many new economic and educational opportunities while helping to ameliorate problems of the aged, the disabled, and the disadvantaged. But simple observation reveals that personal income is spread very unevenly among individuals, groups, and families.

In a very simple model of the economy, the production of goods and services generates income that, in turn, pays for the purchase of these goods and services. Even in a simplified model it should be clear that income will not be distributed evenly to the factors of production—land, labor, capital, and entrepreneurial skill. How much each of these factors will receive depends not only on its abundance or scarcity relative to the demand for it, but on institutional arrangements and social values. Since the actual functioning of economic mechanisms is infinitely more complex than any model can suggest, it is far from easy to explain "who gets what and why." However, it is possible to indicate some major income determinants, some of the ways in which they have changed in this century, and some of the problems they have created.

In constant 1968 dollars, per capita disposable income rose from $853 in 1899 to $2,928 in 1968. By this measure, the nation was better off than it was seventy years earlier, despite the demands placed on the economy by a much larger population. But these statistics do not tell who has benefited and who has suffered in the growth process, or whether the income gap between rich and poor has shrunk.

Income distribution has been affected most by the changed nature of the economy itself and the impact that these changes have had on sources of income. For example, the percentage of unskilled workers and those engaged in agricultural jobs with low cash income has declined significantly in this century. Unskilled labor composed 12.4 percent of the work force in 1900 but less than 2.5 percent in 1970. These changes reflect increased skill demands and the changing emphasis of an industrial economy, which substitutes machines for human labor in production and requires a growing number of semiskilled workers in distribution and services sectors.

Personal income from labor and professional services, compared to other sources of income, has risen substantially. The ratio of wages and salaries to national income rose from about 60 percent in the 1920's to about 70 percent in 1957, and the upward trend has continued. This trend, in part, reflects the movement of workers from the farm to employment where compensation is entirely in cash. It does not mean that these workers are necessarily better off but that their whole income can now be counted in money terms. Also, an increasing number of the highest incomes go to top business executives and professional men, whose compensation is primarily in salaries or their equivalent, rather than in a return on capital.

Between the 1920's and 1957, income received from capital, as a share of national income, declined from 23 percent to 18 percent; yet capital inputs to the economy rose faster than labor inputs. In other words, although earnings per unit of output increased for both capital and labor, labor benefited more than capital from the increase in total productivity. The impact on individual incomes, however, has been uneven because productivity increases have also eliminated jobs in the private sector, especially farm jobs.

The strengthened position of organized labor as a result of New Deal labor legislation and policies did not in itself greatly alter the distribution of income between capital and labor. Labor's functional share of national income rose about 7 percent between 1890 and 1953, but almost half this increase was achieved before 1929 in an era when unions were not a significant factor in wage determination. Wage trends for most union members tend to follow those of nonunion workers, which in turn seem to vary with general economic conditions. Strong unions can raise the earnings of their members relative to the nonunionized by perhaps 15 to 25 percent, but this advantage varies with the industry and other factors. In 1969, amidst inflation, both union and nonunion wages rose about 5 percent, but in 1970 union wages rose 6 percent while nonunion wages increased only 4 percent. Much of the difference between the two years could be attributed to key unions in industries like transportation and construction, which won wage increases double or triple those of other unions. Some unions may seek higher wages by accepting technological changes that reduce employment. In the short run this strategy increases wages for those who keep their jobs, but in the long run it may further reduce labor's aggregate share of income in a given industry by inviting the substitution of capital for labor.

The rise of unions represents only one facet of the effort to alter the distribution of income between possessors of capital resources and labor skills. From its beginning this society accepted private property as socially desirable and relied heavily on private enterprise to promote economic growth. Streams of income from private property and enterprise have therefore received legislative encouragement and legal protection, and at times preferential treatment. Highest incomes have gone to those who possessed capital and entreprenaurial skills. The lowest incomes have gone to those whose "property" consisted primarily of the unskilled labor services that they had to offer. The courts were so thoroughly indoctrinated with the property concept that they treated labor as though it were capable of being capitalized. The United States Supreme Court, for example, refused in 1905 to sustain a state law limiting the hours of work for bakery employees on the grounds that it interfered with their right to dispose of their "property" as they saw fit. In this kind of social, economic, and legal environment, wide disparities of income distribution were to be expected. Thus, in the early years of this century the top 1 percent of income recipients received as much as the bottom 30 percent; just before World War II the top 1 percent of income recipients was still receiving as much as the bottom 11 percent.

At the turn of the century the distribution of income was considered by those with adequate incomes to be the result of personal abilities, competition, and an impersonal market mechanism. In this view, those who made the greatest contribution to the economy, which of course was a matter of definition, were entitled to be the most amply rewarded; those who failed to make an adequate income were held to be the source of their own difficulties. If illness and misfortune seemed to account for an unfortunate state of personal finances, private charity was the answer—but not enough charity to undermine the motivation to work.

As the economy became more interdependent, as employment opportunities hinged increasingly on the stage of the business cycle and the functioning of a complex economic system, such a simplistic rationale for extreme inequalities became less acceptable. One approach was to attribute the wide range of monetary rewards to the system—capitalism, it was said, had to work that way. Alternatively, there were explanations that the problem lay in the malfunctioning of the system, not in its inherent defects. Such malfunctions, originating with the concentration of economic power and the lack of organized labor power, could, it was thought, be corrected by legislation. Thus, more economic opportunity, more flexible prices, might be created by vigorous antitrust enforcement, and income might be distributed more equitably by putting the power of government behind the collective bargaining demands of labor. Income could also be redistributed directly by government through taxation and the allocation of benefits. In the past seventy years all these approaches, and more, have been tried but they have never been carried to the point where they have radically changed income distribution in terms of the relative shares of rich and poor.

Congress first enacted an income tax during the Civil War as a revenue measure. It did so again in 1894, only to have the legislation declared unconstitutional. However, around the turn of the century this type of tax attracted growing attention for social and economic reasons. President Theodore Roosevelt called for both inheritance and income taxes, primarily directed against the very rich, as a means of preserving "a measurable equality of opportunity for the generations growing to manhood." But after the 16th Amendment was adopted in 1913 to overcome constitutional objections to it, the income tax became primarily a source of revenue. Some 45 percent of the federal government's income in 1973 came from personal income taxes, which touch even some of the poorest members of society. But, given the complexities and loopholes in the tax laws, those with very large incomes may pay relatively, or even absolutely less, than those with small incomes. Until 1970 some could even escape income taxes completely.

The depression of the 1930's emphasized the wide disparity that persisted between top and bottom income groups. The top 5 percent of income recipients, for example, received 25 percent of total income in 1933. Given the times, it is not surprising that there were numerous proposals to "soak the rich" for the benefit of the poor. To meet the political pressures generated by proponents of this approach, like Father Charles Coughlin and Senator Huey Long, President Franklin D. Roosevelt gave at least lukewarm support to wealth tax legislation. In 1935 Congress raised estate, gift, and capital stock taxes, as well as the surtax on large incomes. But in the same year, enactment of social security legislation, with financing partially dependent on payroll levies, simultaneously reduced many workers' take-home pay. The relative incomes of rich and poor were, therefore, not greatly altered by these measures.

While all income groups have increased their absolute incomes in this century, the relative shares of families in total family money income measured by quintile, changed very little after World War II. The lowest fifth had a 5 percent share in 1947 and the same in 1967. The middle fifth and the next–to–highest fifth increased their shares 1 percent each, while the top fifth lost 2 percent— from 43 percent in 1947 to 41 percent in 1967.

Because property and state and local taxes tend to be regressive and therefore bear more heavily on low-income groups, after-tax income over a wide range of incomes has tended to be a steady, high percentage of pre-tax income. In 1966, federal income tax as a percentage of income ranged from 3.7 percent for those with annual incomes under $3,000 to 9.7 percent for those with incomes just under $10,000. However, when total taxes, including social security, are considered, the percentage of income paid in taxes by these two income groups was surprisingly close. In fact, as a percentage of income, total taxes paid by those with incomes from $3,000 to $4,999 were only exceeded by those with incomes over $15,000. Total taxes paid by those in the $5,000–$14,999 income brackets differed by less than 1.5 percent of income over the whole range.

In 1969 Congress enacted a tax reform bill that increased, for the first time, after-tax income at the lower end of the scale more than at the upper end. The after-tax effects of this legislation raised incomes below $5,000 about 2.5 percent and higher incomes, up to $50,000, about 1.4 percent. Those with still higher incomes had their after-tax income decreased about 0.1 percent. By comparison, in 1964 a tax cut of 100 percent for incomes below $3,000 only increased these taxpayers' after-tax income by 2.0 percent, while a 16 percent tax cut for taxpayers with incomes of $200,000 increased their after-tax income by 16 percent.

Direct government benefits and transfer payments, many of which date back to the New Deal era, also affect the distribution of income, but it is difficult to isolate these effects by income class. In general, the effect is a redistribution from the upper to the lower end of the income ladder. It was estimated in 1960 that those with incomes under $4,000 had their incomes increased substantially, while those with incomes over $10,000 paid substantially more in taxes than they received in direct benefits from government expenditures.

Government benefits and transfer payments may ease the consequences of inadequate private income, but poverty has remained a persistent problem in an affluent America. The Social Security Administration calculates an annual average money income that officially defines the level of poverty. This definition is based in large measure on minimum dietary requirements. On this basis the poverty level rose from $2,973 for a nonfarm family of four in 1959 to $3,553 in 1968, when the median family income was $8,937 for white families and $5,360 for nonwhite families. Even after considering income from all sources, including welfare, 2.5 million

American families out of a total of 50.5 million still had incomes of less than $3,000 in 1968, which was supposedly a prosperous year. Using the official definition of poverty, poor Americans as a percentage of the total population dropped 9 percent between 1959 and 1968. Statistics can be misleading. The standard of poverty-level income in 1959 was 54 percent of the median income for all families, while it was only 41 percent in 1968. In other words, if the same standard of poverty had been applied, the percentage of poor in the population would not have declined significantly.

Between 1959 and 1968, there were some changes in the composition of poverty-stricken groups. The decline of poverty was least in the groups that are most vulnerable to economic adversity—the aged poor, who comprise about 25 percent of all aged persons, rose from 15 percent of all poor persons in 1959 to 18 percent in 1968. In the same time period, members of poor households headed by women increased from 26 percent of the total poor to 41 percent. However, "poor" children, who include about 15 percent of all children under 18, constituted 42 percent of the total poor population in both 1959 and 1968. The decrease in the percentage of poverty-level incomes for nonwhite families has been more marked than for whites. Nonwhite families constituted 60 percent of the families with incomes under $3,000 in 1947, 41 percent in 1960, and 23 percent in 1968. However, the absolute median incomes of nonwhite families have lagged behind those of whites, and the percentage of total nonwhite families in poverty was still more than twice that of white families as of 1968.

Despite the decline of officially defined poverty in the society during the 1960's, the percentage of the poor receiving public assistance rose rapidly. In 1959 only 15 percent of the 39.5 million poor received some form of public assistance. In 1968, about 40 percent of the 25.4 million poor people received such aid. During the decade, the dollar amount of assistance about doubled, with the federal government providing more than half and state and local governments the remainder.

The federal assistance programs dating from New Deal days include Old Age Assistance, whose beneficiaries have declined in number with the availability of Social Security retirement payments; aid to the blind, whose recipients have also declined; and aid to the permanently and totally disabled, whose numbers more than doubled between 1960 and 1969. General assistance at state and local levels also increased sharply, precipitating major financial crises in metropolitan centers like New York City.

Government expenditures for social welfare, which include aid to education and Medicare, have grown rapidly, especially since 1965. Social welfare expenditures represented 15.0 percent of GNP in fiscal year 1970, compared with 11.8 percent in 1965, and only 2.4 percent in 1899–1900. In relation to other types of governmental expenditures, the upward trend in social welfare has also been marked. In 1960 expenditures for social welfare represented 38 percent of all government expenditures; in 1965 they were 42 percent, and by 1970 the figure had risen to 47 percent. Social insurance, amounting to $54.4 billion in fiscal 1970, was the largest component of social welfare expenditures, amounting to about two-fifths of the total.

Income maintenance and social welfare expenditures alleviate the consequences of poverty, but they do not strike at its causes. For example, technological progress since World War II has made it increasingly difficult for the uneducated and unskilled to obtain jobs. The hope of breaking through barriers of this type led to President Lyndon Johnson's "War on Poverty," launched in March 1964. The resulting Economic Opportunity Act of 1964 was designed to help poor people find their way out of poverty, by education, training, or both. The Job Corps concentrated on providing trainees with skills that they might use in the labor market. The Neighborhood Youth Corps was to furnish unemployed young people between 16 and 21 with work and on-the-job training, and it had a counterpart in federally funded work-study programs for students. Loan programs were established for the rural poor, cooperatives, and small business, while Volunteers in Service to America formed a domestic Peace Corps. Perhaps the most innovative element of the Economic Opportunity Act was Community Action programs, combining public and private efforts in low-income areas. Among these projects are Head Start for disadvantaged children; legal services to aid the poor; and family planning services to help the poor limit the number of their children.

The results of these programs have been important but considerably less than was hoped. For one thing, public assistance programs reach appreciably less than half the poor. Secondly, the resources allocated to the war on poverty have been much fewer than its planners had expected. In its first full year of operation, the Office of Economic Opportunity (OEO) was funded at $1.5 billion; by 1970 the figure had risen to only $2.048 billion. Minimum levels of support contemplated by the planners, however, were more than triple these amounts. Equally important, experience has shown that nonphysical causes of poverty—personal attitudes, motivation, literacy, and the like—are more difficult to change than had been anticipated. In 1973 President Richard Nixon, concerned about the effectiveness of OEO and its cost, ordered its termination despite strong protests from Congress.

Relief of poverty remains a major governmental challenge. For example, assistance to those in poverty is affected by the state in which one resides. Cash aid to families with dependent children in the month of June 1969 averaged $43.85 for the United States, but a family in New Jersey received $66.40, while its counterpart in Mississippi received only $10.20. Such uneven distribution of assistance mocked the 1966 recommendation of the Advisory Council on Public Welfare that the federal government should "set a minimum standard for welfare payments below which no state may fall and below which no family would be required to live."

The movement toward some form of federal government guarantee of minimum family income has made little headway. Such a system would presumably contain incentives to work and greater administrative efficiency than has existed in past programs, and it would aid all persons below the poverty level instead of only those on the welfare rolls. One approach turns on the adoption of a negative income tax. A minimum income level would be established, and for families below that level the government would pay some or all of the difference. As family income passed the minimum level, it would become subject to income tax. A major advantage of this approach is that it can utilize the existing Treasury tax system by extending it. On the other hand, it would be difficult to estimate its cost in advance. A variation of the negative income tax, called the family assistance plan, was placed before Congress in 1969, but was not adopted.

During the twentieth century distribution of income has not changed drastically. The productivity of the economy has lifted the absolute income of all groups, but poverty remains a major problem. Since social values and institutions basically support private initiative and capital accumulation, government's role has been to deal with the consequences of resulting income inequality more than to alter the basic causes of it. The extremes of inequality have been reduced somewhat as a result of governmental policies, especially since 1933, but the relative shares of income groups have remained remarkably stable, despite changes in income tax policy, government programs to improve skills and education, and distribution of direct aid, transfer payments, and the like. In the prevailing type of economic system, income inequality in the last analysis appears to rest as much on personal, sociological, and psychological factors, as on economic factors. In the early 1970's the Republican Nixon administration began to dismantle the governmental apparatus developed by the preceding Democratic administration to war on poverty, which reformers had seen as a major step towards reduction of income inequalities. Meanwhile, attempts to reform the tax structure that perpetuated such inequalities, remained stalled. The revelation in 1974 that President Nixon had paid less in income taxes for several years than many wage workers, focused attention anew on the need for legislative action to reform income taxation.

INTRODUCTION:
POVERTY AND INCOME DISTRIBUTION,
1936–1972

Poverty and income distribution are closely linked, since poverty is associated with low income. But whereas poverty is a social and economic problem, income distribution is more clearly the product of economic and institutional arrangements in a society. Problems of poverty and income distribution, which have a long history in this country, were intensified as the nation became more industrialized and urbanized. Not until the era of the Great Depression in the 1930's, however, did the federal government out of necessity begin to take an active, aggressive role in coping with these problems. The following selections focus on the changes that have taken place since that time, culminating in President Johnson's 1964 proposal for a war on poverty and its results in the early 1970's.

In the first selection Dwight Macdonald reviews what happened to the nation's poor between 1936 and 1963. He points out that while New Deal measures did little to relieve their situation, World War II did a great deal. However, while the percentage of poor families decreased, so did their share of national income. Furthermore, unlike the labor situation during the war years, the constant advance of postwar technology had made worse the plight of unskilled workers. Writing in the midterm of President Kennedy's administration, Macdonald criticizes the federal government's failure to stimulate employment and the economy by increased deficit spending. Above all, given the increased prosperity of most Americans, he stresses the difficulty of organizing the poor or giving their plight visibility.

The next selection, by Gilbert Y. Steiner, takes up a review of suggestions, going back as far as 1925, to provide some form of income maintenance for poor families. Characterizing local and state charity and welfare payments as "crude" relief, Steiner focuses on the "subtle" relief measures of the New Deal and subsequent proposals to provide a minimum income in a dignified way for those unable to work within the economic system or who are surplus to its requirements.

President Lyndon Johnson's proposal for a war on poverty incorporated much of this new thinking about subtle relief. The dimensions of his approach are outlined in the selection from his 1964 message to Congress outlining his program.

Next, Sar A. Levitan evaluates some five years of efforts to implement the war on poverty, concluding that the results had fallen significantly short of what had been hoped. Seeing that the problem involves more than income maintenance, Levitan, nevertheless, believes that poverty could be eliminated in the 1970's if the country gave it priority over other programs. But he sees little likelihood that the American people would accord it such priority.

The final selection by Mitchell I. Ginsberg, Dean of the School of Social Work at Columbia University, reverts to the theme that Americans generally do not understand the welfare problem and have little desire to do so. He outlines major programs undertaken since the 1930's; dispels some of the myths about welfare recipients; and offers several recommendations for welfare reform.

THE INVISIBLE POOR

Dwight Macdonald

The main reason the American poor have become invisible is that since 1936 their numbers have been reduced by two-thirds. Astounding as it may seem, the fact is that President Roosevelt's "one-third of a nation" was a considerable understatement; over two-thirds of us then lived below the poverty line, as is shown by the tables that follow. But today the poor are a minority, and minorities can be ignored if they are so heterogeneous that they cannot be organized. When the poor were a majority, they simply could not be overlooked. Poverty is also hard to see today because the middle class ($6,000 to $14,999) has vastly increased—from 13 percent of all families in 1936 to a near-majority (47 percent) today. That mass poverty can persist despite this rise to affluence is hard to believe, or see, especially if one is among those who have risen.

Two tables in "Poverty and Deprivation" summarize what has been happening in the last thirty years. They cover only multiple-person families; all figures are converted to 1960 dollars; and the income is before taxes. I have omitted, for clarity, all fractions.

The first table is the percentage of families with a given income:

	1935–6	1947	1953	1960
Under $ 4,000	68%	37%	28%	23%
$4,000 to $ 5,999	17	29	28	23
$6,000 to $ 7,499	6	12	17	16
$7,500 to $14,999	7	17	23	31
Over $15,000	2	4	5	7

The second table is the share each group had in the family income of the nation:

	1935–6	1947	1953	1960
Under $ 4,000	35%	16%	11%	7%
$4,000 to $ 5,999	21	24	21	15
$6,000 to $ 7,499	10	14	17	14
$7,500 to $14,999	16	28	33	40
Over $15,000	18	18	19	24

Several interesting conclusions can be drawn from these tables:

1. The New Deal didn't do anything about poverty: The under-$4,000 families in 1936 were 68 percent of the total population, which was slightly more than the 1929 figure of 65 percent.
2. The war economy (hot and cold) did do something about poverty: Between 1936 and 1960 the proportion of all families who were poor was reduced from 68 percent to 23 percent.
3. If the percentage of under-$4,000 families decreased by two-thirds between 1936 and 1960, their share of the national income dropped a great deal more—from 35 percent to 7 percent.
4. The well-to-do ($7,500 to $14,999) have enormously increased, from 7 percent of all families in 1936 to 31 percent today. But it should be noted that the very rich, according to another new study, "The Share of Top Wealth-Holders in National Wealth, 1822–1956," by Robert J. Lampman (Princeton), have experienced a decline. He finds that the top 1 percent of wealth-holders owned 38 percent of the national wealth in 1929 and own only 28 percent today.
5. The reduction of poverty has slowed down. In the six years 1947–53, the number of poor families declined 9 percent, but in the following seven years only 5 percent. The economic stasis that set in with Eisenhower and that still persists under Kennedy was responsible. (This stagnation, however, did not affect the over-$7,500 families, who increased from 28 percent to 38 percent between 1953 and 1960.) In the New York Times Magazine for last November 11th, Herman P. Miller, of the Bureau of the Census, wrote, "During the forties, the lower-paid occupations made the greatest relative gains in average income. Laborers and service workers . . . had increases of about 180% . . . and professional and managerial workers, the highest paid workers of all, had the lowest relative gains—96%." But in the last decade the trend has been reversed; laborers and service workers have

gained 39% while professional-managerial workers have gained 68%. This is because in the wartime forties the unskilled were in great demand, while now they are being replaced by machines. Automation is today the same kind of menace to the unskilled—that is, the poor—that the enclosure movement was to the British agricultural population centuries ago. "The facts show that our 'social revolution' ended nearly twenty years ago," Mr. Miller concludes, "yet important segments of the American public, many of them highly placed Government officials and prominent educators, think and act as though it were a continuing process."

The post-1940 decrease in poverty was not due to the policies or actions of those who are not poor, those in positions of power and responsibility. The war economy needed workers, wages went up, and the poor became less poor. When economic stasis set in, the rate of decrease in poverty slowed down proportionately, and it is still slow. Kennedy's efforts to "get the country moving again" have been unsuccessful, possibly because he has, despite the suggestions of many of his economic advisers, not yet advocated the one big step that might push the economy off dead center: a massive increase in government spending. This would be politically courageous, perhaps even dangerous, because of the superstitious fear of "deficit spending" and an "unbalanced" federal budget. American folklore insists that a government's budget must be arranged like a private family's. Walter Lippman wrote, after the collapse of the stock market last spring:

There is mounting evidence that those economists were right who told the Administration last winter that it was making the mistake of trying to balance the budget too soon. It will be said that the budget is not balanced: it shows a deficit in fiscal 1962 of $7 billion . . . . But the budget that matters is the Department of Commerce's income and product accounts budget. Nobody looks at it except the economists [but] while the Administrative budget is necessary for administration and is like a man's checkbook, the income budget tells the real story . . . .

[It] shows that at the end of 1962 the outgo and ingo accounts will be virtually in balance, with a deficit of only about half a billion dollars. Thus, in reality, the Kennedy administration is no longer stimulating the economy, and the economy is stagnating for lack of stimulation. We have one of the lowest rates of growth among the advanced industrial nations of the world.

One shouldn't be hard on the President. Franklin Roosevelt, a more daring and experimental politician, at least in his domestic policy, listened to the American disciples of J. M. Keynes in the early New Deal years and unbalanced his budgets, with splendid results. But by 1936 he had lost his nerve. He cut back government spending and there ensued the 1937 recession, from which the economy recovered only when war orders began to make up for the deficiency in domestic buying power. "Poverty and Deprivation" estimates that between 1953 and 1961 the annual growth rate of our economy was "only 2.5 percent per annum contrasted with an estimated 4.2 percent required to maintain utilization of manpower and other productive resources." The poor, who always experience the worst the first, understand quite personally the meaning of that dry statistic, as they understand Kipling's "The toad beneath the harrow knows/Exactly where each tooth-point goes." They are also most intimately acquainted with another set of statistics: the steady postwar rise in the unemployment rate, from 3.1 percent in 1949 to 4.3 percent in 1954 to 5.1 percent in 1958 to over 7 percent in 1961. (The Tory Government is worried because British unemployment is now at its highest point for the last three years. This point is 2.1 percent, which is less than our lowest rate in the last fifteen years.)

It's not that Public Opinion doesn't become Aroused every now and then. But the arousement never leads to much. It was aroused twenty-four years ago when John Steinbeck published "The Grapes of Wrath," but Mr. Harrington reports that things in the Imperial Valley are still much the same: low wages, bad housing, no effective union. Public Opinion is too public—that is, too general; of its very nature, it can have no sustained interest in California agriculture. The only groups with such a continuing interest are the workers and the farmers who hire them. Once Public Opinion ceased to be Aroused, the battle was again between the two antagonists with a real, personal stake in the outcome, and there was no question about which was stronger. So with the rural poor in general. In the late fifties, the average annual wage for white male American farm workers was slightly over $1,000; women, children, Negroes, and Mexicans got less. One recalls Edward R. Murrow's celebrated television program about these people, "Harvest of Shame." Once more everybody was shocked, but the harvest is still shameful. One also recalls that Mr. Murrow, after President Kennedy had appointed him head of the United States Information Agency, tried to persuade the B.B.C. not to show "Harvest of Shame." His argument was that it would give an undesirable "image" of America to foreign audiences.

CRUDE AND SUBTLE RELIEF SYSTEMS

Gilbert Y. Steiner

The call for reform that would emphasize subtle over crude relief is more intense now than at past periods in modern American history, but it is not a new call. Paul Douglas made it in 1925 when his studies of income distribution led him to rethink the principle of the living wage and to conclude that family allowances for dependents should be paid separate from and complementary to a worker's basic compensation.[1] The Townsend Plan of the early 1930's called for a $150 monthly pension, financed by a national sales tax, for everyone over sixty. At the same time, Huey Long was espousing a campaign to "share our wealth." In response to the political threat Long represented, a national program to forestall indigency and to provide support for the indigent was enacted by the New Deal. After a hundred and fifty years of only local or state and local public charity administered crudely and sparingly, development of a federal-state program to provide support for the needy was a landmark accomplishment: the old age assistance, aid to dependent children, and aid to the blind titles of the Social Security Act properly are regarded as the basic element in the

---

[1] Paul H. Douglas, *Wages and the Family* (University of Chicago Press, 1925). The discussion in the next several pages of the development of the guaranteed income idea borrows from a paper by Judith Heimlich Parris of the Brookings Institution. "The Guaranteed Annual Income as a Political Issue" (August 1967).

country's welfare program. (Significantly, it was originally expected that subtle social insurance would ultimately drive out crude public assistance.) Other key measures also date to the New Deal period: public housing, both surplus commodity distribution and food stamps, public employment of the poor, special youth programs, and the insistence on need as a condition for veterans' pensions.

Proposals to use the tax system as a welfare device are found with increasing frequency after World War II. One of the first, from Lewis Meriam, suggested that an income tax return serve in lieu of a conventional means test in determining eligibility for welfare benefits.[2] A tax lawyer who was later to become assistant secretary of the treasury for tax policy, Stanley S. Surrey, in 1948 began writing articles noting that the income tax was already being used as a welfare device, although those whose welfare was being benefited from the existing law were generally the nonpoor.[3] In 1950 Senator Hugh Butler, a Republican stalwart from Nebraska, called for a basic federal pension of $50 a month to all citizens with less than $600 a year in income. He would have used the income tax return as the device for establishing eligibility.[4] Byron L. Johnson, a professional economist and later a Democratic congressman from Colorado, pointed out in 1955 that income tax deductions serve as a de facto family allowance. He urged that benefits be extended to those below the income tax line as well.[5]

Family allowance—subtle relief in the form of unrestricted cash payments for children—had their supporters during the same period. Noting that larger family size correlates with lower family income, not to mention per capita income, several Roman Catholic welfare specialists called for family allowances as an alter-

[2] *Relief and Social Security* (Brookings Institution, 1946), pp. 850–51.

[3] "The Federal Income Tax Base for Individuals," *Columbia Law Review*, Vol. 58 (June 1958), pp. 815–30, and "Federal Taxation of the Family—The Revenue Act of 1948," *Harvard Law Review*, Vol. 61 (July 1948), pp. 1097–1164.

[4] *Congressional Record*, Vol. 96, Pt. 7, 81 Cong. 2 sess. (1950), pp. 8768–71, and Vol. 96, Pt. 18, pp. A7284–86.

[5] *Low-Income Families*, Hearings before the Subcommittee on Low-Income Families of the Joint Committee on the Economic Report, 84 Cong. 1 sess. (1955), p. 144.

native to limiting family size.[6] The family allowance idea was raised also by some witnesses at two sets of hearings held by the congressional Joint Economic Committee prior to its important 1968 hearings on income maintenance programs. In 1949 the committee heard testimony on low income families. John L. Thurston, acting administrator of the Federal Security Agency, termed family allowances like the Canadian program "a sound idea" for the United States. At the same hearing, Maurice J. Tobin, secretary of labor, said it would be "desirable" for states to "pay minimum additional [unemployment insurance] allowances for dependents."[7] When the committee had more hearings on the same topic in 1955, a distinguished economist, President Howard R. Bowen of Grinnell College, suggested that the applicability of foreign family allowance systems to the United States should be explored. Princeton economist Richard A. Lester and Professor Eveline Burns of the New York School of Social Work also endorsed such an investigation in their statements to the committee.[8] That same year, Democratic Senator Richard L. Neuberger of Oregon introduced a resolution to create a select Senate committee to undertake a study of the Canadian family allowance system and its possible application to the United States.[9] The resolution died in committee. By 1958 James C. Vadakin could publish a comprehensive analysis entitled simply *Family Allowances*.[10] It was clear that he believed on balance that some measure of this sort was desirable.

[6] Francis J. Corley, S.J., *Family Allowances* (St. Louis: Institute of Social Order, 1947); Robert and Helen Cissell, "The Case for Family Allowances," *America*, Oct. 16, 1954, pp. 65–67; R. A. Lassance, S.J., "Economic Justice for Families," *Eagle*, June 1955, pp. 9 ff. On Dec. 5, 1968, Msgr. Leo J. Coady, president of the National Conference of Catholic Charities, wrote the *Evening Star* (Washington), "The concept of guaranteeing a minimum of income is not new or revolutionary; it is completely consistent with programs already enacted, such as Social Security."

[7] *Low-Income Families*, Hearings before the Subcommittee on Low-Income Families of the Joint Committee on the Economic Report, 81 Cong. 1 sess. (1949), pp. 62, 138.

[8] *Low-Income Families*, Hearings, 84 Cong. 1 sess. (1955), pp. 50, 138, 713.

[9] S. Res. 109, *Congressional Record*, Vol. 101, Pt. 11, 84 Cong. 1 sess. (1955), p. 709; see also Richard L. Neuberger, "Family Allowances," *America*, May 11, 1957, pp. 189–91.

[10] With the renewal of interest in income maintenance a decade later, Vadakin published a new version, *Children, Poverty, and Family Allowances* (Basic Books, 1968).

Taking a different approach to welfare policy, Milton Friedman, a professor of economics at the University of Chicago, called for what he termed a "negative income tax" in *Capitalism and Freedom*, publishd in 1962.[11] The book was a general exposition of laissez-faire liberalism, and discussion of the negative income tax occupied only part of one slim chapter. However, Friedman's proposal to eliminate all existing welfare programs and replace them with payments equal to unused income tax deductions and other credits generated particular interest when the author became an economic policy adviser to Barry Goldwater's presidential campaign in 1964.

The view from the Right was quickly followed by a view from the Left. In 1963 Robert Theobald, an Englishman who described himself as a "socioeconomist," produced *Free Men and Free Markets*, in which he urged a guaranteed annual income to sustain demand on the part of those who would be inevitably displaced from their jobs as a result of automation.[12] Theobald contended that the United States, and probably the Western world generally, was now in the dawn of an age of cybernetics. Machines, he said, would take over most of the commonplace work of man, and no program of job development could reconstruct the preexisting market. To meet this challenge, the link between jobs and income should be broken. The government must provide two sorts of payments to maintain demand. To the former working class would go "basic economic security" in lieu of gainful employment. To the former middle class would go something called "committed spending," payments at a rate higher than to the erstwhile workers but less than their own former white collar salaries. Theobald kept the idea of income maintenance alive in a report made public in 1964 by a group in which he was a leading force, the Ad Hoc Committee on the Triple Revolution. Its membership, concerned with the implications for society of the threefold changes in race relations, cybernation, and weaponry, recommended a variety of new policies, including establishment of a federally guaranteed annual income.

But all of this was small stuff from which policy change is not

[11] (University of Chicago Press, 1962), especially pp. 190–95.

[12] "We need to adopt the concept of an absolute constitutional right to an income." *Free Men and Free Markets* (New York: Clarkson N. Potter, 1963), p. 184.

fashioned. Intellectuals' musings do not surface as public policy questions until political leaders find it necessary or desirable to take stands on them. By early 1964 some stands were being taken on income maintenance and on poverty. In March, Labor Secretary Willard Wirtz told the United Auto Workers that a guaranteed annual income was the "wrong answer" to the unemployment problem. "I don't believe that the world owes me a living," Wirtz said, "and I don't believe it owes anybody a living."[13] He added that he thought society owed an opportunity to work to all its members, in part by the provision of adequate educational facilities.

President Johnson's decision to support a war on poverty in 1964 first pushed income maintenance close to the forefront of policy issues. Those actively engaged in the poverty effort included some who had already endorsed subtle relief proposals and who now achieved a new respectability. Other poverty workers, forced to contend with a revolution of rising expectations as the widely publicized poverty program failed to bring quick change, became interested in new solutions to persistent problems. Supporters of the guaranteed income took advantage of the chance to gain a forum for discussion. Thus, reform of the relief system came to be discussed with increasing seriousness in policy-making circles at the same time as civil disorder in American cities accelerated the search for equality in American life.

Public policy decisions to make war on poverty by emphasizing community action and economic opportunity did not carry with them any immediate instructions about the categorical aids for the old, the young, the blind, or the underfed. The war on poverty engendered attacks on the deficiencies in the older relief programs by many who realized that the old programs did not do enough, rather than only by those who thought public welfare did too much. It became routine to hear categorical assistance referred to as bankrupt because it cannot meet its obligation to relieve human need, to hear public housing characterized as a failure because it houses too few people and houses them cheerlessly, to hear food relief programs deplored as demeaning handouts and inadequate ones at that.

[13] *Congressional Quarterly Weekly Report,* March 27, 1964, p. 632.

Relief compatible with minimum standards of health and decency are available without regard to prior work history or presumptions about current employability was elevated to national issue status by Johnson's belated appointment of an income maintenance commission in 1968. In calling for an examination of all alternatives, however unconventional, Johnson invited public attention to income maintenance techniques and to the idea of radical change in the public assistance mechanism.[14] Toward the end of the 1960s, a decade of tinkering could be shown to be without results. Concluding that the existing welfare policy was a failure and had to be changed, President Nixon proposed a family assistance plan that is a start at restructuring the whole crude relief apparatus, albeit less than comprehensively.

The family assistance system comes down for work relief over honorable dependency: "Under this proposal," said the President, "everyone who accepts benefits must also accept work or training provided suitable jobs are available either locally or at some distance if transportation is provided."[15] Family assistance would never pay a nonworking family more than the total income available to a working family of comparable size—"benefits would be scaled in such a way," explained the President, "that it would always pay to work"[16]—although the actual needs of the nonworking unit might be greater than those of the working family. In this respect the plan shies away from need as a determinant of benefit level and tends instead to keep even the involuntary nonworker (for example, a female heading a household of small children) in a less advantageous position than the worker.

President Nixon's proposal was designed both to provide additional help to some already assisted poor families and to add to the whole number of assisted poor by putting a federal floor under the income of all working as well as nonworking families with children. The Nixon plan introduces improved financing by providing federal funds to insure families in every state at least half a poverty level income. Since the basic federal benefit would presumably be paid automatically on receipt of a valid application, immediate relief would be provided, and it would be provided

[14] *Economic Report of the President, January 1967*, p. 17.
[15] *Congressional Quarterly Weekly Report*, Aug. 15, 1969, p. 1518.
[16] *Ibid.*

independently of social casework (if not of job counseling) services. Still, differences between states in total family assistance benefits will continue to be possible; some lucky families will continue to benefit from more than one program (for example, family assistance and public housing) while other similarly situated families will not; unattached individuals and childless couples who are neither aged, blind, nor disabled will be left no better protected than before. And if "more workfare and less welfare" became a program that coerced poorly educated blacks into menial service jobs in urban areas under threat of loss of benefits, the consequences could be socially unsettling.

In any event, as the cost, the inadequacies, and the inequalities of public poor relief have been exposed and publicized, it has become clear that these programs that started in the New Deal have become a poor deal. We have come to a period of great doubt about most of our crude relief programs. Self-help, community organization, and education and training of the poor are newly emphasized, but these and other brave new words and phrases of the sixties—rehabilitation, model cities, sweat equity, outreach—are not easily translated into sure shot programs that overcome the need for relief. While the effort continues to universalize economic opportunity, there is a widespread demand for massive changes in the old crude relief system, a demand sustained by President Nixon's conclusion that "our studies have demonstrated that tinkering with the present welfare system is not enough."[17]

THE WAR ON POVERTY

Lyndon B. Johnson

We are citizens of the richest and most fortunate nation in the history of the world.

One hundred and eighty years ago we were a small country struggling for survival on the margin of a hostile land.

[17] Message to the Congress, April 14, 1969.

Today we have established a civilization of free men which spans an entire continent.

With the growth of our country has come opportunity for our people—opportunity to educate our children, to use our energies in productive work, to increase our leisure—opportunity for almost every American to hope that through work and talent he could create a better life for himself and his family.

The path forward has not been an easy one.

But we have never lost sight of our goal—an America in which every citizen shares all the opportunities of his society, in which every man has a chance to advance his welfare to the limit of his capacities.

We have come a long way toward this goal.

We still have a long way to go.

The distance which remains is the measure of the great unfinished work of our society.

To finish that work I have called for a national war on poverty. Our objective—total victory.

There are millions of Americans—one fifth of our people—who have not shared in the abundance which has been granted to most of us, and on whom the gates of opportunity have been closed.

What does this poverty mean to those who endure it?

It means a daily struggle to secure the necessities for even a meager existence. It means that the abundance, the comforts, the opportunities they see all around them are beyond their grasp.

Worst of all, it means hopelessness for the young.

The young man or woman who grows up without a decent education, in a broken home, in a hostile and squalid environment, in ill health or in the face of racial injustice—that young man or woman is often trapped in a life of poverty.

He does not have the skills demanded by a complex society. He does not know how to acquire those skills. He faces a mounting sense of despair which drains initiative and ambition and energy.

Our tax cut will create millions of new jobs—new exits from poverty. But we must also strike down all the barriers which keep many from using those exits.

The war on poverty is not a struggle simply to support people, to make them dependent on the generosity of others.

It is a struggle to give people a chance.

It is an effort to allow them to develop and use their capacities, as we have been allowed to develop and use ours, so that they can share, as others share, in the promise of this Nation.

We do this, first of all, because it is right that we should.

From the establishment of public education and land-grant colleges through agricultural extension and encouragement to industry, we have pursued the goal of a nation with full and increasing opportunities for all its citizens. The war on poverty is a further step in that pursuit.

We do it also because helping some will increase the prosperity of all.

Our fight against poverty will be an investment in the most valuable of our resources—the skills and strength of our people.

And in the future, as in the past, this investment will return its cost manyfold to our entire economy.

If we can raise the annual earnings of 10 million among the poor by only $1,000 we will have added $14 billion a year to our national output. In addition we can make important reductions in public assistance payments which now cost us $4 billion a year, and in the large costs of fighting crime and delinquency, disease and hunger.

This is only part of the story.

Our history has proved that each time we broaden the base of abundance, giving more people the chance to produce and consume, we create new industry, higher production, increased earnings, and better income for all.

Giving new opportunity to those who have little will enrich the lives of all the rest.

Because it is right, because it is wise, and because, for the first time in our history, it is possible to conquer poverty, I submit, for the consideration of the Congress and the country, the Economic Opportunity Act of 1964.

The act does not merely expand old programs or improve what is already being done. It charts a new course. It strikes at the causes, not just the consequences of poverty. It can be a milestone in our 180-year search for a better life for our people.

The act provides five basic opportunities:

- It will give almost half a million underprivileged young Americans
  the opportunity to develop skills, continue education, and find
  useful work.
- It will give every American community the opportunity to develop
  a comprehensive plan to fight its own poverty—and help them
  to carry out their plans.
- It will give dedicated Americans the opportunity to enlist as volunteers in the war against poverty.
- It will give many workers and farmers the opportunity to break
  through particular barriers which bar their escape from poverty.
- It will give the entire Nation the opportunity for a concerted
  attack on poverty through the establishment, under my direction,
  of the Office of Economic Opportunity, a national headquarters
  for the war against poverty.

This is how we propose to create these opportunities.

First, we will give high priority to helping young Americans
who lack skills, who have not completed their education or who
cannot complete it because they are too poor.

The years of high school and college age are the most critical
stage of a young person's life. If they are not helped then, many
will be condemned to a life of poverty which they, in turn, will pass
on to their children.

I, therefore, recommend the creation of a Job Corps, a work-
training program, and a work-study program.

A new national Job Corps will build toward an enlistment of
100,000 young men. They will be drawn from those whose background, health, and education make them least fit for useful work.

Those who volunteer will enter more than 100 camps and centers
around the country.

Half of these young men will work, in the first year, on special
conservation projects to give them education, useful work experience and to enrich the natural resources of the country.

Half of these young men will receive, in the first year, a blend
of training, basic education and work experience in job training
centers.

These are not simply camps for the underprivileged. They are
new educational institutions, comparable in innovation to the
land-grant colleges. Those who enter them will emerge better
qualified to play a productive role in American society.

A new national work-training program operated by the Department of Labor will provide work and training for 200,000 American men and women between the ages of 16 and 21. This will be developed through State and local governments and nonprofit agencies.

Hundreds of thousands of young Americans badly need the experience, the income, and the sense of purpose which useful full or part-time work can bring. For them such work may mean the difference between finishing school or dropping out. Vital community activities from hospitals and playgrounds to libraries and settlement houses are suffering because there are not enough people to staff them.

We are simply bringing these needs together.

A new national work-study program operated by the Department of Health, Education, and Welfare will provide Federal funds for part-time jobs for 140,000 young Americans who do not go to college because they cannot afford it.

There is no more senseless waste than the waste of the brainpower and skill of those who are kept from college by economic circumstance. Under this program they will, in a great American tradition, be able to work their way through school.

They and the country will be richer for it.

Second, through a new community action program we intend to strike at poverty at its source—in the streets of our cities and on the farms of our countryside among the very young and the impoverished old.

This program asks men and women throughout the country to prepare long-range plans for the attack on poverty in their own local communities.

These are not plans prepared in Washington and imposed upon hundreds of different situations.

They are based on the fact that local citizens best understand their own problems, and know best how to deal with those problems.

These plans will be local plans striking at many unfilled needs which underlie poverty in each community, not just one or two. Their components and emphasis will differ as needs differ.

These plans will be local plans calling upon all the resources available to the community—Federal and State, local and private, human and material.

And when these plans are approved by the Office of Economic Opportunity, the Federal Government will finance up to 90 percent of the additional cost for the first 2 years.

The most enduring strength of our Nation is the huge reservoir of talent, initiative, and leadership which exists at every level of our society.

Through the community action program we call upon this, our greatest strength, to overcome our greatest weakness.

Third, I ask for the authority to recruit and train skilled volunteers for the war against poverty.

Thousands of Americans have volunteered to serve the needs of other lands.

Thousands more want the chance to serve the needs of their own land.

They should have that chance.

Among older people who have retired, as well as among the young, among women as well as men, there are many Americans who are ready to enlist in our war against poverty.

They have skills and dedication. They are badly needed.

If the State requests them, if the community needs and will use them, we will recruit and train them and give them the chance to serve.

Fourth, we intend to create new opportunities for certain hard-hit groups to break out of the pattern of poverty.

Through a new program of loans and guarantees we can provide incentives to those who will employ the unemployed.

Through programs of work and retraining for unemployed fathers and mothers we can help them support their families in dignity while preparing themselves for new work.

Through funds to purchase needed land, organize cooperatives, and create new and adequate family farms we can help those whose life on the land has been a struggle without hope.

Fifth, I do not intend that the war against poverty becomes a series of uncoordinated and unrelated efforts—that it perish for lack of leadership and direction.

Therefore this bill creates, in the Executive Office of the President, a new Office of Economic Opportunity. Its Director will be my personal chief of staff for the war against poverty. I intend to appoint Sargent Shriver to this post.

He will be directly responsible for these new programs. He will work with and through existing agencies of the Government.

This program—the Economic Opportunity Act—is the foundation of our war against poverty. But it does not stand alone.

For the past 3 years this Government has advanced a number of new proposals which strike at important areas of need and distress.

I ask the Congress to extend those which are already in action, and to establish those which have already been proposed.

There are programs to help badly distressed areas such as the Area Redevelopment Act, and the legislation now being prepared to help Appalachia.

There are programs to help those without training find a place in today's complex society—such as the Manpower Development Training Act and the Vocational Education Act for youth.

There are programs to protect those who are specially vulnerable to the ravages of poverty—hospital insurance for the elderly, protection for migrant farmworkers, a food stamp program for the needy, coverage for millions not now protected by a minimum wage, new and expanded unemployment benefits for men out of work, a housing and community development bill for those seeking decent homes.

Finally there are programs which help the entire country, such as aid to education which, by raising the quality of schooling available to every American child, will give a new chance for knowledge to the children of the poor.

I ask immediate action on all these programs.

What you are being asked to consider is not a simple or an easy program. But poverty is not a simple or an easy enemy.

It cannot be driven from the land by a single attack on a single front. Were this so, we would have conquered poverty long ago.

Nor can it be conquered by government alone.

For decades American labor and American business, private institutions and private individuals have been engaged in strengthening our economy and offering new opportunity to those in need.

We need their help, their support, and their full participation.

Through this program we offer new incentives and new opportunities for cooperation, so that all the energy of our Nation, not merely the efforts of Government, can be brought to bear on our common enemy.

Today, for the first time in our history, we have the power to strike away the barriers to full participation in our society. Having the power, we have the duty.

The Congress is charged by the Constitution to "provide . . . for the general welfare of the United States." Our present abundance is a measure of its success in fulfilling that duty. Now Congress is being asked to extend that welfare to all our people.

The President of the United States is President of all the people in every section of the country. But this office also holds a special responsibility to the distressed and disinherited, the hungry and the hopeless of this abundant Nation.

It is in pursuit of that special responsibility that I submit this message to you today.

The new program I propose is within our means. Its cost of $970 million is 1 percent of our national budget—and every dollar I am requesting for this program is already included in the budget I sent to Congress in January.

But we cannot measure its importance by its cost.

For it charts an entirely new course of hope for our people.

We are fully aware that this program will not eliminate all the poverty in America in a few months or a few years. Poverty is deeply rooted and its causes are many.

But this program will show the way to new opportunities for millions of our fellow citizens.

It will provide a lever with which we can begin to open the door to our prosperity for those who have been kept outside.

It will also give us the chance to test our weapons, to try our energy and ideas and imagination for the many battles yet to come. As conditions change, and as experience illuminates our difficulties, we will be prepared to modify our strategy.

And this program is much more than a beginning.

Rather it is a commitment. It is a total commitment by this President, and this Congress, and this Nation, to pursue victory over the most ancient of mankind's enemies.

On many historic occasions the President has requested from

Congress the authority to move against forces which were endangering the well-being of our country.

This is such an occasion.

On similar occasions in the past we have often been called upon to wage war against foreign enemies which threatened our freedom. Today we are asked to declare war on a domestic enemy which threatens the strength of our Nation and the welfare of our people.

If we now move forward against this enemy—if we can bring to the challenges of peace the same determination and strength which has brought us victory in war—then this day and this Congress will have won a secure and honorable place in the history of the Nation, and the enduring gratitude of generations of Americans yet to come.

POVERTY IS HERE TO STAY: IS OEO?

Sar A. Levitan

A decent provision for the poor is the true test of civilization.

SAMUEL JOHNSON

The Economic Opportunity Act sought to remedy the causes of poverty rather than merely to mitigate its symptoms. Its goal was not to ease the burdens of poverty by providing cash benefits but to offer the poor the opportunity to lift themselves out of poverty. In practice, income support was often a necessary adjunct to "rehabilitation," but the thrust of the EOA programs was essentially one of self-help.

The various Economic Opportunity Act efforts have in one way or another helped millions; and new approaches were tried for age-old problems. However, because of the orientation, these efforts bypassed many who could not benefit from the self-help approach, and they failed to reach additional millions because of limited funds. Even for those who were helped, the assistance was frequently minor, and there was rarely immediate or perceptible improvement. Thus, though poverty sharply declined during the years of the Great Society, the most ardent friends of the EOA would not credit its programs with contributing much to this improvement.

An Evaluator's Lot

The uncertain impact of the EOA programs is not necessarily a reflection of their worth but rather a recognition that there are no reliable measurements that one can use to make conclusive judgments about program effectiveness. Since it takes time for opportunities to be realized and effects to be felt, most EOA programs are still too new to permit appraisal of their value as antipoverty tools. For example, the first participants in Head Start have barely reached their tenth birthday, and it would be premature to anticipate the lasting impact of the children's experience in the antipoverty program. If Head Start is to produce long-term results, society will have to provide other compensatory opportunities as the children progress in their school careers.

An evaluator finds it hard to determine which programs have been successful enough to warrant expansion and which could be cut back or eliminated without undue loss. The dearth of reliable data, mentioned earlier, adds to the evaluator's difficulties. But even if the results of a program were measurable and quantified so as to determine its effectiveness, consideration would have to be given to its relationship to the total antipoverty effort. Thus, while the Job Corps may be expensive and produce few successful graduates, it could be the only measure to help some enrollees. And the selection of priorities and the rejection of existing programs must remain largely a matter of value judgment and gut feeling, all model building and computer-generated data notwithstanding. Formulas have yet to be devised which permit "scientific" judgment about the relative superiority of a million dollars expended on locally planned and designed cultural projects for the poor compared with an equal amount for a job creation project devised in Washington. If self-determination is an essential ingredient in combating poverty, then locally planned and administered programs might have and added intrinsic value that should be properly considered and weighted in evaluating antipoverty efforts. An effective antipoverty design might include apparent in-efficiencies and "frills" which in the long run could prove effective in motivating the poor.

The difficulties of evaluating the EOA programs and comparing their effectiveness does not mean that once a program has started it should continue indefinitely. The worth of specific programs can as assessed, and judgments on their effectiveness can be made, in light of explicitly stated assumptions. Thus Upward Bound is a poor program if securing maximum feasible participation by parents and community action agencies is considered a higher priority than helping youths from poor homes to enter college. Legal Services may be important to instill dignity and self-reliance in the poor and to help protect their rights, even if some legal aid activities do not have any bearing on raising the income of clients. VISTA can be criticized for frittering away much of its resources on a lot of small projects in many large cities, but there is no way to measure the total impact of the "good works" performed on hundreds of VISTA projects. Rural loans appear to be a poor investment if the goal is achieving economic independence, but it may be an ac-ceptable means of providing income maintenance under the guise of self-help. In assisting rural migrant and seasonal labor, OEO could not decide whether its programs should concentrate on "keeping 'em down on the farm" or on aiding farm laborers to move into urban areas where the jobs are. Similar issues re-mained unresolved in Indian assistance programs. The significance of participatory democracy as an antipoverty tool is impossible to measure. Participation of the poor is closely intertwined with other forces that operate slowly and by indirection.

It is not surprising, therefore, that the General Accounting Office, after spending more than a year on a detailed examination of the Economic Opportunity Act programs, despaired of carrying out its mandate to recommend to Congress the future direction of the Act. The GAO report, while evaluating individual programs, did not indicate priorities. The Senate Subcommittee on Employ-ment, Manpower, and Poverty undertook a similar exercise in 1967 but also failed to spell out program priorities.

The public may demand a more definitive judgment about the impact of the Economic Opportunity Act, and Congress must determine again the future scope of the legislation and the magnitude of its programs. Given the immensity of the needs and the paucity of funds, this evaluator would conclude that the funds expended on EOA self-help programs have been a worthwhile investment, but this is only a subjective testimonial, and proof is lacking. However, available evidence mixed with a dose of value judgment indicates the need for expansion of some programs and the curtailment of others.

The adage that "an ounce of prevention is worth a pound of cure" seems to be the case with the EOA programs. On the basis of cost effectiveness criteria, the birth control program appears to be the best investment of antipoverty dollars. Economic considerations are not enough, however; opposition to this program has come from another quarter. Thus, OEO has rationalized its timidity in funding birth control projects on the ground that excessive zeal in this area would bring criticism upon the agency and place its other programs in jeopardy. The argument does not appear persuasive in light of the demonstrated effectiveness and increased public acceptance of the birth control program. Efforts to prevent poverty with "the pill" should be substantially increased.

OEO programs have contributed important insights about approaches to the solution of old social problems. The Head Start experience has indicated that we start public education too late, at least for children from poor families. By the time they reach public school age, many of these children are already "retarded" compared with children raised in a more favorable environment. There is evidence that these disadvantages can be overcome, or at least minimized, by providing child development programs at age three and earlier. But even this popular program has its detractors. Some cautious scholars have warned about the "fade-out" effects of a short summer program. The failure of the program to leave lasting results should not be surprising, since it is unrealistic to expect the debilitating effects of living in poverty for four or five years to be overcome by an eight-week summer project. This suggests the need for universal nursery and kindergarten, supplemented by nutritional and health programs, for all poor children.

Recommendations for retrenchment are more difficult. Obviously there is fat in almost all EOA programs, but it is more pronounced in the Job Corps than in the others. President Nixon joined in a favorite pastime of OEO critics when he condemned the Job Corps as being too expensive an effort. The President's criticism was not merely campaign rhetoric, though he exaggerated the annual cost per enrollee in Job Corps centers. With the wisdom of hindsight it can be concluded that much of the billion dollars allocated to the Job Corps during its first four years could have been more wisely spent elsewhere, particularly the funds expended on conservation and women's centers. At an annual cost of $7,400 per youth, it is difficult to justify assigning enrollees to conservation work; the Job Corps should concentrate instead on the needs of the youth. Another statutory provision requiring that Job Corps enrollment be equally divided between the sexes also needs reexamination. It is not that females should be given less consideration than males, but experience shows that they do not utilize Job Corps training. Past performance does not seem to justify the expenditures, and the savings from reducing the scale of the program should be allocated to other programs.

After four years of experience it is also time for OEO to take a hard look at the community action programs. A good place to start is with the decision to spread CAP funds among more than a thousand areas. While the poor, regardless of where they live, deserve OEO help, it does not follow that OEO can reach them all. With current funds, CAP can expend only about $45 a year per poor person. While it may be difficult for OEO officials to exclude poor people from CAP just because they reside in the "wrong" place (where there are few poor people), the cause of antipoverty is not served by spreading CAP's meagre resources thin. At the local level, some CAA's might better concentrate on designing effective new systems for delivering services to the poor than on rhetoric favoring transformation of society. Neighborhood centers have been a useful rediscovery of CAP, but CAA's have not had the muscle or the know-how to secure from old-line agencies in the communities cooperation in the delivery of vital services.

Restructuring OEO

Whatever the allocation of funds within and between programs, a question that remains unanswered is whether the Office of Economic Opportunity is the proper mechanism for administering antipoverty dollars. Should OEO survive, or should its resources be allocated to other agencies? If the elimination of poverty is to remain a prime national goal, then there is room, indeed a necessity, to include in the federal establishment an agency dedicated to its realization.

Experience indicates some basic faults in the initial design, however. The Act charged OEO with two distinct responsibilities: (1) planning, coordinating, and mobilizing antipoverty efforts; and (2) operating several programs established under the Act. OEO assumed direct responsibility for operation of the Job Corps, Community Action Program, migrant and seasonal labor programs, and VISTA, while delegating administration of the remaining programs to other federal agencies. Even advocates of OEO cannot claim that the agency has made a serious effort to plan and monitor federal antipoverty efforts and to mobilize federal, state, and local resources to aid the poor. Preoccupied with day-to-day operational responsibilities, OEO is another illustration of Senator Jacob K. Javits' observation: "Program operations drive out planning and innovation."

Congress recognized these failures and tried to remedy them. However, congressional attempts to secure information about OEO's long-range planning have been frustrated. What planning was done has been pigeonholed within the federal executive establishment and has been unavailable to the public because of "executive privilege." The Johnson Administration apparently decided that neither Congress nor the public was ready to be exposed to grand plans aimed at eradicating poverty by huge federal expenditures. Congress also sought to strengthen the capability of the executive branch to coordinate antipoverty efforts by empowering the cabinet-level Economic Opportunity Council, which has this role, to hire its own staff; but President Johnson ignored this legislative initiative. As a result, the Great Society's effort to coordinate antipoverty programs was assigned to a special assistant in the White House, who performed the task on a part-time basis. In the claims for budget allocations, OEO was just another agency in the Executive branch and had little influence on setting priorities.

In the Nixon Administration, coordination of federal antipoverty efforts is apparently to be carried out by the Urban Affairs Council in the Executive Office of the President. While it is too early to pass judgment on this arrangement, experience with welfare programs argues against this mechanism if antipoverty efforts are to remain a major goal of the administration. The Urban Affairs Council will be concerned with the numerous pressing problems of our cities, and in its jurisdiction are measures which help all sectors of the population. Experience has shown that institutions that serve the rich and the poor normally tend to ignore the needs of the poor and aid their more affluent clients. Even with the best intentions, it is likely that before too long the Urban Affairs Council will focus upon the needs of the majority and will ignore the poor, who have little political clout. The case for funding special programs in aid of the poor and for establishing a special council in the Executive Office of the President charged with the responsibility of planning, coordinating, and evaluating antipoverty efforts is persuasive. If added prestige is desired, it might help to require the advice and consent of the Senate in appointing the members of such a council. This idea was first proposed by the Republican Opportunity Crusade of 1967. President Nixon has apparently chosen to ignore the proposal, as did his predecessor.

Once the planning, coordinating, and evaluating functions of OEO are separated from its operating responsibilities, the scope of the reconstituted agency must be determined. There is little to be said for continuing the present arrangement whereby OEO indefinitely delegates programs to other agencies. Once a program is entrusted to another agency and appropriate guidelines have been established that guarantee the rights of the poor under the measure, OEO's responsibility should cease. Funneling funds through OEO complicates, rather than solves, administrative problems. Thus the manpower programs under Title IB of the Economic Opportunity Act could be transferred altogether to the Labor Department, and a revised Job Corps might be added as part of a comprehensive manpower package. This would leave OEO with a number of operating responsibilities.

The present organization of CAP is a product of happenstance, and the role of CAA's in Model Cities is ambiguous. As programs evolved, CAP assumed certain responsibilities and funded selected activities while it neglected or delegated others. A sound arrangement would be to transfer all proven and established programs to other agencies for administration. OEO (or whatever the antipoverty agency might be called) could then focus its resources on demonstration and experimental projects, transferring successful ones and abandoning those falling short of their mark. CAP has proven a useful tool in developing and testing innovative approaches and in nourishing participation by the poor, even if it was not "maximum." There are signs, however, that it is growing less flexible with age. If CAP becomes another bureaucracy with a specified set of functions, its major contribution will diminish. If it is to remain a viable agency it should concentrate on experimental programs in aid of the poor.

One experimental program that is an excellent candidate to be added as a major CAP effort is support of community development corporations. CAP has already funded a few such projects; given additional funds, it could experiment with more community-based development programs. Where feasible, experimental community-centered projects that are aimed at the rehabilitation of slum areas or at helping their poor residents should be part of the community action program. The challenge to the federal community action agency would be to encourage and fund worthwhile programs and to continue only those that gain acceptability. If it fails in this mission, it may as well wither away.

Consideration should also be given to overhauling the distribution and allocation of community action funds. The federal government does not operate community action agencies; its role should be to fund activities of these agencies within broad guidelines and not to dictate operational details. The experience of OEO has indicated that funding on a project-by-project basis is wasteful and tends to impose federal judgments on details best left to the communities. OEO practice has led to a proliferation of disjointed projects and efforts, frequently just for the sake of encouraging participation, without improving services to the poor. Conceptually, it would appear that OEO can best discharge its responsibilities to a community by providing the funds, leaving the community to decide the structure of their organizations as well as the programs they undertake.

This begs the question of the role of the state, city halls, court houses, and community groups in administering CAP funds. In rural areas, states will have to play an important part since smaller rural communities rarely possess the technical expertise and institutions needed to develop viable programs. But in urban areas, a case can be made for direct funding to city hall or local groups, although state agencies control significant sources of funds and vital services. On balance, it appears desirable to include the states as partners in a federal effort. Since there is also a need for funding specific experimental projects, and for helping communities where states are recalcitrant, it might be practical to distribute a fixed percentage, say 70 percent, of total funds to states on the basis of predetermined formulas, using the remainder for experimental projects or for direct help where states or communities fail to carry out federal objectives.

The states would then be faced with choosing between city halls and local community groups to administer their funds. This is not as difficult a choice as one might expect from the image of constant friction between CAA's and city halls. This friction was more a creation of the mass media looking for the man-bites-dog story than a reflection of reality. Where conflicts did exist, they have usually been resolved. Some communities have created semi-public or private community action agencies, others have operated through their elected officials; but in most cases at least a moderately successful accommodation has evolved, and there is no apparent reason to disturb this arrangement.

What Would It Take To Eliminate Poverty?

The discussion thus far has been limited to the EOA programs. However, Congress and the Nixon Administration do not have to settle for merely streamlining the administration of the 1964 antipoverty law and improving program operations. Society could raise its sights and focus on the elimination of poverty, an undertaking that would require a sustained effort involving allocation of vast resources. It would call not only for expansion of self-help programs but also for income maintenance programs. The crucial question is whether the American people consider the elimination of poverty a high priority goal.

Few would disagree that the United States has the capacity to raise the income of all its poor above the poverty threshold. The aggregate poverty gap of the 22 million poor in 1967 was "only"

$10 billion, based on current poverty income criteria. Latest available data would support a poverty threshold about one-third higher than that used by the government. A plan that would guarantee a poverty-threshold income for all, with realistic incentives to keep the poor and near-poor wage earners in the labor force, might carry an annual price tag of $20 billion to $25 billion.

Whatever the income deficit of the poor, an effective antipoverty effort must provide more than income maintenance. Since the government has assumed the responsibility of providing many social services which are currently taken for granted, raising the income of the poor would not reduce this responsibility. In addition, the services provided by EOA programs would have to be radically expanded if the antipoverty effort were to be accelerated.

Over a century ago it was decided that free schooling would be made available to all. While publicly supported education has continually expanded, little attention has been given to lowering the entry age. With present funds, Head Start can provide year-round facilities for one of every fifteen poor children and for one in five during the summer months. Universal Head Start is only a first step. Considerably more needs to be done to improve the quality of education throughout the primary and secondary schools, particularly in poverty areas. Since a college sheepskin is possibly the best insurance against poverty, children from poor homes with the required intellectual capacity would benefit from special help in getting into college and from financial assistance in remaining there.

While additional expenditures for education will undoubtedly prepare more students for work, there will remain many youths who will fail in school—or, some would say, whom school fails—and they will need remedial education, pre-vocational training, and employment opportunities. There is a need for expanded community skill centers to make remedial training accessible to all, and residential facilities must also be provided to homeless youths or those in isolated rural areas.

There is also a variety of community services, some of which are provided by OEO funds. Health care is increasingly becoming a responsibility of government. The government's health care bill for the poor is already about $10 billion per year and rising rapidly. Considering the vast expansion of medical services in aid of the poor in recent years, the most crucial public policy consideration is a more efficient utilization of the resources allocated to health programs. OEO's neighborhood health centers offer one example of a promising effort to improve the delivery of health services to the poor. Finally, planned parenthood and birth control programs need additional funds from the present, or in any expanded, war on poverty.

Although this discussion focuses on the development of human resources, environmental factors cannot be ignored. The housing needs of the poor require no elaboration, and the physical rehabilitation of our cities goes hand-in-hand with investment in human resources. Metropolitan problems are not exclusively those of income, jobs, and welfare services.

This oversimplified catalogue of programs for fighting poverty would cost about $20 billion, so that the annual bill for an effective antipoverty war would be in the vicinity of $40 billion, about equally divided between income maintenance and outlays for goods and services. The nation could afford these expenditures without added taxes by utilizing the additional revenue generated by normal economic growth. This assumes, however, that a major proportion of the extra taxes collected by the federal government in the 1970's would be allocated to aid the poor, and that other national programs would remain at about their present level or expand only slightly.

There is little evidence that the American people are willing to assign a top priority to a real war on poverty. Realism would dictate that in the years immediately ahead it would be more useful to concentrate on a gradual expansion of the modest antipoverty efforts initiated by the Great Society and to make the best use of on-going efforts and resources. Admittedly, in the long run this piecemeal approach will involve greater costs than an "unconditional war on poverty." The application of a systems approach should be helpful. The task of Head Start and compensatory education becomes increasingly difficult if the child is brought up in a family where the father is unemployed or the family lives on a dollar a day per person, the level of relief provided in the majority of states. It would be unthinkable to send a soldier to fight in Vietnam without providing him with ammunition, housing, medical aid, and a myriad of other supportive services. We should apply the same standards to the domestic war. However, given the current climate, talk about the imminent elimination of poverty is indulgence in exhortation rather than a practical guide for action.

As long as society continues grudgingly to provide help to the poor, as manifested by the poor laws over the centuries, we must settle for improving the administrative efficiency of the 1964 poor law and augmenting its operations. Therefore, the continuance in the federal Establishment of an agency whose sole mission is to help the poor and to help design new exits from poverty is appropriate. For the foreseeable future it appears that the biblical admonition that "the poor shall never cease out of the land" will hold for our society.

WELFARE: THE PROGRAM NOBODY WANTS
Mitchell I. Ginsberg

Welfare remains the most difficult and complicated problem for which there are no simple, easy, quick and inexpensive solutions. But, no significant progress can even begin until we recognize the realities, unpopular though they may be, rather than the myths that are so widely believed.

Welfare itself is neither the basic cause of, nor the solution to, the poverty problem. Welfare is the result of the failure of so many other systems in America.

People end up on welfare primarily because of poor education, inadequate health care, chronic and substantial unemployment and discrimination of all kinds. The average educational level of AFDC family heads is about 10 years. School dropouts increase as educational requirements for jobs become consistently higher. Poor health is the reason given most frequently for applying to welfare. The number who are physically incapacitated and unable to work grows steadily as adequate health care becomes less available and much more expensive. Unemployment remains officially around 6 percent, but for some groups it is much higher, particularly in areas where welfare groups are concentrated. Automation and other changes in production have been reducing and in some cases eliminating the unskilled jobs formerly available to people with limited education and experience.

To do something really substantial for poor people would mean making changes in education, health and employment policies and programs. Most of us and the government are not anxious to face up to this because of the time, cost and effort involved. But the truth is that while welfare reform can help, no real anti-poverty program will make major progress without doing something about these basic problems. The belief that millions of welfare clients are cheating the taxpayers and receiving help illegally is another myth shared by a large majority of the American people. Of course, there is cheating and dishonesty among welfare clients; it is ridiculous to claim otherwise. Among 15 million welfare clients there are bound to be some that will try to take advantage of the system. In that sense, welfare clients are like many of the rest of us.

Although exact figures on welfare fraud are hard to determine in such a complex system—not enough objective research has been carried on; the best available evidence indicates that actual fraud—intent to cheat—is less than 3 percent. Actually, HEW figures suggest less than 1 percent. Add to fraud another 2 percent to 3 percent ineligibility due to misunderstanding or technical mistakes and there may be a total of 5 percent to 6 percent either completely or partially ineligible.

Fraud of any kind and degree is indeed a serious problem and to the maximum extent possible should be prevented; but cheating and mistakes in income tax payments are also extremely serious and would seem to deserve at least equal attention. What has to be understood is that cheating, while a problem, is not a major factor in the increase in the welfare rolls.

A third myth is about the large number of employable men on welfare who won't work—which most people believe. Of the almost 15 million people on welfare, about 8 million are children, over 2 million are aged and well over 1 million are totally and permanently disabled or blind. Almost 3 million are mothers and a few unemployed fathers, and less than 1 million—including some working poor—are receiving General Assistance or Home Relief.

Thus there are less than 150,000 so-called able-bodied, employable men on welfare. Many of them are well along in years, are uneducated and suffer a number of physical and emotional ailments. This does not mean that many mothers cannot and would not work; but that requires substantially more day care for their children, training opportunities and above all, jobs.

Still another widely held—though less often discussed—belief is that most welfare clients are black. Non-whites do make up a disproportionate share of most welfare categories, but the largest group—49 percent—is white, with blacks at 46 percent and all others at about 5 percent. These figures must be viewed in the light of what we know about discrimination in employment, health care and education.

The facts do not support the common belief that millions of welfare clients go from place to place looking for higher welfare payments. In New York, for example, less than 2 percent of new clients have lived in the state for less than a year and more than 85 percent of all recipients have had residence for over five years. Poor people, like the rest of us, move around mainly to find better job opportunities and to be close to relatives and friends.

Illegitimacy is also generally believed to be a major factor in the welfare increase. Illegitimacy is a problem, but certainly in other groups as well as those on welfare. Whether we agree with them or not, attitudes toward sex and family life have substantially changed. The fact is that in recent years the average size of a welfare family has been declining and for the AFDC category it is now under four. This is true even though family planning information and help have all too often been unavailable for this group.

Many, if not most Americans, also are convinced that welfare payments are too high and that somehow welfare clients live too well. Actually, in no state does the average payment bring a family up to the poverty level. Payments for a family of four range from about $700 a year in Mississippi to $3,600 to $3,700 for a family of four in New York, New Jersey, Massachusetts and Connecticut. This means that an AFDC client receives an average of about $1.68 a day with a range from 48 cents to $2.58. These payments take on a different light in view of recent increases in the cost of living.

Along with these other myths have recently come claims that increases in welfare are largely due to poor management and administration. Of course, welfare programs can be better administered by making use of more efficient management techniques.

Given a fantastically complicated system full of variations in regulations, methods of determining eligibility and levels of payment, plus the political and public pressures involved, it is a wonder welfare operates at all. Imagine, having the federal, state and local governments all involved in the same program at the same time. In addition to the federal government, welfare has 54 state and territorial units participating and over 1,100 on the city and county level.

These administrative difficulties will not really be solved by better management techniques, although these are needed, nor by the introduction of business methods, whatever they may be. Given some of the recent performances by many businesses, they hardly seem to offer much of an example for welfare. I believe strongly in the need for better management and administration, but it is a myth to believe and a disservice to suggest that this is the way to solve such basic social problems as poverty. The increase in welfare roles and costs helped bring about unanimous feeling that something drastic had to be done. The heavy and indeed impossible financial burdens placed on some cities and states and the resulting political pressures were key factors in this development.

In 1969, when President Nixon announced that welfare reform was his No. 1 domestic priority, he sent his Family Assistance Plan to Congress. The President's proposal was modified substantially by the House Ways and Means Committee under the leadership of its chairman, Rep. Wilbur Mills (D-Ark.), and some of his colleagues.

As proposed by the President and modified in the House, the plan did include a number of significant and helpful changes. It provided a federal program that would cover all needy families with children, including those where the head of the family was working full time but earned less than the state's welfare level. This would have extended coverage to the working poor in all the states. It also meant at least a minimum floor for payments that would be applicable in all the states. It made some progress toward federal administration with more uniform regulations and eligibility requirements. Increased federal financing would have provided some fiscal relief for cities and states. The plan also offered some financial incentives for working and made available limited but increased funds for day care and public service jobs.

But the program as originally proposed and as modified in the House had several serious disadvantages:

> While the idea of a federal floor of payments was sound, the level set at $1,600 a year for a family of four was clearly too low, well below the existing level in most states. There was no guarantee that the states would even continue the present, inadequate level of payments.
> The basic inequity in not covering single adults and childless couples was continued.
> The program had been publicized by the Administration as "work fare" rather than welfare and thus a whole series of compulsory and often inequitable work requirements were included. Even many Administration supporters did not claim these would be effective, but justified them on the basis of winning public and congressional support.
> Likewise, a number of unfortunate changes were made in reducing the legal rights of recipients and their "due process" protections.

Some major objections to the bill were not based solely on its specific provisions but on its tone and attitude. All too much of the rhetoric re-emphasized the popular belief that welfare clients were mainly cheaters and that compulsions and restrictions are necessary.

The original Administration proposal with its subsequent revisions was never adopted by Congress. For many it went too far to include more people on welfare, especially the working poor. For others, it did not go far enough in expanding the level of payments and changing eligibility and other regulations. The Senate Finance Committee, under the leadership of Senators Russell Long (D-La.) and John J. Williams (R-Del.), was basically opposed to most of the program and the bill died in the Senate.

CHAPTER 4

The Role
of Private Enterprise

PRIVATE PROPERTY and private enterprise are twin cornerstones on which the American economic system was built. Both are under unprecedented attack in a world where state planning and collective ownership of productive resources challenge the effectiveness of decentralized economic decision making of the traditional American variety. Public opinion polls of the early 1970's showed a sharp decline from the mid-1960's in Americans' confidence in business. The situation at home and abroad raises the question of how competitive and effective the American enterprise system is. How "private" is it? Has the very success of the system outmoded the assumptions and resulting reliance on private enterprise that made business so dynamic and productive in American economic development?

From its beginning, the United States has relied primarily on private, profit-motivated initiative to get its economic work done. In part, this was inherited from its European background, where the spirit and institutions of mercantile capitalism had gained a firm hold by the seventeenth century. Acquisitiveness, rationality, and competitiveness had acquired positive social sanction, and rising national monarchies seeking to extend their power across the seas recognized the potential benefits to national and monarchial ambitions of harnessing the appetite for private profit. Much of the initial colonizing on these shores was conducted by companies seeking a return on the investment of their shareholders. Vast undeveloped land and opportunity relative to the labor supply further encouraged private enterprise. An environment of personal freedom, protected by political institutions and a legal system that recognized private property rights, made the search for private gain a logical basis for American economic growth. These unleashed forces of private creativity contributed to the drive for independence from Great Britain and then to the rapid conquest of the American West. By 1900 vast business empires had been created and had transformed the economy but had also challenged the authority and power of federal and state governments that had eagerly encouraged their development. By the 1970's, government and business roles had become so closely intertwined that the relationship of 1900 had virtually been reversed; government has assumed responsibility for the survival of large firms that would have collapsed if they had been left to their own devices.

In this century, much of the controversy over the relationship of public and private goals and interests has focused on the uses and abuses of the corporation. Little used in the colonial era except for projects of obvious public importance, the corporation gained popularity in the middle of the nineteenth century when the demand mounted for an organization that could tap a wide range of capital sources, continue its operations whatever happened it its organizers and, at the same time, enjoy legal privileges and immunities like those of an individual. Chartered by individual states, corporations rapidly replaced the proprietorship and partnership for organizing major private economic activity. Movement in this direction was accelerated by the rapid growth of the national market. Early experience gained while organizing, financing, and managing railroad corporations was transferred to new mining and manufacturing industries that developed after the Civil War.

The emergence of the corporation took place within an ideological framework that supported private property, competition, and profit making as socially desirable. The personal relationship of ownership and management in that earlier era was in effect carried over into the new corporate era, at least so far as the formal rationalization went. As owners of the corporation, the shareholders were vested with the legal authority to determine how it should be operated. Management was an agent of the owners, who, so the theory went, determined overall policies and strategies through elected directors.

Where ownership was closely controlled, theory and practice coincided. But as corporations grew larger and ownership of shares became more widely dispersed, it became increasingly difficult for shareholder "owners" to exercise the authority legally vested in them. Under the direction of professional managers, whose stake in the corporation was represented primarily by salary, bonuses, and fringe benefits, the large corporation took on an identity and life of its own. The "owners" consisted of a shifting group of shareholders tied to the corporation by a piece of paper that entitled the holder to dividends or the choice of selling this evidence of "ownership" to the highest bidder.

The power and potential of this type of business enterprise was greatly increased in the late nineteenth century by the development of the trust and then the holding company. Both were means of exercising control over a group of companies, usually related functionally to one another, through ownership of a controlling interest in their shares. This pyramiding of power and control quickly became suspect. The trust, pioneered by Standard Oil in 1882 and thereafter widely imitated, proved vulnerable to state antitrust action. Beginning in 1890, the existence of a federal antitrust statute posed an additional potential legal threat to combinations that dominated their markets. With states like New Jersey and Delaware competing in the leniency of their incorporation laws, the holding company soon became the preferred means of controlling subsidiary companies. The desirability of the holding company was enhanced by the U.S. Supreme Court's decision in the case of E. C. Knight *v.* The United States (1895) that mergers or "close" combinations did not, like pools or "loose" combinations, constitute an automatic violation of the federal antitrust law.

This decision cleared the way in the late 1890's for an unprecedented wave of merger activity, fired by rising stock market prices, promotional activity, and the desire to reduce or stabilize competition in a wide range of industries. Within a comparatively short time, American big business emerged in its distinctive twentieth century form—corporate in organization, bureaucratic in structure, and oligopolistic in behavior.

The United States Steel Corporation (USS) was the premier creation of the holding company era of private enterprise. Organized in 1901 by combining the properties of Carnegie Steel, Federal

Steel, and other leading producers, the new corporation (holding company) had a capitalization of well over one billion dollars. In 1909 it represented 22.32 percent of the total assets of the nation's 100 largest industrial companies. In terms of total assets it remained number one until the 1930's. Managers and committees operated the company, the size of which made their decisions a matter of critical importance to smaller concerns that produced iron and steel. Stockholders willingly delegated their authority to management. In 1912, when USS labor policies were adversely highlighted by a report of John Fitch of the New York State Department of Labor, a concerned stockholder succeeded in having management solicit the views of 15,000 "owners." Of these shareholders, less than 1 percent bothered to reply. Only a dozen of them indicated that they would be willing to accept a cut in dividends as the price of reducing working hours. In the view of the vast majority of U.S. Steel's shareholders, management's job was to run the corporation profitably, and they were content to leave it up to management to decide how this should best be done.

With few exceptions, such as the Ford, DuPont, and A&P companies where family control persisted, the separation between ownership and management was much the same in America's largest companies as in U.S. Steel. Standard Oil is a case in point. After the Standard Oil combination was broken up by a 1911 Supreme Court decision, the Rockefeller family continued to hold very substantial interests in the constituent companies. But in 1929 when John D. Rockefeller, Jr., determined to oust the head of Indiana Standard, he was able to achieve his objective only by a massive effort to win the proxies of other stockholders.

A few years later in a classic study of the ownership and management of the nation's 200 largest nonfinancial corporations, Adolph Berle and Gardiner C. Means reported that the managements of these corporations had become virtually self-perpetuating. To be sure, stockholders still had a legally defined role as owners, but in fact effective control was exercised by management, who were salaried employees.

Not only dispersion of stockholding but its changing character contributed to this situation. As insurance companies, mutual funds, and pension trusts grew, so did investment by professional portfolio managers acting in a fiduciary capacity for individuals who were concerned only with the return on their money. In 1970, for example, pension funds held $40 billion worth of New York Stock Exchange listed stock and were adding to it at the rate of $5 billion a year. Institutional investors tend to move into or out of "situations" rather than developing a deep interest in or continuing involvement with the actual operations of the companies in which they invest. This has further strengthened the power of management. Boards of directors, theoretically representing stockholders, in practice often come to be the nominees of management and in many cases are wholly or partially composed of managers. This practice is facilitated where corporate retained earnings are sufficiently large to finance expansion with little or no resort to the money markets. And in the 1960's, 80 percent of the gross capital expenditures in manufacturing come from internal financing.

Given this situation, the large corporation has become a virtually self-contained political, governmental, and social system, as well as an economic engine of great effectiveness in the production and distribution of goods and services. Management has become professionalized and institutionalized. Individuals climb the corporate ladder successfully by accepting and successfully discharging the obligations that a bureaucratic organization places on them. The corporate executive, therefore, has had to make his mark not as a "businessman" in the nineteenth-century sense but increasingly as a financial or legal specialist, sales manager, personnel expert, engineer, or in other special areas in the large corporation. In the heyday of the senior Rockefeller, Andrew Carnegie and Gustavus Swift, "big" business decisions were essentially individual decisions, though they might be informed by contributions from many sources. Overall business strategy was determined by powerful individuals, whose names—for better or for worse—were familiar to the general public. Although this type of decision making by no means disappeared in the twentieth century—the first Henry Ford's close control of Ford Motor Company is a case in point—it has become far more characteristic in most large corporations for committees to assume the authority and responsibility that once rested on a single pair of shoulders. Today, with few exceptions, the names of the top executives of even the largest corporations are unknown to the public.

With the rise of big business, the quantity and variety of products available to Americans have increased beyond comprehension, and the nature of competition has been shaped thereby. National and international marketing requires carefully devised advertising and product planning. Brand names and trademarks differentiate the products of one company from those of another, though their differences, in terms of consumer utility, may be small. Even by 1900, competition in some industries was being shifted away from price to quality, service, and other nonprice phenomena.

Since 1900, significant segments of the private sector have become dominated by industries composed of a few large companies. In these industries the costs of producing comparable items tend to be much the same in terms of capital equipment, labor, materials, and the like. Therefore, price tends to be determined by cost plus a predetermined rate of return on the investment. Target budgeting and target rates of return were introduced in the 1920's by Donaldson Brown at General Motors, making it possible after World War II for GM to raise automobile prices by about $3.75 for every dollar of increased labor cost and to target a 20 percent return on capital after taxes.

This quantitative approach to the use of corporate resources has provided a ready yardstick for measuring the performance of managers. Failure to produce an acceptable rate of return on the resources entrusted to them becomes a mark of unacceptable managerial performance in the absence of unusual extenuating circumstances. This type of measurement has further increased the pressures for professional job competence and the demand for professionally trained managers. The widespread introduction of computers in the 1960's not only expanded the range and precision of information with which managers must deal, but was typical of the accelerated pace of business decision making.

The traditional rule-of-thumb approach to management was challenged as early as the 1880's when Frederick W. Taylor showed that there were "scientific" ways to organize shop and factory work. In the same decade the Wharton School of the University of Pennsylvania began to offer instruction in business management. In 1908 the Harvard Graduate School of Business Administration was established as a professional school to train future businessmen. From that time, college and university trained managers have mounted in number. Given a broader perspective on the role of business than their predecessors and equipped with a wider variety of management tools, including many derived from the social sciences, new generations of managers have recognized that the corporation is not merely an instrument for making profit through economic service to society, but is a major system of power with obligations to many publics in the society. But the question remains whether even the best-intentioned management is, or should be expected to be, capable of policing itself.

Many of the classical assumptions about the self-policing roles of profit and private enterprise have been challenged by the growth of the large corporation. For example, the simplifying assumption that the goal of businessmen is to maximize profit is subject to important qualifications. In fact, contrary to public belief, as expressed in one recent poll, average after-tax profit in manufacturing companies is closer to 5 than 28 percent of sales. Profit is essential for a business to survive, but it is only one of a broad constellation of goals that top management must consider. Desires or imperatives for security, power, or freedom from governmental attack may significantly qualify the unalloyed pursuit of profit. Calculated restraint in the use of economic power in favor of achieving one or more of these goals has indeed characterized the management of most large corporations. As far back as the turn of the century, Judge Elbert Gary, chief executive of the newly formed U.S. Steel Corporation, recognized that the size of his company made it particularly vulnerable to attack by government responding to public and industry pressures. He, therefore, adopted a policy of cooperation with government and with smaller firms in the industry. The policy of restraint was profitable, but it also exemplified concern for protecting a position of private economic power.

This sketch of the rise of large-scale private enterprise differs substantially from the simple competitive model with which it is so often explained. As Adolph Berle has put it, "We have come to believe our own repeated declarations that our society is based on individual initiative—whereas, in fact, most of it is no more individual than an infantry division. We assume that our economic system is based on 'private property.' Yet most industrial property is no more private than a seat in a subway train, and indeed it is questionable whether much of it can be called 'property' at all."[1] While private enterprise has remained private in name and form, it has become increasingly more public in ownership and, to a lesser extent, in the range of its enforced and acknowledged responsibilities. However, the nineteenth century capitalist, competitive rationale, which fitted the corporate system loosely even in that era, has continued to be articulated by business spokesmen (and, until recently, widely accepted by the public) with sincerity and in the knowledge that even a century ago, the exceptions, such as protective tariffs and land-grant subsidies, challenged rather than confirmed the rule. The American business system has become so complex, its interaction with the public sector so confusing, yet basic, that it defies satisfactory reduction to a simple model. Therefore, it has continued to be popularly described in the outmoded terms of "individual enterprise and market competition," because the assumptions of that model hue closely to familiar, comfortable, and traditional values in American life.

Perhaps Adolph Berle went too far in criticizing the contemporary adequacy of the traditional enterprise model. Individual initiative has not disappeared, even in the large corporation; it has been harnessed to team effort. In some instances the creators of modern conglomerates have displayed initiative, ingenuity, and entrepreneurial ability akin to that of the early industrialists. Furthermore, the business system is still "private" in the sense that most decisions about what and how much to produce are still made by private individuals and companies, rather than by the state. However, government increasingly determines, at the least, the environment in which such decisions are made. In the old sense that stockholders "own" the capital assets used in production, the popular concept of "property" has been outmoded. But both the individual and the corporation can still exercise ownership rights and generally can buy or sell them without permission from the government. And it is significant that private financial power is still concentrated in stockholdings. For example, it has been estimated, though probably too generously, that in 150 "supercorporations" as few as 200 or 300 families still own controlling shares.

[1] Adolph A. Berle, Jr., *Power Without Property* (Harvest Book, New York, 1959), p. 27.

Unquestionably, the role of government in providing direct and indirect assistance to private enterprise has steadily increased in this century, especially since the 1930's. In the process, the terms of the relationship have changed to favor the state. As economist John Kenneth Galbraith has pointed out, government has assumed the role of insuring an adequate overall level of demand in the economy, becoming, in effect, the guarantor of private enterprise as the senior partner, rather than as the junior partner of the pre-1930 era.

Direct governmental assistance to private enterprise has had a long history, exemplified in the charters of the first (1791) and second (1816) U.S. Banks, local and state assistance to railroad construction, and federal land grants to railroads. Recognition of the government's obligation to protect and promote private enterprise ranges from favorable tax treatment, to protection of the domestic market by import quotas and the distribution of government loans, credit, or contracts based on demonstrated or assumed need.

In the recent past the federal government rescued the Penn-Central Railroad, the nation's largest, from financial collapse. The same was true for Lockheed, the nation's largest defense contractor. The importance of these corporations to the economy and nation provided an obvious rationale for government guarantees of their credit, but equally significant, these large private corporations were treated like public institutions, which indeed they had become in many respects. While small companies have had access to governmental assistance also, collectively and individually, their fates seem to have considerably less interest for Washington than those of the corporate giants.

In the post-World War II period, the ties of the private and public sectors—especially between large corporations and government—have been strengthened by national defense and foreign policy. The sheer magnitude of the financial risks involved in pioneering modern high technology has required that government assume a major portion of the risks. For example, between 1950 and 1965, research and development expenditures by the Department of Defense increased from $652 million to $7 billion; space exploration research rose from $54 million to $5 billion, and atomic energy from $221 million to $1.5 billion. Comparable developments took place in federally funded scientific, health, education, and welfare research programs.

The largest companies are, by and large, the largest recipients of prime defense contracts, though they also filter down to thousands of subcontractors. These corporations tend to be the direct participants and the greatest beneficiaries of major government-financed research and development contracts. But the large companies have the resources and personnel to push forward in these areas. Logically, the benefits of commercial applications of new technical knowledge should fall first to them. Although thousands of small firms act as subcontractors for the large ones, the resulting dependent relationship has little resemblance to the free market model of classical competition.

The barriers to entry to existing industries that confront new firms have been raised further as already large corporations have consolidated and expanded. The conglomerate movement of the 1960's was the third major merger movement of this century, and in many respects it built on those of the turn of the century and the 1920's. However, where the earlier merger movements tended to unite firms in the same industry under single control, the 1960's merger wave has emphasized acquisitions in related and non-competitive markets. Today the 200 largest corporations are active in some 2200 industrial categories. United States Steel, for example, organized in 1901 as a combination of firms in the iron and steel industry, today is engaged in such diverse fields as plastics, fertilizer, real estate, and jet plane leasing, while it remains a key firm in its original industry. Other large corporations, like United States Rubber Company, also the product of the turn-of-the-century merger movement, changed their names and shifted their activities away from the industry that gave them birth.

A concentration of the control of manufacturing has accompanied the 1960's movement. From 1948 to 1968, the 200 largest manufacturing corporations acquired some 600 companies with assets over $30 billion. In this process, much of which took place in the 1960's, the 100 largest corporations acquired more of the nation's manufacturing assets than the 200 largest had held in 1950.

Behind these mergers has been the search for continued growth and profitability, an awareness that continued growth in a single industry might invite antitrust action, and a belief that a highly skilled, small management group can direct diversified, decentralized operations to produce more profit than would otherwise be possible. In some instances, the lure of pyramiding stock market profits and of financing acquisitions by ingenious financial arrangements has played an important role. The national economic downturn after 1968 left some of these schemes and empires in ruins, as in the case of James Ling of Ling-Tempco-Vought. Other conglomerates like International Telephone and Telegraph (ITT), which made 250 acquisitions between 1961 and 1971 before it met antitrust constraints, have come under serious public and congressional scrutiny and criticism. But the trend towards increasing size has not been reversed.

The shifting of operations overseas and the rise of the so-called multinational company have accompanied these developments. Multinational companies directly own and manage businesses in two or more countries rather than simply making a portfolio investment in a foreign concern. With the rise of big business in the nineteenth century, American firms went overseas, generally following a pattern of marketing or searching for raw materials, and eventually setting up manfacturing there. After World War II, and especially since the 1950's, the exodus overseas accelerated. The creation of the European Common Market in the late 1950's gave it added impetus, but American companies in partnership with one another, through subsidiaries, or in cooperation with foreign nationals, have increasingly sought low-cost production, expanded markets, and increased profits through worldwide operations.

In part this role has been forced on the large corporation. The magnitude of contemporary technical and managerial resources requires a world stage to utilize them most effectively. When Alfred Sloan set up the organization for General Motors in the 1920's, the emphasis was almost completely on domestic operations. But when the corporation was reorganized in 1967, top management was deliberately separated from any particular geographical area, and the top executive group contained representatives from the major areas of GM's worldwide operations. Multinational operations are not limited to American firms, of course, but in the late 1960's American-based companies dominated the field. There were over 200 of them compared to 30 in other countries, and the American multinationals were growing at twice the rate of domestic corporations.

The American multinational corporations have swelled the transfer of funds from underdeveloped areas to the United States and Europe. But sales of foreign-made goods in the U.S. market, ranging from cameras to automobiles, by the early 1970's had reached such proportions that imports exceeded exports and the repatriation of multinational corporation profits did not begin to offset claims on American dollars. Since 1958, the United States' share of world exports of electrical machinery has shrunk by almost a third, chemicals by a one-fourth, and nonelectric machinery by almost one-fifth. Only U.S. transport equipment increased its share of the world market between 1964 and 1970, but even there the rate of gain slowed in 1968–1970. There was good reason to question whether U.S.-made goods could compete with foreign-made products in the domestic market, and it was small comfort to unemployed workers that American multinational corporations were profiting from the influx. This situation raised new questions about equating private, profit-oriented decisions with the public interest.

While American enterprise remains private, it is far from "free" in the sense that it was seventy years ago. One approach to government regulation of private enterprise, since about 1900 and particularly since 1933, has been the use of antitrust laws to maintain competition. But implementation necessarily has been selective and has produced only limited results. When the Supreme Court decided in 1911 that there could be reasonable restraints of trade, in effect it confirmed that an enforced return to competition of the classical type among many small firms was no longer possible. Although those disenchanted or adversely affected by the power and practices of large firms continued to demand their dissolution, even during the depression years of the 1930's no drastic restructuring of American industry took place through antitrust action, despite some wide-ranging prosecutions undertaken by Assistant Attorney General Thurman Arnold. In the post-World War II era, some successful actions have been taken to prevent further concentration of economic power in specific industries, but they have reversed no basic trends. To say that antitrust enforcement has been a complete failure would be inaccurate, but its significance appears to lie more in its potential to regulate competitive practices than in its potential to restructure private enterprise.

The federal government's regulatory powers have given it a direct role in the licensing and policing of private enterprise that is obviously affected by a public interest, such as broadcasting and interstate common carriage; and, in some cases, a role of direct participation in pricing and type-of-service decisions. Since 1887 with the first federal regulation of interstate railroads, the regulatory function has expanded, particularly under the two Roosevelts, to a wide range of industries. The most drastic step came in August 1971 when Nixon's revised economic strategy subjected, for the first time, all significant wage and price decisions to peacetime governmental review. In addition, of course, the government controls employment and other practices of private firms that hold government contracts or benefit from government-financed research.

As national goals and values began to undergo searching reexamination and redefinition in the late 1960's, a young lawyer, Ralph Nader, rekindled doubt about corporate power and practices that had been largely dormant since the depression years of the 1930's. He has also raised questions about the effectiveness of government regulatory bodies. On his own, as an individual, he demonstrated that even a corporate giant like GM, with worldwide sales in 1968 of nearly $23 billion, was vulnerable to a determined attack.

During and since the 1960's, old assumptions about the allocation and use of natural resources by private, profit-oriented decisions have come under renewed fire. As the nation's waters became more polluted with industrial wastes and the air blackened with smoke and gases, the consensus that the treatment of the physical environment was a matter for individual and private rather than public and collective decisions lost ground. By 1971 state and federal legislation distinctly limited freedom of managerial decision making concerning plant locations and methods of operation. The government has begun to insist that the social costs of protecting the natural environment be borne by those who create them. Environmental protection measures cost business over $9 billion in 1970, and they are rapidly becoming part of the overhead costs of even small firms. Size and power in the marketplace are obviously important determinants in how these increased costs can be passed on. Small firms appear to be at a comparative disadvantage in facing this challenge, although government has softened the blow by making provisions for depreciating the cost of pollution control equipment. But most important, another obstacle has been placed in the path of potential entrepreneurs who, in classical theory, should be free to enter any market that gives promise of profit.

In the last analysis, it is probably correct to say that, for the economy as a whole, political decisions currently predominate over private economic decisions, whereas in 1900 the reverse was true. Even new job formation has become a public function. The public sector or private not-for-profit activities have been responsible for generating most new jobs since 1950. In the mid-1960's about a third of the labor force worked for employers other than private business, whereas only 15 percent did so in 1929. Because America's priorities have shifted to areas where policy decisions based on profit expectations are no longer relevant—e.g., poverty, civil rights, urban renewal, and population control—the prestige and influence of businessmen will most likely continue to decline. Concern over the public's adverse image of private enterprise was spreading rapidly through the business community in the early 1970's.

In summary, few major business decisions are made presently that do not involve some consideration of governmental attitudes, policies, and powers. In some isolated instances since World War II, the chief executive has seized private property, or used governmental power, to reverse private business decisions; President Truman seized the nation's steel mills in 1952, and President Kennedy used all the power at his command to pressure U.S. Steel to revise a 1962 pricing decision that he believed to be unjustified. In addition, the federal government, through such multipurpose regional development projects as the Tennessee Valley Authority (1933) and its associated public electric power projects, has competed directly with private enterprise. Thus, American private enterprise is not only supported and encouraged but also supervised, regulated, disciplined and, in some cases, competed with by the federal government. In this respect and in the changed terms of business ownership and competition, private enterprise is no longer "free" or even "private" in the same sense that it was in 1900.

INTRODUCTION:
BUSINESS AND AMERICAN SOCETY,
1901–1971

American business has contributed to significant change in the economy and in the society. These changes have, in turn, raised important questions about the relationships between business and the society it serves. Inevitably such questions turn on issues of corporate power and responsibility, which are stressed in the following selections. By the turn of this century, large corporate enterprise in transforming the economy had raised major issues concerning the effects of concentrated, private economic power. There was serious doubt then whether government possessed the power to cope with such questions. President Theodore Roosevelt, in the first selection, emphasizes the good that had come from reliance on private enterprise, but at the same time he asserts the need for the federal government to supervise and regulate interstate corporations.

The next selection emphasizes the many changes that took place in American industry between 1900 and 1925. The rewards of innovation in a relatively free enterprise system outmoded traditional industries, while creating new industries that underpinned the national prosperity of the 1920's. When the report from which this selection is drawn was published in 1929, however, the nation's economy was already on the brink of a collapse that was to alter significantly the freedom of enterprise and the brisk optimism of the business community.

A substantial amount of federal regulation of business was enacted during Theodore Roosevelt's administration and in the period immediately preceding World War I. But enforcement during the 1920's was weak. New Deal legislation of the 1930's expanded the regulatory role of government, including efforts to reduce the amount of concentration in various industries. The selection from A. D. H. Kaplan's post-World War II analysis of big enterprise in a competitive system acknowledges the importance of very large companies but points out that small business and noncorporate enterprise had remained surprisingly significant. Further, Kaplan maintains that to stay on top, even the largest companies had to be innovative, abandoning traditional products and business procedures in response to changed conditions.

As ownership and management of corporations became separated, working control of large corporations passed increasingly into the hands of professional managers, who had to satisfy a wide range of publics yet were frequently in a position to define their own responsibilities. The next selection, from the August 1960 issue of *Fortune,* suggests that both the rate of concentration growth and, more important, the absolute size of business firms were matters for serious concern. In this context, the selection examines several contemporary analyses of the problem, with particular emphasis on the question of corporate responsibility. It concludes that a satisfactory answer lay neither with managers nor government, but with an insistence on the maintenance of market mechanisms.

While *Fortune* was concerned about the effects of oligopoly in the early 1960's, a movement had already started towards another form of concentration—the conglomerate. Companies with very large assets could be built up by acquisitions in various industries, with none of the individual acquisitions large enough to attract serious antitrust attention. In 1972 a Ralph Nader Study Group published a report that considered what had happened to an economy where antitrust had not stemmed the movement away from marketplace competition. The selection from that report included here deals with the conglomerate "explosion," as the Nader group saw it.

In the next selection, written in the mid-1960's, Robert Heilbroner argues that labor and small business had not suffered at the hands of large business as much as was commonly supposed, but the consumer's position had not been improved. However, he argues that the power of big business was being diminished by a shift in national priorities that downgraded the role of the business elite and increased those of professional consultants, the military, and government administrators. Accordingly, he predicts decreased power for business to guide national policy, domestically or in foreign affairs.

In the following selection, James M. Roche, chairman of General Motors Corporation, reviewed in 1971 the attacks of the critics of free enterprise and their damaging effects. In his view, unless businessmen are willing to "stand up and be counted," the ability of business to meet its economic and social responsibilities may be seriously impaired.

In the final selection, Daniel Bell looks ahead. He views the traditional concept of the corporation as outmoded by developments reported in this chapter and prior selections. He has no clear prediction of what future change in the role and powers of the corporation may involve, but, he is very clear that the national shift away from "free enterpirse," as understood by Mr. Roche, is very much in progress. He sees it as involving the substitution of politically determined decisions on major economic matters for the operation of the private enterprise-market system.

NATIONAL REGULATION OF INTERSTATE CORPORATIONS, 1901

Theodore Roosevelt

During the past five years business confidence has been restored and the nation is to be congratulated because of its present abounding prosperity. Such prosperity can never be created by law alone, although it is easy enough to destroy it by mischievous laws. If the hand of the Lord is heavy upon any country, if flood or drought comes, human wisdom is powerless to avert the calamity. Moreover, no law can guard us against the consequences of our own folly. The men who are idle or credulous, the men who seek gains not by genuine work with head or hand but by gambling in any form, are always a source of menace not only to themselves but to others. If the business world loses its head, it loses what legislation can not supply. Fundamentally the welfare of each citizen, and therefore the welfare of the aggregate of citizens which makes the nation, must rest upon individual thrift and energy, resolution and intelligence. Nothing can take the place of this individual capacity; but wise legislation and honest and intelligent administration can give it the fullest scope, the largest opportunity to work to good effect.

The tremendous and highly complex industrial development

which went on with ever accelerated rapidity during the latter half of the nineteenth century brings us face to face, at the beginning of the twentieth, with very serious social problems. The old laws, and the old customs which had almost the binding force of law, were once quite sufficient to regulate the accumulation and distribution of wealth. Since the industrial changes which have so enormously increased the productive power of mankind, they are no longer sufficient.

The growth of cities has gone on beyond comparison faster than the growth of the country, and the upbuilding of the great industrial centres has meant a startling increase, not merely in the aggregate of wealth, but in the number of very large individual, and especially of very large corporate, fortunes. The creation of these great corporate fortunes has not been due to the tariff nor to any other governmental action, but to natural causes in the business world, operating in other countries as they operate in our own.

The process has aroused much antagonism, a great part of which is wholly without warrant. It is not true that as the rich have grown richer the poor have grown poorer. On the contrary, never before has the average man, the wageworker, the farmer, the small trader, been so well off as in this country and at the present time. There have been abuses connected with the accumulation of wealth; yet it remains true that a fortune accumulated in legitimate business can be accumulated by the person specially benefited only on condition of conferring immense incidental benefits upon others. Successful enterprise, of the type which benefits all mankind, can only exist if the conditions are such as to offer great prizes as the rewards of success.

The captains of industry who have driven the railway systems across this continent, who have built up our commerce, who have developed our manufactures, have on the whole done great good to our people. Without them the material development of which we are so justly proud could never have taken place. Moreover, we should recognize the immense importance to this material development of leaving as unhampered as is compatible with the public good the strong and forceful men upon whom the success of business operations inevitably rests. The slightest study of business conditions will satisfy any one capable of forming a judgment that the personal equation is the most important factor in a business operation; that the business ability of the man at the head of any business concern, big or little, is usually the factor which fixes the gulf between striking success and hopeless failure.

An additional reason for caution in dealing with corporations is to be found in the international commercial conditions of to-day. The same business conditions which have produced the great aggregations of corporate and individual wealth have made them very potent factors in international commercial competition. Business concerns which have the largest means at their disposal and are managed by the ablest men are naturally those which take the lead in the strife for commercial supremacy among the nations of the world. America has only just begun to assume that commanding position in the international business world which we believe will more and more be hers. It is of the utmost importance that this position be not jeopardized, especially at a time when the overflowing abundance of our own natural resources and the skill, business energy, and mechanical aptitude of our people make foreign markets essential. Under such conditions it would be most unwise to cramp or to fetter the youthful strength of our nation.

Moreover, it can not too often be pointed out that to strike with ignorant violence at the interests of one set of men almost inevitably endangers the interests of all. The fundamental rule in our national life—the rule which underlies all others—is that, on the whole, and in the long run, we shall go up or down together. There are exceptions; and in times of prosperity some will prosper far more, and in times of adversity some will suffer far more, than others; but speaking generally, a period of good times means that all share more or less in them, and in a period of hard times all feel the stress to a greater or less degree. It surely ought not to be necessary to enter into any proof of this statement; the memory of the lean years which began in 1893 is still vivid and we can contrast them with the conditions in this very year which is now closing. Disaster to great business enterprises can never have its effects limited to the men at the top. It spreads throughout, and while it is bad for everybody, it is worst for those furthest down. The capitalist may be shorn of his luxuries; but the wage-worker may be deprived of even bare necessities.

The mechanism of modern business is so delicate that extreme care must be taken not to interfere with it in a spirit of rashness or ignorance. Many of those who have made it their vocation to denounce the great industrial combinations which are popularly, although with technical inaccuracy, known as "trusts," appeal especially to hatred and fear. These are precisely the two emotions, particularly when combined with ignorance, which unfit men for the exercise of cool and steady judgment. In facing new industrial conditions, the whole history of the world shows that legislation will generally be both unwise and ineffective unless undertaken after calm inquiry and with sober self-restraint. Much of the legislation directed at the trusts would have been exceedingly mischievous had it not also been entirely ineffective. In accordance with a well-known sociological law, the ignorant or reckless agitator has been the really effective friend of the evils which he has been nominally opposing. In dealing with business interests, for the government to undertake by crude and ill-considered legislation to do what may turn out to be bad, would be to incur the risk of such far-reaching national disaster that it would be preferable to undertake nothing at all. The men who demand the impossible or the undesirable serve as the allies of the forces with which they are nominally at war, for they hamper those who would endeavor to find out in rational fashion what the wrongs really are and to what extent and in what manner it is practicable to apply remedies.

All this is true; and yet it is also true that there are real and grave evils, one of the chief being over-capitalization because of its many baleful consequences; and a resolute and practical effort must be made to correct these evils.

There is widespread conviction in the minds of the American people that the great corporations known as trusts are in certain of their features and tendencies hurtful to the general welfare. This springs from no spirit of envy or uncharitableness, nor lack of pride in the great industrial achievements that have placed this country at the head of the nations struggling for commercial supremacy. It does not rest upon a lack of intelligent appreciation of the necessity of meeting changing and changed conditions of trade with new methods, nor upon ignorance of the fact that combination of capital in the effort to accomplish great things is necessary when the world's progress demands that great things be done. It is based upon sincere conviction that combination and concentration should be, not prohibited, but supervised and within reasonable limits controlled; and in my judgment this conviction is right.

It is no limitation upon property rights or freedom of contract to require that when men receive from government the privilege of doing business under corporate form which frees them from individual responsibility and enables them to call into their enterprises the capital of the public, they shall do so upon absolutely truthful representations as to the value of the property in which the capital is to be invested. Corporations engaged in interstate commerce should be regulated if they are found to exercise a license working to the public injury. It should be as much the aim of those who seek for social betterment to rid the business world of crimes of cunning as to rid the entire body politic of crimes of violence. Great corporations exist only because they are created and safeguarded by our institutions; and it is therefore our right and duty to see that they work in harmony with these institutions.

The first essential in determining how to deal with the great industrial combinations is knowledge of the facts—publicity. In the interest of the public the government should have the right to inspect and examine the workings of the great corporations engaged in interstate business. Publicity is the only sure remedy which we can now invoke. What further remedies are needed in the way of governmental regulation, or taxation, can only be determined after publicity has been obtained, by process of law, and in the course of administration. The first requisite is knowledge, full and complete—knowledge which may be made public to the world.

Artificial bodies such as corporations and joint stock or other associations, depending upon any statutory law for their existence or privileges, should be subject to proper governmental supervision, and full and accurate information as to their operations should be made public regularly at reasonable intervals.

The large corporations, commonly called trusts, though organized in one State, always do business in many States, often doing very little business in the State where they are incorporated. There is utter lack of uniformity in the State laws about them; and as no State has any exclusive interest in or power over their acts, it has in practice proved impossible to get adequate regulation through State action. Therefore, in the interest of the whole people, the

Nation should, without interfering with the power of the States in the matter itself, also assume power of supervision and regulation over all corporations doing an interstate business. This is especially true where the corporation derives a portion of its wealth from the existence of some monopolistic element or tendency in its business. There would be no hardship in such supervision; banks are subject to it, and in their case it is now accepted as a simple matter of course. Indeed, it is probable that supervision of corporations by the National Government need not go so far as is now the case with the supervision exercised over them by so conservative a State as Massachusetts, in order to produce excellent results.

When the Constitution was adopted, at the end of the eighteenth century, no human wisdom could foretell the sweeping changes, alike in industrial and political conditions, which were to take place by the beginning of the twentieth century. At that time it was accepted as a matter of course that the several States were the proper authorities to regulate, so far as was then necessary, the comparatively insignificant and strictly localized corporate bodies of the day. The conditions are now wholly different and wholly different action is called for. I believe that a law can be framed which will enable the National Government to exercise control along the lines above indicated, profiting by the experience gained through the passage and administration of the Interstate Commerce Act. If, however, the judgment of the Congress is that it lacks the constitutional power to pass such an act, then a constitutional amendment should be submitted to confer the power.

CHANGES IN NEW AND OLD INDUSTRIES

Dexter S. Kimball

Every observer of American industry is impressed with its size and rate of growth. In a later chapter, Dr. Mills presents a table showing economic movements in the United States from 1922 to 1927. According to these figures, primary production has increased each year 2.5 per cent; production of manufactured goods, 4 per cent; and ton-miles of freight carried, 4 per cent.

We are producing more than two-fifths of the world's supply of coal, about seven-tenths of all the petroleum, practically all the natural gas, and more than one-third of the water power.

An outstanding fact has been the improvement in the efficiency of fuel consumption which has tended to check the growth in demand for coal, while other sources of energy were expanding, notably those of water power and of oil and gas. Bituminous and anthracite coal, which contributed 85 per cent of the world's total energy in 1913, furnished but 71 per cent in 1927, and but 64 per cent in the United States.

The growth of the electric light and power industry has also been phenomenal; about one-half of the total world capacity is in this country. The consumption of electric energy has been increasing at a rate about three and three-quarters times the increase in population. Production of electric current in 1927 was about 676 kilowatt-hours per inhabitant, as compared with 630 kilowatt-hours in 1926. The percentage of electrification of manufacturing industries was about twice as large in 1927 as in 1914.

In the production of iron and steel the United States has an annual output representing approximately half that of the entire world, the greater portion of which is consumed in this country. The production for 1927 was about 51 per cent greater than the average for the years 1910–1914.

Not only have most of our industries greatly increased in size, but there has also been a rapid increase in the size of industrial equipment and industrial structures. Buildings, engines, locomotives, steamships, and bridges have increased in size at a rapid rate in recent years. The new bridge over the Hudson River at One Hundred Seventy-first Street, New York, with a clear span of 3,500 feet, towers 625 feet high, and four supporting cables 36 inches in diameter, is without doubt the greatest and most difficult construction ever undertaken by man. And it should be remembered that the basic tools by means of which these great undertakings are built have increased proportionately in size and capacity.

Another fact of great importance for industry as a whole is the increase in the size and variety of consumer demands. These changes have helped to create and to quicken the constant flow of new materials and new products, some of them, like rayon, of startling economic significance, others like radio, appearing at present as mainly another addition to the crowded field of personal amusement. And a more searching examination of this flow of new things would uncover scientific research activities and applications of the results of research far in advance of anything existing a few years ago.

In addition to the more tangible and visible changes in size of industries and products, there has been a great advance in the last few years in what may be called the theoretical side of production. One of the most outstanding of these movements, and one that is intimately related to mass production, is standardization. The economic advantages of standardized products are now so fully recognized as to make the problem of standardization not only a national problem but also an international one. Our largest manufacturing plants produce largely standardized products and the lowest unit costs are found in connection with standardized production.

These varied phenomena have been much more in evidence since the World War than prior to that event. Yet the war developed no new basic productive processes. In this respect it differed from the Civil War which was instrumental in developing modern automatic machinery. The basic mechanical productive processes in use today are in general those in use before the World War. Chemical processes have come into more extended use in connection with the production of certain new materials, and processes like electric and oxyacetylene welding have appeared; but there have been no radical advances in the basic industrial processes.

The war, however, did focus attention upon the advantages of mass production. In the preparation of war material, many plants were narrowly specialized and many "single purpose" plants were organized. The Hog Island shipyard, with its many feeder plants, was in some respects the largest attempt at mass production that has ever been attempted, and the influence of this effort in calling attention to the advantage of mass production must have been considerable. The war also greatly expanded our industrial equipment, and the effort to keep this equipment in operation has been one influence in the vast production of recent years.

In any case there has been a decided movement toward the use of semiautomatic and automatic machinery wherever this is warranted, and in the larger industries some highly developed special machinery has resulted.

The last few years have witnessed a tremendous effort upon the part of factory managers to lower productive costs. This effort is twofold in character. First, close scrutiny has been given all methods and processes, and, second, an effort has been made to check avoidable wastes. The movement to check industrial wastes inaugurated by Herbert Hoover, when Secretary of Commerce, is of wide scope and great economic significance. American industry has been proverbially wasteful, and the gains that have already been made in some industries by waste elimination would indicate that we have here a hitherto neglected factor of great importance to industry.

The last ten years have also witnessed a fuller appreciation of industrial research and many interesting and important applications of the results of research. Many new materials have appeared and a number of new industrial processes. We are probably somewhat behind some European nations in this respect, but the realization of the importance of industrial research is growing rapidly.

One of the important influences has been the change in efficiency of rail transportation.[1] In 1927, goods were moved with the greatest rapidity in history, gross ton-miles per train-hour increasing 47.5 per cent as compared with 1920, and ton-miles of revenue freight carried exceeding by 42 per cent the performance of 1913. Between 1901 and 1913, the ton mileage of the carriers had practically doubled. Employee productivity showed an important increase, the index of traffic units handled per employee, based on 1913, being 134.4 in 1927.

An important element in the increase in output has been the rapid abandonment of inefficient plants. In a recent survey of the merchant blast furnace industry, it is reported that "of the 37 plants furnishing data for the prewar years 1911–1914, 15 were both hand filled and sand cast, while only 8 were mechanically filled and machine cast. But in 1926, out of 49 plants furnishing data, only 3 were both hand filled and sand cast, while 34 were both mechani-

[1] See *Recent Economic Changes in the United States* (1929), Vol. I Chap. IV, Transportation, Part I, p. 285.

cally filled and machine cast."[2] The significance of the record lies in the fact that in 1911–1914, the modern methods were known but were applied in but three plants. In 1926, nearly three-fourths had adopted the improved machinery.

Until comparatively recent times, the problem of industry was to produce in sufficient quantity to supply the demand. To-day the problem of industry is largely that of disposing of its products. If manufacturing industry should devote all of its energies to the production of *necessities* alone, it would be difficult to dispose of the output intelligently. The problem of industrial production has been temporarily solved, and as a consequence we have passed from a "sellers' market" to a "buyers' market."

These rapid glances at industrial changes suggest the significance of shifts in consumer demands and the importance of technical improvements in recent years. Without mass consumption there could not be mass production.

Mass production necessitates mass financing and mass management. Large enterprises are comparatively more difficult to organize and manage than small ones and, as a result, a great deal of thought and experiment have been expended in recent years upon the problems of management. It is significant that these problems are now sufficiently crystallized to form the nucleus of instruction in colleges of high standing. The growth in the size of industrial plants, and the consequent advantage that may be taken of the principles of standardized quantity production, will depend to no small degree upon our ability to finance and manage large plants upon sound economic principles.

Out of these changes has developed the astonishing increase in productivity which is discussed in Part 2 of this chapter. But it is obvious that not all industry is prosperous nor all industrial leaders progressive. Anyone well acquainted with industry knows that there is much inefficiency in both management and production. The fact remains that the field of industry as a whole has made marked advances during the last decade, and the productivity per worker in most industries has been advanced markedly. Never before has the human race made such progress in solving the problem of production. If poverty and industrial distress still exist, it is because

[2] United States Bureau of Labor Statistics, "Productivity of Labor in Merchant Blast Furnaces." *Bulletin* No. 474. Washington, 1928.

of our inability to keep our industrial machinery in operation and to distribute equitably the resulting products. It is not sufficient to be able to produce abundantly; we must also be able to distribute intelligently.

In recent years the developments in new productive methods have been so startling as to force themselves upon the attention of all men. But these developments are the result of changes which began many years ago, and which have gathered such momentum during the last few decades as to raise serious questions as to their present influences and probable future effects. For the purpose of this discussion these changes may be listed as follows:

a. Disappearance of old industries and callings
b. Changes in character of old industries
c. Growth in size of old industries without change in character
d. Development and growth of new industries and callings[3]

It would be superfluous to recount the advent of the Industrial Revolution with its constantly increasing tendency to undermine and eliminate handicraft production. It should be noted, however, that the growth of modern factory methods[4] in the United States was comparatively slow during the nineteenth century, handicraft production either by individuals or in handicraft factories predominating until about 1850, and production by these methods was quite common as late as fifty years ago in some callings.

By the year 1900 the value of manufactured goods exceeded that of agricultural products, and therefore the census of 1900 may be taken as a datum from which to measure industrial changes. Furthermore, this census contains certain comments upon the new industrial methods, then just assuming great importance, which are

[3] A new industry is one which is producing a new product, such as rayon, or which involves a new process or technique, such as electric welding. A new trade or calling is one which requires a new body of knowledge or a new specialized skill on the part of the worker. Thus electric welding and chauffering may be considered as new callings, whereas there are probably no new trades involved in the production of radio apparatus.

[4] The term "modern factory methods" is used here to define production by the use of "transfer of skill" and extended division of labor. The most important machine tools upon which modern manufacturing depends are the turret lathe, the automatic screw machine, and the milling machine. These appeared in America about the middle of the nineteenth century and gave a tremendous stimulus to manufacturing. Grinding machinery, which has become almost as important as these machines, was a later development.

most illuminating in view of recent developments and which will be alluded to later on. The biennial census of manufactures for 1925 is the latest corresponding document, and since no marked changes have occurred since then, comparisons between these two statistical reports are enlightening.[5]

Disappearance of Old Industries and Callings

A comparison of the industries listed in the census of 1900 with the corresponding list given in the biennial census of manufactures for 1925 shows that few industries have actually disappeared. Nearly all of those listed in 1900 appear also in the list of 1925. There are some interesting exceptions. Thus, blacksmithing and wheelwrighting, which in 1900 employed over 5,800 men, is not mentioned in the 1925 list. Distilled liquor is, of course, not included in the 1925 list but appears as ethyl alcohol, and there are a few smaller industries, such as lock and gun smithing and watch and clock repairing, which are not considered important enough for the 1925 list. But, in the main, the list of industries cited in 1900 is included in some form in 1925.

Some of the industries listed in 1900 and 1925 have declined greatly. Thus, in 1900 there were 7,632 establishments employing 62,540 workers making carriages and wagons. In 1925 there were only 152 establishments employing 4,833 persons in this industry. As might be expected, saddlery and harnessmaking show a corresponding decrease.[6]

[5] It should be remembered that the population of the United States increased from 74,607,225 in 1890 to over 113,493,000 in 1925. Also, all such statistics as are expressed in dollars must be interpreted with reference to the relative value of money at the two dates discussed.

[6] It has been suggested that an inventory of the idle manufacturing plants might be something of an index to industrial change. The writer is skeptical as to the value of such a survey, except as it would show that industry has been and is now in a state of flux. Idle plants should not be confused with the disappearance of trades and industries. Plants become idle for a variety of reasons, such as exhaustion of resources, bad management, supercession of other products or processes, and migration of industry as a whole to other localities. American industry presents, and will probably present for some time to come, just such a picture. Some reasons for this phase of industry are to be found in certain basic changes in our manufacturing methods which are discussed in a succeeding section and with which this report is primarily concerned. As a

The development of factory methods during the period under review has practically eliminated some handicraft callings. Thus the 1900 census distinguished between custom or hand-made shoes and the factory-made product. The census of 1925 makes no such distinction, practically the entire product being factory-made. In a similar way, other callings, such as custom-tailoring, village blacksmithing, cooperage, and cabinet making, have succumbed almost, if not entirely, to factory processes. There are, of course, survivals of some of these handicraft callings to-day, but their total output is negligible compared to the factory-made articles. However, the basic building trades, such as carpentry and bricklaying, have survived, though they have been supplemented by many other building trades. The basic machine crafts, such as machinist, boiler maker, foundryman, and pattern maker, are still important and to a certain degree unchanged, though their places in industry have been changed and their tools greatly improved. These callings, as will be seen from a later discussion, must necessarily survive since upon them rests the entire industrial fabric. Comparatively few industries, as such, have disappeared, though many of them have greatly changed.

Changes in Character of Old Industries

While many industries which are listed in the 1900 census appear under the same name in 1925, it is well known that they have been greatly changed as to methods and process. In some instances they bear little relation to the industries of the same name of 50 years ago. As an illustration, consider the men's clothing industry. The census of 1900 lists 28,014 establishments employing 191,043 persons with an output valued at over $415,000,000. The 1925 census lists only 4,000 establishments employing only 174,332 persons but with an output valued at over one billion dollars. Again, in 1900, there were 23,560 custom shoemaking establishments employing 9,689 persons as compared to 1,900 factories, so-called,

---

corroboration of this statement, the census of 1900 gives a detailed list of the idle plants at that date. They numbered 3,864 with a total capitalization of about one million dollars and included 188 different industries. No doubt a similar survey at any time will show similar results. . . .

employing 143,000 persons. In 1925, there were only 1,460 establishments, but they employed 206,992 persons and their output was valued at $925,383,422. This industry has been almost completely changed from handicraft to machine production with corresponding changes in the workers involved. Practically all of the older industries which have survived have been affected more or less in a similar manner, either by the introduction of new processes or new methods of production.

Growth in Size of Industries without Change in Character

Many of the industrial plants of the old type have greatly increased in size for three reasons. First, the size of the product needed has greatly increased. Engines, locomotives, ships, bridges, for example, have all increased enormously in recent years, necessitating corresponding increase in the size of the physical equipment of the producing plants. Or the size of the productive units has been increased so as to secure greater economy of operation. A blast furnace of 500-ton capacity is much more economical than one of 100 tons; and it requires no more men to operate a 4,000 horse power locomotive than it does to operate one of 400 horse power. Many old industrial plants, however, have expanded in size with no marked changes in product, solely to secure the benefits of quantity production in the matter of productive costs.

Development and Growth of New Industries and Callings

By far the most interesting and important development is the rise of new industries and new callings. For it is in the character of the productive methods by which new industries have been built that we must look for the answer to some of our industrial problems. Some of these new industries, like the automobile and the airplane, are built upon and are extensions of old trades and callings. Others, like the electrical industries, while resting primarily upon old trades and callings, have developed many ramifications and adaptations of these old trades into what are practically new callings. Others again, while having their genesis in chemical processes, must necessarily be constructed through the use of the old mechanic arts. And all of them have been affected by modern productive methods. The magnitude of some of these new industries is impressive. Thus the automotive industry, not mentioned in the 1900 census, is credited in the 1925 census with employing over 400,000 men, with an output valued at over $4,000,000,000. Rayon, mentioned specifically for the first time in the census of 1925, employed 19,128 workers, and the product of radio manufacture, an enterprise only a few years old, was valued in 1927 at about $191,000,000. The value of the telephone and telegraph apparatus produced in 1927 was estimated at over $119,200,000. The chemical industry, a new growth, employed 38,075 workers, with an output valued at $6,438,027,000.

A new industry that produces a product which tends to supplant the product of an old industry does not necessarily eliminate the old industry, even though the new product may be superior in many ways. The new product may find an enlarged field, leaving the old product to do the same and to hold part of its old field. The telephone did not supplant the telegraph nor does the radio supplant either of them. The electric light did not eliminate gas any more than oil has entirely supplanted coal, and the motor truck and autobus seem to be progressing toward co-ordination with older methods of transportation. By similar procedure, rayon is making its own place, and probably will not eliminate cotton and linen. We shall no doubt witness the development of many new synthetic products to supply the lack of natural animal and vegetable products as the supply of these diminish, and we may expect to see many new products to satisfy new or old needs.

BIG ENTERPRISE IN A COMPETITIVE SYSTEM

A. D. H. Kaplan

The big industrials, with which this study is mainly concerned, share the production of goods and services in a diversified economy of more than 60 million persons gainfully employed in public, quasi-public, and private activities, in agriculture and the professions, in government and nonprofit organizations, in domestic services and in small- and medium-sized business enterprises, proprietary and incorporated. Among the 4 million business firms—all but 35,000 of which have fewer than 100 employees—the 2,000 large industrials with (1,000 or more employees each) had an aggregate of 10 million employees on their payrolls.

The number of independent enterprisers, as given in the 1950 census figures of employers and self-employed, was 10.6 millions or 18 per cent of the total labor force. This figure would be increased by another 300,000 if the owners and managers of the smallest business corporations were recognized as being really self-employed enterprisers who had incorporated their businesses.

Outside of agriculture, self-employment has more than kept pace with total gainful employment since 1929. The great decline in the percentage in agriculture has been matched by an increase mainly in trade and services, both typically small business areas. Opportunities for the entrepreneur are reflected also in the numbers of business firms in operation, since the vast majority are proprietorships. The rate of increase in the number of businesses has exceeded that of population over the past fifty years—from 15.4 to 17 per thousand persons, according to the Dun and Bradstreet Directory. According to more comprehensive figures of the Department of Commerce, the number rose from 25 in 1929 to more than 26 in 1949.

Businesses generally have been growing larger, and the number in the higher-size brackets may be expected to increase. There were 6,400 businesses with 500 or more employees in 1948, against 4,900 in 1940; but the 6,400 accounted for between 39 and 40 per cent of total business employment in 1948, while the 4,900 accounted for nearly 41 per cent in 1940. The giant industrials—those with 10,000 or more employees –numbered about 200 in 1948. In manufacturing, 163 such firms accounted for nearly 5 million employees; in retail trade 26 accounted for 840,000. The concentration of employment in firms of this size is impressive. So, too, is the fact that the predominant portion of gainful employment (over 70 per cent in 1948) is still in the smaller business units or in the nonbusiness field. Thus both concentration and opportunity for self-employment have persisted side by side in the American economy.

Concentration of Output

Concentration of employment figures show that big business growth has not prevented the growth of small business, but they tell little about the vigor of competition. Light is thrown on this subject by examining the number of sellers in individual markets.

A significant factor brought out by consideration of the data is that an industry does not have to be large-scale to be large. In manufactures, five of the 12 leading industries are organized predominantly in small-scale units, with from 60 to nearly 100 per cent of their output in firms of less than 500 employees. Although the exceptions are numerous enough to preclude a sweeping generalization, it may be safely affirmed that concentration is most typical where capital requirements are large and that a large part of American industry flourishes in small units. Concentration among a few large companies in a number of key industries has not prevented an increase in the number and the output of small firms. Big business has, in fact, by demanding specialties and special services that a large organization cannot easily provide, frequently been responsible for the birth of small enterprises.

Even where an industry consists of large numbers of small enterprises, competition is not necessarily assured. A small enterprise may enjoy a monopoly in a localized market. Indeed, a big business spreading into local markets may do more to break up the power of local monopolies than to cement its own. But is the typical big business, with multiplant operations on a vast scale, immunized by its very size from the impact of competition?

The one comprehensive study of the numbers of sellers of a product, made by the TNEC in 1937, revealed that four or fewer firms controlled 70 per cent or more of the output of over half of 1,807 manufactured product groups. This has been regarded as major evidence of the "ubiquity of oligopoly" in American manufacturing.

Acceptance of these concentration ratios at their face value would ignore the limitations of the basic data from which they were drawn, particularly the combination of products according to the materials of which they were made rather than according to whether they competed with each other. It would ignore also the relative insignificance of the output of many products in the highly concentrated group, where the high concentration ratio was frequently due to possession of a patent. Above all, it would ignore the dynamics of the markets concerned.

The inability of the Department of Commerce to compare more than one third of the census industries of 1935 with those of 1947 is a striking indication of the fluidity of market situations. Newcomers have steadily penetrated markets dominated initially by patents or mergers. Substitutes from other industries exert continuing pressure upon conventional markets. The leading aluminum company stood alone in the industry for many years, but aluminum waged a constant fight for markets with other metals, with glass and with building materials. It replaced steel in the automobile industry and was in turn replaced by steel. Linoleum, a product found by the TNEC to have a concentration ratio of over 80 per cent, competes with an ever-growing list of floor coverings, and rivals of linoleum companies include powerful companies in apparently unrelated industries such as that of rubber. Pressure to compete may be exercised by distributive organizations, and powerful buyers force competition in markets where producers are few. There is no substitute for tires, yet even the tire industry, with 75 per cent of new tire output controlled by four firms, is not immune from this kind of competition. It is not the number of participants producing the bulk of a single product but the number of participants in the market in which the product must compete that determines the validity of an apparent concentration ratio.

With well-defined products, in which total demand is inelastic, oligopoly may, as in the cigarette industry, lead to stagnation of product and process development, to monopolistic pricing, and to wasteful methods of competition. It would be difficult, however, to draw up an appreciable list of oligopolistic industries that have in fact been monopolistically stagnant over the years.

There is probably no aspect of big business growth that suggests concentration of economic power as dramatically as the increase in the financial resources of the large industrials. By comparison, the percentage of total assets attributable to the smaller units of business enterprise appears very small. Despite an increase in the assets figures of small-scale enterprise during the recent years of impressive corporate growth, the assets of unincorporated businesses are estimated to be as little as one tenth of the assets of the corporate.

The figures for unincorporated enterprise can be obtained only by an indirect method and are not considered reliable. Large and small enterprises have such different capital requirements that asset figures are misleading as a measure for comparing the economic importance of the corporations—particularly the giants—and the many proprietorships. The large corporations are the very firms that require the pooling of investments because they operate in industries requiring heavy capital investment—steel, petroleum, transportation equipment, electrical machinery, etc. The small business is typically one that does not require a large investment to achieve relatively high sales and income and in which entrepreneurial skill is an important but not a bookkeeping asset. More significant than the size of corporate assets as a measure of financial power is the extent to which the concentration of these assets has affected the distribution of income across the economy. In terms of relative contribution to national income and its share in that income, the dominance of the corporate sector is less marked. Corporations have generally originated slightly over half of the national income and nearly two thirds of the national payroll over the past quarter century. The payrolls of unincorporated business (including the unincorporated farms and professions) have amounted to about 30 per cent of the corporate, and their net income has consistently exceeded that of the corporations before taxes.

The noncorporate area has maintained its relative position with striking success. In 1951 corporation payrolls were 232 per cent, and noncorporate 227 per cent, above 1929 levels; corporate profits were almost four times their 1929 levels; while entrepreneurial income had increased threefold. Entrepreneurial profits have held their own despite the rising share of national income generated by the government and the rise in the share of income going to wages and corporate profits. Moreover, since income tax was $1.4 billion out of the corporate income of $9.8 billion in 1929 and $24.2 billion out of $41.6 billion in 1951, the net income of corporate enterprise after taxes has actually increased less than that of noncorporate enterprise.

There has been a slight increase over the last two decades in the percentage of the total national income produced in the corporate income sector—an increase traceable to the change in the wage and salary component of the corporate totals. The distribution of corporate incomes as reported by large and small corporations over the last two decades indicates an increasing share of the total corporate income for the firms in the small and intermediate-size classes. The rise in the financial power of big business has apparently been accompanied by at least comparable gains in the rest of the economy.

Composition of the Corporate Sector

Undoubtedly the corporation is the predominant form of business organization in the economy. Yet the corporate sector is anything but homogeneous. Of the 537,000 corporations submitting balance sheets to the Bureau of Internal Revenue in 1948, nearly half had total assets under $50,000 and an average net worth of $10,000. These small businesses are really independent entrepreneurs using the corporate form. This suggests that the foregoing figures noting the continued importance of the entrepreneurial sector of the economy may well be increased to include these hundreds of thousands of corporations "in name only." In the category of industrial enterprises, the total financial resources of the small, medium-sized, and giant firms are approximately equal. Of the $230 billion of total assets for all industrial firms (that is, excluding public utilities and financial institutions), it is estimated that a third, or $76 billion, is held by the vast majority of proprietorships and corporations having less than $500,000 in assets. The 361 industrials with $50 million or more of assets held $72 billion, slightly less than one third of the total. The middle group of 34,000 corporations, with assets ranging from $500,000 to $50 million, held the largest segment, its assets totaling $82 billion.

The 100 largest industrials in 1948 accounted for about 12 per cent of all income originating in American private business and about 10.6 per cent of the total national payroll, private and governmental. Their assets amounted to nearly $49.2 billion. These figures fell short by a wide margin of the degree of preponderance of the giant corporations suggested by projecting the findings of Berle and Means. But the fact that decisions bearing on the disposition of roughly $50 billion of business resources depend on 100 managements, with some ties of long standing among them, would be cause for concern if this area of centralized managerial control showed a tendency to engulf more and more of the economy.

Fortunately the 100 largest do not form an integrated whole. They represent many branches of industry, from retail trade and motion pictures to foods and petroleum. Nevertheless, if the list of the ranking members remained substantially unchanged over a long period, there would be much greater reason for alarm than if the group exhibited fluidity in its membership and evidence of turnover in leadership. Comparison of the list of the 100 largest industrials of 1909 with the largest at various periods down to 1948 discloses a substantial turnover in ranking. The 1948 list contained only 36 companies that were among the 100 largest in 1909. Of the first 10 in 1948, 5 were not among the 100 of the earlier list. The lists for three intervening years, 1919, 1929, 1935, similarly showed numerous replacements and marked changes in the rank of those who remained.

Industries heavily represented in big business in the early part of the century—coal, shipping, leather—have yielded to more recently developed industrial areas, including automobile and aircraft, motion pictures, chain retailing, and electrical equipment. The companies that have retained their positions of leadership are those that have not hesitated to embrace opportunities in growing industries. Few that have limited production to their traditional lines, and none that have adhered to traditional methods, have increased their stature in the family of the 100 largest or in the economy as a whole. The outstanding companies have helped to revamp their industries and have even created new ones. There is no reason to believe that those now at the top will remain there unless they keep fully abreast of competitive products and processes.

HAVE CORPORATIONS A HIGHER DUTY THAN PROFITS?

Fortune Magazine Editors

The present debate over corporate responsibilities goes back to the publication in 1932 of *The Modern Corporation and Private Property* by Adolph A. Berle Jr. and Gardiner C. Means. At that time the authors noted a two-fold development, which was increasingly concentrating capital assets in the hands of salaried managers and depriving the stockholders of any effective control over their property. Thus, while a centrifugal force was dispersing ownership and thinning out the power of the individual stockholder, a centripetal force was bringing together great aggregations of wealth and bestowing economic power upon a new class of managers. Long before, the classical economists had demonstrated that the capitalist, in seeking his private advantage in competitive markets, contributed indirectly to the public good. But the manager had no property interest in the capital he controlled, hence no claim on profits. At the same time, the concentration of economic means in his hands gave him power over prices and the ability to extort a disproportionate share of the consumer's income.

More recent statistical research has not borne out the thesis that industrial concentration is increasing. Berle himself is willing to admit that there has been no significant change in the ratio of concentration over the last fifty years. But his thesis concerning the separation of ownership from control is widely accepted today in one form or another. This has led Berle, in *Power Without Property*, to shift his ground and lay emphasis on absolute size and the fact of concentration itself, rather than the growth of concentration. Indeed, concentration and the absolute size of the business firm are formidable to contemplate. According to the *Fortune* directory of leading U.S. industrial corporations, the 500 biggest firms accounted last year for more than half the sales of all manufacturing and mining companies, and for over 70 percent of the profits. The fifty biggest accounted for 28 percent of all manufactured or mining output and 40 percent of profits. This represents an enormous concentration of economic power in the hands of a small class of professional managers. They are presumed to be working for their more numerous but less influential stockholders. They are said to be freed from the constraints of the competitive market, and responsible to no one. "What Mr. Berle and most of the rest of us are afraid of," writes Mason, "is that this powerful corporate machine, which so successfully grinds out the goods we want, seems to be running without any discernible controls. The young lad mastering the technique of his bicycle may legitimately shout with pride, 'Look, Ma, no hands,' but is this the appropriate motto for a corporate society?"

The Financial Mix

At least, one might argue, the corporate managers must assure a flow of profits to the stockholders high enough to facilitate additional financing and the flotation of new stock issues. But Berle points to the large proportion of new capital which is internally generated—that is, retained from earnings or drawn from depreciation allowance. Thus it would seem that corporations have become independent not only of the individual suppliers of risk capital but of the money markets controlled by large banks and other lending institutions.

Berle estimates that from 1947 to 1957 capital accumulated by corporations amounted to $292 billion, 60 percent of which was internally financed, 20 percent drawn from bank credit, and another 20 percent from capital markets. But more than half of this last percentage was money handled by the investment staffs of insurance companies and pension trusts. Berle is of the opinion that only 5 percent of the vast total capital accumulation was supplied from the voluntary savings of individuals.

Private Civil Servants

The important new development, from the point of view of Berle's thesis, is the growth of pension trusts with large sums invested in common shares carrying voting rights. It is here that the "fission of property" becomes complete; for the beneficiary of the funds held in trust has no voice at all in the affairs of the corporation in which the trust owns stock. The fund trustees, who could exercise the voting rights to sway management, tend to go along with the incumbency or sell out. Nevertheless, the situation is appreciably changed. While the power of the individual stockholder continues to wane, there has been a reconcentration of common-stock holdings, and in the hands of institutional investors. Where power exists, Berle thinks, men will sooner or later use it:

"In point of present fact, trust fund custody is held by a dozen large banks, chiefly in New York, and by ten or twelve large insurance companies. It would be easy to say that this handful of banks and insurance companies will wield the power nucleus looming over the economic horizon; certainly this is the best forward guess one can make. . . . A relatively small oligarchy of men operating in the same atmosphere, absorbing the same information, moving in the same circles and in a relatively small world, knowing each other, dealing with each other, and having more in common than in difference, will hold the reins. These men by hypothesis will have no ownership relation of any sort. They will be, essentially, non-statist civil servants—unless they abuse their power to make themselves something else."

Berle makes no recommendation to pass on the voting rights to the beneficiaries of the pension funds or to break up the actual or potential power in the hands of trustees. He tends to believe in some kind of mechanism of countervalence whereby power engenders its own limitation. The discretionary power for good or ill, now vested in corporate managers and shortly, if Berle is right, to be shared with fiduciary agents, will be limited by the moral restraints of what he calls the "public consensus," that body of settled moral principles of which public opinion is the fluctuating expression. Moreover, he believes that the boards of publicly held companies have already developed a "corporate conscience" and are primarily concerned with their good reputation in the business community and in the eyes of the public at large.

But Berle's argument does not stop at an appeal to moral principle. The public consensus is the breeding ground of "inchoate law" —the seeds of legal growth that may reach the stage of statutory enactment or administrative law. His final solution to the problem of concentrated economic power would be a national planning agency to coordinate the existing regulatory bodies. Berle does not think that the number of present government agencies needs to be greatly augmented, but their powers should be extended in some cases and action should be taken in conjunction with institutions of business society. Thus the civil servants of the state would act in concert with the civil servants of the corporate bureaucracies.

The Other-Directed Corporation

In *The Meaning of Modern Business* Richard Eells rounds up much material on corporate responsibility and kindred subjects and tries to build it around what he calls three models of the large-scale business enterprise: the "traditional corporation," the "metrocorporation," and the "well-tempered corporation." The first is an instrument for making money for its stockholders. Any moral obligations or social responsibilities it may assume flow from this primary imperative to make money. If its directors and managers assume a wide range of responsibilities, they do so because, under the circumstances, it is the most prudent policy for the corporation. On the other hand, the metrocorporation is a quasi-public body that mediates between the interests of a large number of "contributor-claimant" groups: security holders and customers, employees and suppliers, competitors, local communities, the general public, and governments. The well-tempered model is a mean between these two extremes, but it is hard to see how it differs from the metrocorporation, which Eells condemns. The only clear difference that *seems* to emerge is that, whereas the directors of the metrocorporation regard profits as secondary, for the well-tempered model they are still primary but relative to "coordinate" functions, such as "controlling the economic process," "participating in the governmental process," and "contributing to the cultural process." But this distinction turns out to be elusive, if not illusory. For it is impossible to attach a definite meaning to the expression "profits are secondary" or even to "profits are primary but coordinate with other functions." If profits are secondary, then they can *always* be sacrificed for the sake of fulfilling obligations that are primary; but since profits are an indispensable condition of the corporation's existence, this is tantamount to saying that the corporation can sacrifice its existence and at the same time fulfill its obligations to the community. Again, to say that profits are a primary function, coordinate with other functions, amounts to saying that these other functions are also primary and hence of equal importance. So what does the corporation do in the event of a conflict?

Eells's well-tempered corporation is nothing but David Riesman's "other-directed" personality writ large. "What is required," says Eells, "is a sensing operation in which the antennae are delicately attuned to many wave lengths and pointed in many directions. Investors, customers, suppliers, competitors are obvious groups from which incoming messages have to be assessed. But the *potential* suppliers of equity capital, goods, and services, the *potential* customers, the *potential* competitors, as well as the 'public at large' and especially its representatives in local, state, national, and international governments, are all extremely important sources of intelligence about the reputation of the company and its impact upon social institutions."

How the corporation is to introduce order into this babel of voices, Eells does not exactly say. With a multitude of voices demanding now this, now that, is it not more honest, and for that matter simpler, to do one's duty and steer by rational self-interest?

Abstaining from Profit

Eugene V. Rostow, dean of the Yale Law School, obviously thinks that the old theory is preferable to the new. He writes in his contribution to *The Corporation in Modern Society:* "The law books have always said that the board of directors owes a single-minded duty of unswerving loyalty to the stockholders, and only to the stockholders. The economist has demonstrated with all the apparent precision of plane geometry and the calculus that the quest for maximum revenue in a competitive market leads to a system of prices, and an allocation of resources and rewards, superior to any alternative, in its contributions to the economic welfare of the community as a whole. To the orthodox mind, it is therefore unsettling, to say the least, to have the respected head of the Standard Oil Co. of New Jersey [he means Frank Abrams] equating the management's duty to stockholders with its obligations to employees, customers, suppliers, and the public at large."

Rostow's argument turns, of course, on the key term, "competitive market." Writers like Berle and Eells think this term is largely inapplicable to the present capitalist economy in America. They contend that capitalism has entered a new phase, and under conditions incompatible with the classical assumptions of Adam Smith and Ricardo. It is true that in markets where there are many traders, or at least to which many traders have easy access, the forces of competition will bring prices down to a point where they just cover costs and thus eliminate monopoly profits. And to be sure, in oligopolistic markets, where one big company exercises price leadership, it is possible that profits may represent an extortionate levy on the consumer's purchasing power. The question of whether or not corporations should assume social responsibilities and become arbiters of social justice largely resolves itself into a question about the effective functioning of the market mechanism. If the market is functioning and regulating the flow of income to different functional classes within society, then attempts to find an equitable distribution, based on a notion of just prices, wages, and profits, can only wreck the mechanism. And this is Rostow's view of the present situation. "If, as is widely thought, the essence of corporate statesmanship is to seek less than maximum profits, postwar experience is eloquent evidence that such statesmanship leads to serious malfunctioning of the economy as a whole."

Rostow is arguing here that the market will regulate the flow of income to different groups, and that modern corporate "statesmanship" is attempting to reroute funds against the current. No doubt if capital does move in response to changes in the structure of relative prices, then a policy of holding prices down, motivated by public benevolence or whatever, can lead to misallocation of resources and widespread diseconomy. The question then is: to what extent is the rate of investment actually sensitive to changes in prices and resultant profits?

The Invisible Hand of Oligopoly

There is some evidence that oligopolistic markets are allocating resources with tolerable efficiency. Numerous buyers and sellers, acting independently, are but one criterion of competitive performance. Free entry into markets and the fact that capital, labor, and other resources actually do move into areas where profits are higher indicate that the economy is still performing in a relatively healthy manner. And this would seem to be the case in many industrial sectors dominated by oligopoly. John Lintner sums up the latest findings in his contribution to *The Corporation in Modern Society*: "An impressive recent study [*The Investment Decision* by John R. Meyer and Edwin Kuh] investigated the factors determining the plant and equipment expenditures of approximately 700 firms in the early postwar period. The study included virtually all the companies, large and small, listed with the Securities and Exchange Commission, in seventeen different manufacturing industries accounting for the bulk of plant and equipment expenditures in all manufacturing. The authors found that the rate of profitability, the level of sales, and the degree of pressure of sales upon current capacity were uniformly the most important factors determining the current rate of investment outlays among these firms—we may add, just as would be expected, if market mechanisms were functioning efficiently. . . . Other things being the same, the amount of new investment was not only correlated with profitability and increasing sales, but the reliance on the financial markets for outside capital was also closely associated with the rate of growth of the firm."

This evidence that the market still does its work should not incline us, however, to assume that there is no danger from oligopoly. Antitrust prosecutions, or the threat thereof, are needed to spur competitive performance. But even if our markets worked less well than they do, we should beware of any shift in fundamental theory that would assign either to corporation managers or to government the functions now assigned to the market. Once we subordinate the market, either a businessman must become a public official or a public official must become a businessman. Either way, the principle of a division of labor between government and market will be violated. From this point of view, managerialism is the worst solution of all; for it is highly repugnant that a corporate manager, not publicly elected and hence not subject to popular recall, should have a special responsibility for what the managerialists call the process of government. At least a socialist government can be defeated at the polls.

THE CONGLOMERATE:
WHERE DOES IT STAND?

Ralph Nader Study Group

The superconcentration caused by the recent conglomerate explosion also inflicts economic costs, though of a different and more subtle nature. While an oligopolist is a huge firm in an industry with a few big firms, a conglomerate is a huge firm with holdings and subsidiaries in *many* industries. It is the modern form of the old trust and holding company, only instead of securing controlling shares in many companies, they own the companies outright. Textron, with 1970 sales of $1.6 billion, is a fast-growing new conglomerate with octopal interests: textiles, aircraft and parts, electronic equipment, iron and steel castings, bathroom fixtures, machine tools, plastic products, car parts, boat building, agrochemicals, pharmaceuticals, shoes, zippers, and golf carts. Ling-Temco-Vought, with sales of $3.7 billion in 1970, is into aerospace and missiles, sporting equipment, telephone and power cables, pharmaceuticals and chemicals, processed foods, electronic equipment, steel, domestic airplane service, and meats. Consequently, while oligopolies involve concentration in one industry, conglomerates affect overall, economy-wide concentration.

With little antitrust law established to contest this growth—most cases and statutes aim at actual horizontal or vertical competitors —the conglomerate boom took off in the late 1960s. As noted, 80% of the recent merger wave was conglomerate; and high frequency combined with large size. Of 698 manufacturing and mining firms acquired in 1965–69 with assets over $10 million, 561 were conglomerate. The assets involved in manufacturing and mining mergers jumped from an average of $2.8 billion a year in 1960–66 to $10.8 billion per year in 1967–69.

Conglomerates have little redeeming competitive value. They are fueled by and exploit financial gimmicks, leading even *Forbes* magazine to complain that for some "the corporation was no longer primarily a vehicle for conducting business; it had become a machine for compiling an earning record." They are classic examples of empire-building by aggressive managers, indifferent to the inefficiencies of too-large scale, as sprawling, diverse companies are "connected by a common financial heart and a common financial brain." Five separate economic studies, have all concluded that there was no relationship between conglomeration and efficiency.

It is true that a conglomerate merger *can* help generate competition. When a conglomerate acquires a small company in a sluggish, concentrated industry, called a "toehold acquisition," and infuses new capital and an innovative energy, the oligopoly can be shaken up into a state of competition. Although by definition conglomerates do not involve direct competitors, they are anticompetitive in several ways. First, since a Procter & Gamble might have gone into bleach production via internal expansion, there is a loss of *potential competition* when it merges with Clorox; such a threat of potential entry can be a significant check on the abuse of monopoly power by the dominant firms in an industry. Second, there is a heightened danger of *reciprocity*, when a firm takes its business to firms who buy from it. Such interrelationships foreclose the market to more efficient competitors, who lose out not to a superior product but to a back-scratching relationship. Oligopoly would be magnified by a kind of circular integration, and "the U.S. economy might end up completely dominated by conglomerates," complained *Fortune*, "happily trading with each other in a new kind of cartel system." Third, when a conglomerate buys a leading firm, it can *entrench* the firm's dominant position; conglomerate backing, plus large advertising outlays, can intimidate small competitors and potential entrants. Finally, there is, in the words of Willard Mueller, "conglomerate interdependence and forbearance." A conglomerate merger, greatly increasing size and diversification, concomitantly increases the number of contact points shared with competitors, suppliers, and customers. While competition in any one line of commerce is not severely diminished, "aggregate" competition can be. Communities of interest among major industrial decision makers arse, and a situation of cartel-like deferral, or soft competition, replaces real competition. "Management difficulties with newly acquired companies," concluded the *Celler Conglomerate Report* in September, 1971, "indicate that combination frequently had an injurious effect on efficiency, on productivity and upon corporate values."

Conglomerates seem to be falling of their own weight. The "high flyers," as they were called in 1967 and 1968, saw their glamour-stock reputation wane as their stock prices tumbled. By mid-1969 the average price of conglomerate stocks had fallen 40–60%, while the composite market index itself was down only about 10%; there was some recovery through early 1971, but it was far from complete. The political and social power held by conglomerates, however, will not wither away as easily as its dividends.

A combination of mismanagement, a depressed stock market, tight money, and government lawsuits brought these trendy consolidations down, one hopes disproving the frank prediction of one conglomerate president that in 10 years there would be only 200 industrial companies left in the United States. By 1970 no less than eight agencies and Congressional committees were studying the conglomerate meteor, the proper initial response to a phenomenon of such widespread impact. Yet when this problem and response are compared to the more continuous and generic costs of shared monopoly, and the official indifference expressed toward it, the policy mispriority becomes evident. If LTV or ITT creates economic and political problems by concentration of assets, what of AT&T and Standard Oil (N.J.), both of which are bigger? "I suggest it is bizarre," said Edwin Zimmerman, a recent Antitrust Assistant Attorney General, "to concoct a particular antitrust doctrine in order to contain the emerging political power or social impact of a Northwest Industries but not a General Motors . . ."

There are large blocks of our industrial economy which are characterized by "workable competition," where firms follow the laws of supply and demand to compete for the sovereign consumer's dollar. Given the earlier data on market concentration, one feels about these competitive sectors as Dr. Samuel Johnson did of the dog who could walk on his hind legs: marveling not that he could do it well but that he could do it at all.

What of the monopolized sectors of our economy? In the name of free enterprise, up to two-thirds of American manufacturing has been metamorphosed into a closed enterprise system. While businessmen spoke the language of competitive capitalism, each sought refuge for himself. Price-fixing, parallel pricing, mergers, excessive and deceptive advertising, tariffs, quotas, subsidies, loan guarantees, political favoritism, and preferential tax treatment—all have created a system of what Senator Estes Kefauver aptly labeled "corporate socialism—a collective run by business, not government." It is a business collective with staggering consumer and public costs: lost GNP *alone* of $60 billion is enough to cover our annual crime bill ($32 billion), the removal of major sources of pollution ($415 billion) and the elimination of poverty ($11 billion for a $3,000 minimum income). The reality of Big Business is—like sex in Victorian England—our big dirty secret. Occasional reference is made to the obvious pretense. As Michael Harrington ironically states in his *Accidental Century*, "Adam Smith has been stood on his head. . . . The capitalist destruction of the capitalist ethic took place primarily through the private collectivization of the Western economy for minority profit. The dominance over large blocks of industrial production by huge enterprises free from the restraints of the competitive marketplace presents the challenge to the antitrust agencies: enforcement must confront the competitive and consumer costs of this giantism, to avoid the charge it is a "charade" (J. K. Galbraith) or mere "folklore" (Thurman Arnold).

THE PLACE OF BIG BUSINESS
IN AMERICAN SOCIETY

Robert L. Heilbroner

The elusive problem of the "power" of the business ideology leads us toward a problem that we have as yet failed to engage squarely. That is the over-all importance of big business in society today. What are the limits of its sway? Is its influence diminishing or increasing?

These questions plunge us still deeper into the seas of uncertainty and conjecture. But we can at least begin to discuss the problem objectively by focusing on one aspect that is fairly open to observation and empirical judgment. This is the oldest and purest exercise of economic power—the market exploitation of the weak.

Among those whom big business has exploited, the classic victim has been labor. For example, as late as 1919 the workweek at United States Steel consisted of a twelve-hour day and a seven-day week, with a 24-hour swing shift every other week—a schedule that was, according to Judge Gary and other steel officials, impossible to change. And then there is the familiar, if dreary, chronicle of the Ford assembly-line speedups and the Colorado Fuel and Iron company towns, of antiunion discrimination, yellow-dog contracts, and the like.

In point of fact, big business was never the only or the most culpable oppressor of labor. The most terrible sweatshops were in trades such as garment making where competition among numerous small entrepreneurs led to pitiless practices of cost cutting, or in agricultural fringe industries where poverty, fierce competition, and rural cruelty joined to create small hells of labor conditions. Yet throughout the late nineteenth and early twentieth centuries, the practices of big business toward its labor force—in the great mills, on the railroads, in the mass production factories—were harsh and indifferent at worst, patronizing at best.

Merely to call to mind this chapter of the past is to remind us that it has been written finis. Few would deny, I think, that the power relationship between big business and labor has been fundamentally changed, and that however fiercely labor may attack big business—and it is not very fiercely any more—it is not any longer afraid of the big corporation as it once was. Partly because of changes in labor legislation, itself testimony to a diminution of business influence, partly because of the greater ease, in today's market structure, in extracting more profit from a sales check than from a pay check, big business no longer exercises its market power over labor as in the past.

A second locus of big business power on the marketplace has been in regard to small business. We think, for instance, of Standard Oil who forced the railroads to charge its smaller competitors higher freight rates, the additional revenues from which were then turned over to Standard Oil. Indeed, it often comes as a surprise to recall that the original pressure for the containment of big business by antitrust laws came not from labor or from "the public," but from small businessmen who were being driven to the wall.

Here too is unmistakable evidence of a decline in the power of big business—not, as in the case with labor, because of a growth in the countervailing power of the other party, but through the operation of laws such as the Fair Trade acts and the repeated strengthening of antitrust legislation. In some areas the elimination of small business under the pressure of big business continues— as, for example, in the independent grocery field, or with independent filling station, or drug stores. But the elimination takes place under the aegis of impersonal market forces and rarely, if ever, through the deliberate maneuvering of the larger companies. Typically, when a merger takes place between a small firm and a large one these days, it is not because the small firm has been forced to sell out but because there are substantial tax advantages of which the small businessman is eager to take advantage.

Small business still continues to manifest a latent anti-big business sentiment that bubbles up from time to time—for instance, in the revolt of the General Motors dealers or in the recurrent discovery by the Small Business Committee of Congress that the large companies get the overwhelming bulk of defense contracts. But such sporadic and mild protests aside, it is surely fair to maintain that the fiery anti-big business feelings prevalent fifty years ago among the small business community have today largely been dissipated.

It is less easy to make an unambiguous finding with respect to the third traditional target of big business power in the marketplace—the consumer. Certainly the consumer is much more ardently wooed than in the public-be-damned days, when it was said that he was born to the profit of the Milk Trust and died to the profit of the Coffin Trust. The big corporation today falls all over itself in its efforts to depict itself as the servant of the public. It must be said, however, that this ardent wooing is sometimes accompanied by breach of promise. Cagily phrased advertisements, dubious testimonials, outright deception in television "demonstrations," glittering packaging and shoddy contents are all too familiar elements in consumer selling. From time to time these instances make the newspapers, as when the Federal Trade Commission found that General Foods was charging more, per unit of weight, for its "economy-sized" packages than for its regular packages. But leafing through the pages of *Consumer Reports* at any time hardly leaves one with a sense of overwhelming corporate solicitude for the consumer.

If it is uncertain that the big corporation really caters to the modern customer with all the zeal that it advertises, so it is also uncertain that the consumer is no longer plucked on the market as badly as ever in the old days. Long-term comparisons are difficult to make, since the higher bite of corporate tax laws has brought an increasing sophistication to corporate accounting, and many profits that were once proudly announced are now "charged off" in various ways. But certainly there is no evidence that corporate profit margins as a whole have declined over the past half century. Indeed, in certain lines of goods profit margins are higher than ever. General Motors, for example, makes almost as much profit per car as it pays out for wages on the car, and for every dollar of increased labor costs since 1947 it has raised automobile prices by about $3.75. Its profit "target" is 20 percent on capital *after* taxes—on the assumption that it will operate its plants only thirty-six weeks out of fifty-two. This goes a long way to explain its after-tax profits for 1965 or $2,125,606,440.

The only force that can be counted on to keep consumer prices down is competition. It is arguable that product competition has increased since the days of the breakup of the Trusts, but no one would contend that price competition has sharpened. Hence, while the power of the big company vis-a-vis the consumer may be more genteelly used, it has not noticeably diminished nor does it seem likely to do so.

Thus if we conclude that the exploitative capability of big business toward labor and small business has weakened, this cannot be echoed with respect to the consumer. But that does not yet fully satisfy our inquiry. For everyone knows that market exploitation, however bad, is not all of what we mean by the power of big business within society. In fact what the words usually bring to mind are not so much these instances of market abuse, but larger and subtler kinds of influence—for example, business's use of the national government to create new domains of private profits, as in the enormous landgrabs of the railroad era, or the insinuation of business ends into foreign policy, such as the banana republic diplomacy that once made the world safe for United Fruit, or the blind deference to business views characteristic of the 1920's when Calvin Coolidge could say in earnest that the business of America was business.

It is not easy to assay the trend of this varied and immensely important form of power. Certainly, when we are alerted to some new insinuation of business influence into the Pentagon, or when we remember the tidelands oil steal, or when we learn about the perversion of the income tax for the benefit of the very rich, we cannot airily dismiss the influence of big business on the nation's affairs as a thing of the past. Anyone who has read Robert Engler's *Politics of Oil*, or who has followed the course of efforts to write a stronger Pure Food and Drug Act, or to require admonitory labeling of cigarettes, or who has probed into the operations of the Federal Communications Commission or the Federal Power

Commission, or who notes the parade of business chieftains into the White House, knows that big business continues to exercise a very important influence on the formulation and administration of the nation's policies, including not least those policies that are supposed to regulate business itself. Of all the interest groups in the nation, no other is so potent as business.

Nevertheless, I would hazard the opinion that the power of big business to shape legislation or to have its way in the determination of national policy is on the wane. What one needs here, above all, is a sense of historic perspective that will enable us to weigh the present degree of business penetration with that characteristic of the 1920's and the 1900's. One has to judge the ease of access to the President and Congress by business leaders, the weight accorded their opinions, the countervailance of nonbusiness institutions, and not least the ability of newspapers and broadcasting stations to influence electoral opinion today and in the days of T. R. Roosevelt, Taft, Harding, Coolidge, Hoover. Here precise judgments are largely impossible and subjective evaluations inescapable. I can only say that my own judgment leads me to believe that business has experienced a considerable diminution in its ability to influence the immediate course of events, comparing the pre-Depression era with our own.

I would rest this case not alone on a subjective estimate of the degree of business influence in general, but also on some observable aspects of American society. One of these we have noted already— the slowdown in the rate of expansion of big business within the economy and the change in the character of its leadership. Another perhaps even more important development, to which we must now pay heed, is the rise within our society of new elites, whose importance in and competence for the direction of national affairs is clearly on the increase, compared with that of the business elite.

One of these new groups is the military, whose emergence into national prominence during the Second World War has never been followed by a normal eclipse. The military forces of the nation not only constitute an enormous semi-independent bureaucracy aggregating half the employees in the federal government (which does not include the three million in the armed forces), but high-ranking military personnel have increasingly emerged as counselors of the over-all political, as well as military, strategy of the United States.

Ever since President Eisenhower's surprising reference to the "military-industrial" complex there has been considerable discussion as to the relationship of business to the military machine. There is little doubt that a military-industrial-political interpenetration of interests exists, to the benefit of all three. Yet in this alliance I have seen no suggestion that the industrial element is the dominant one. It is the military or the political branch that commands, and business that obeys; and although company officials have offered lavish entertainment, high post-retirement positions, and other inducements to the political and the military, the role of business in the entire defense effort is essentially one of jockeying for favor rather than initiating policy.

A second elite that has risen relatively to the business elite is the professional expert—the advisor from the academic world, and in particular from the areas of social and natural science. In part this is also a by-product of the enormous increase in military activity—between 1950 and 1965, research and development expenditures by the Department of Defense grew from $652 million to $7 billion, research in space exploration from $54 million to $5 billion; and in atomic energy from $221 million to $1.5 billion.

But the tremendous jump in the demand for scientists was not confined to military of quasi-military purposes alone. The National Science Foundation spent $1 million in 1952 and $204 million in 1965; health, education, and welfare research budgets grew from $40 million to $796 million in the same years. These figures reflect not only the explosive growth of technical expertise within the United States but its virtual pre-emption by nonbusiness sectors. The direction of this vast flow of research effort is now a matter of the highest national priority—but it is a matter that is largely determined by the military, political, and scientific communities, rather than by the business community.

A third elite, also rising rapidly in national prominence and importance, is the government administrator. The moving force here, of course, is the increasing importance of the public sector in the operation of the over-all economy. Between 1950 and 1960, for example, private enterprise accounted for only one out of every ten new jobs that were created in the economy. All the rest were generated by the public or the private not-for-profit sectors (university, hospital, philanthropic, etc.). Today a third of the labor force works for some employer other than a private business- man, compared with only 15 percent in 1929. This very consider- able displacement of the business world clearly points to a cor- responding shift in the importance and influence of public officials in the determination of the course of national affairs.

Thus the years since the Great Depression have seen the rise of at least three new elites to challenge the previously uncontested dominance of the business elite—four, if we add the much larger role played by labor unions. The military, the professional advisor from the field of physics, medicine, economics, foreign affairs, the career administrator in the fields of agriculture, public health, trans- portation, housing, collective bargaining, and the labor union of- ficialdom are among them responsible for the delineation and review of programs affecting the social, economic, and political life of the nation to an unrecognizably larger degree than before the Depression. What is more, I think we can expect their influence relative to that of business to increase still further.

The reason is not far to seek. If the nation at large were to draw up a list of those matters that appeared of the greatest urgency for the future, I suspect that on every list—including those of businessmen—we would find defense, economic stability and growth, foreign relations, poverty, civil rights, urban renewal, education, unemployment, mass transport, population control, and the like. The lists would undoubtedly have different priorities and each list might not include the items of every other, but there would be, I think, a wide consensus as to the most important challenges facing the nation in the future. There would also be a striking common denominator to the problems on the list. All of them are problems in which the initiatory impulse, the financial support, the essential policy determinations, and the day-to-day guidance of programs would have to come largely from nonbusiness elites. To put it differently, the thing at which businessmen are best— the production and sale of marketable goods and services—is no longer the thing that stands at the head of America's list of needs. No doubt for an effective discharge of our nonbusiness programs we depend on a vigorous productive foundation, but that requires not so much the indiscriminate encouragement of output as its re-direction.

Thus it seems to me that the trends of the present, which are far from halted, portend a continuation of the general elevation of nonbusiness elites and a general compression of the influence of business leadership itself. To put my prognostication as concretely as possible, I expect to see fewer big businessmen in positions of power in Washington and more educators, career administrators, scientists, or soldiers; to see fewer big businessmen as trustees of universities or on the boards of the largest foundations, and more of the new men of influence there; to hear less about the sanctity of foreign investment and more about economic development; to find less attention paid to the rhetoric of laissez faire and more to that of Neo-Keynesianism and Input-Output Tables. In a word, I believe that the slowly fading presence of the big businessman as an originator of policy or as a counselor in the determination of foreign and domestic affairs will fade further, and that his place will be increasingly taken by new men, largely from nonbusiness backgrounds.

Always, in long-run historical comparisons of this sort one runs the risk of overstating the case. Hence let me repeat my earlier emphasis on the power that big business still commands. Of all the various centers of influence and direction within America, the business community is still unquestionably the single most important as regards the shaping of national policy. Nonetheless, I think it is an unavoidable conclusion, once one takes a line of sight into the past, that this power, however formidable, is markedly less than was the case in the not so very distant era prior to the Great Depression.

AMERICAN BUSINESS IS PLAINLY IN TROUBLE

James M. Roche

Notwithstanding that America is the envy and the aspiration of the world, there are those who maintain our economic system is not the best and ask, "Is there not a better way?"

Some who question our society and its achievements are young. Some are well-intentioned. Some are sincere. But there are others. Their final objectives are not what they first profess. Their beliefs, their purposes run contrary to the principles of the majority of our people. They question many of our institutions, including our economic system. They crusade for radical changes in our system of corporate ownership—changes so drastic that they would all but destroy free enterprise as we know it. Deliberately or not, they are also weakening our free competitive system.

Many observers have noted the recent growth of a group of critics who have launched, and have pressed, an assault on the reputation of America. It has already diminished the idea of America in the eyes of many people, at home and abroad. The damage they do is greatest among our young, who are no longer even given the time to judge our system by their own experience. Instead, their ideals are aborted at an age and often in a place—in our schools—where ideals ought to be instilled rather than destroyed.

The current disparagement of America holds many ironies. One is that the country is criticized for the relatively narrow area of shortcoming, without credit for the broad range of achievement. For example, the nation is credited less with a superior system of public higher education than it is criticized for not making it freely available to all, even the unqualified. The nation is credited less with an incomparable transportation system than it is faulted for its traffic jams. The nation is credited less with having two thirds of its families own their own homes than it is condemned for its slums.

Another irony is that many of today's problems are an outgrowth of yesterday's progress. They are marks of a society that, on the whole, has had extraordinary success in meeting the aspirations of earlier generations. Yet some who criticize our system would substitute other systems which have fallen far short of ours. In most other countries, the quality of our daily life is still no more than a hopeful vision. In those places, such criticisms as we hear would be mere frivolities—idle pastimes of the academic. Where there are no roofs, there are no leaks.

Nevertheless, in our country this climate of disparagement and doubt is real. Its depressing impact upon the national mood is affecting the attitudes and values of our younger generation. All of us with a concern for our society's future must recognize and deal with what is really a kind of national malaise.

To the extent that doubt and disparagement are directed toward free enterprise, they are of direct and immediate concern to us as businessmen. And it is all too evident that, in too many cases, the climate of criticism is highly adverse to free enterprises. The equating of profit with immorality is spreading a cloud of suspicion and distrust over all we have achieved and hope to achieve.

To those of us in business, progress is both our goal and our habit. We understand that progress means change. We never expect or want things to stay as they are, much less to turn back to simpler days.

Progressive change has brought our country to its present high position. Competitive enterprise has been a principal engine of change and progress. Business has not only responded to change but has caused change. Out of this process of competitive innovation comes progress. . . .

American business today has no lack of challenges. The list is long and familiar to all of you. It includes inflation, foreign competition, unsatisfactory productivity, urban rebuilding, minority opportunity, pollution control and, in many areas, increasing government regulation.

Some of these challenges—inflation, foreign competition, unsatisfactory productivity—are tied together. Our rising costs and lagging productivity have damaged our country's competitive position. They have lessened the ability of many industries to compete in world markets. They have also resulted in an influx of imported merchandise never before experienced in the United States.

American business, from the perspective of the world, is plainly in trouble. . . .

Those critics whose aim is destructive are following a basic tactic of divisiveness—and with considerable success. They are endeavoring to turn various segments of our society—government, labor, the universities—against business. They are trying to make America in the 1970s a society at war with itself.

Their ultimate aim is to elienate the American consumer from business, to tear down long-established relationships which have served both so well. They tell the consumer he is being victimized. New products are being foisted upon him, whether he wants them or not. These products are not as good as they should be—that is, they are less than perfect. Businessmen are greedy and uncaring. Corporations are beyond reach and above response to the consumer's needs. Advertising is false. Prices are padded. Labels are inaccurate.

Therefore, the consumer—many would have us believe—is helpless and unprotected when he shops and is really not responsible for what he buys.

This delusion—that the consumer cannot trust his own free choice—strikes at the very heart of our free competitive system. The system is founded on the conviction that in the long run the consumer is the best judge of his own welfare. The entire success of free enterprise can be traced to the vitality it gains by competitive striving to satisfy the discriminating customer. To destroy the concept of consumer supremacy is to destroy free enterprise. If the consumer can be convinced that he really does not know what is good for him—and this is what the critics try to do—then freedom leaves free enterprise.

In other words, if the consumer cannot protect his own interest, then someone else must do it. That someone else will then dictate what can be made, what can be sold, and at what price. That will surely mark the end of free enterprise. The greatest of our economic freedoms—the freedom to decide our purchase—will be gone.

This cannot happen, many will say. To them we should reply, "Look back." Look back at only the past decade to see how rapidly we have expanded the role of government in the marketplace.

To protect the consumer, a new aspect of bureaucracy, "consumer affairs," has been created, not only in Washington but in State capitals and local communities. Since 1900, Congress has passed 39 major consumer laws, but two thirds of these have been enacted in only the last eight years. To the extent that new laws and new officials do protect the consumer against fraud and deception, and safeguard his health and safety, they are good. But too much of this new development is unnecessary and does not deliver a value to the consumer commensurate with the potential cost in higher taxes and higher prices.

Also to protect the consumer, it has been mandated that many of the products he buys be altered. In this way, too, consumer choice is sometimes unnecessarily reduced, and costs are added without equivalent increase in value. For these unwanted products as well, it is the consumer who pays.

Harassment Adds to Cost of Doing Business

Make no mistake, the results of irresponsible harassment have added significantly to the cost of doing business. The higher taxes are costly. Adapting products to new regulations is costly. Meeting daily harassments, answering criticism, defending against public attack—all these carry costs, in time and energy as well as dollars.

Yet the fashion is still to call for these new controls of business. The regulations and inspections of administrative agencies have their harassing counterpart in the legislative halls, where there are also those who seek to devise new means to impair the free workings of our economic system.

Individuals and agencies have competed—sometimes blindly— to be on the crest of the wave of consumer protection. In the 1960s, consumer legislation came into political vogue. Much of this was necessary and serves our society well. Yet the short-term political advantage offered by spectacular but unsound consumer legislation can do lasting damage to the very consumers it purports to help.

The consumer—that is, all of us—is the loser when irresponsible criticism and ill-conceived legislation break down faith in our economic system, when harassment distracts us from our modern challenges, when the very idea of free enterprise is diminished in the eyes of the young people who must one day manage our businesses.

Every unwise impairment of free enterprise carries some additional costs to 200 million individual Americans. It carries other great collective costs to the extent that it further reduces the ability of American industry to compete in the markets of the world.

With U.S. Losing Its "Technological Edge"—

America no longer enjoys the technological edge over other advanced countries that we once did. This is especially true in the case of such industrialized nations as Germany, Japan, France and Italy.

They are enjoying substantial annual increases in productivity as opposed to the slower rate of increase in our own economy. They too are experiencing inflation but, because we start from a higher base, the gap in dollars-and-cents costs is widening in many industries.

This growing competitive disadvantage against America is an important fact of international economic life. Yet it is little acknowledged by some of the critics. They demand that American business be more socially responsible, but give too little consideration to the costs of meeting social aspirations.

Yet the costs must be considered when business is directed to achieve the social as well as the economic aspirations of a society. The costs of meeting these social aspirations are superimposed upon our present very high cost base. They simply compound the difficulty of competing with foreign manufacturers whose economies have not yet lifted their societies to the level of ours, and consequently have not experienced the same demands for still further social advances.

"Corporate responsibility" is a catchword of the adversary culture that is so evident today. If something is wrong with American society, blame business.

Business did not create discrimination in America, but business is expected to eliminate it. Business did not bring about the deterioration of our cities, but business is expected to rebuild them. Business did not create poverty and hunger in our land, but business is expected to eliminate them.

Business as a Vehicle of Social Reform

As citizens and Americans, we heartily endorse all these objectives.

No thoughtful American can be opposed to equal opportunity, to better housing and education, and to the elimination of poverty from our land. But every thoughtful American must face the fact that new aspirations entail new costs. We should also recognize that business is not always the best vehicle for their accomplishment, although there is much business can contribute.

Business nevertheless is often a convenient scapegoat; but blaming business—or government, for that matter—does not excuse us from our own personal responsibility as citizens, as parents, as teachers.

These considerations pose questions which should be much on the mind of every American, because if our society does not give them a satisfactory answer—and soon—whatever capacity American business does have to influence social change for the better may be severely impaired. Business, burdened by new and unnecessary social costs, may find itself hard-pressed to maintain the economic progress that has so distinguished our history.

The climate of criticism and disparagement has dulled the reputation of business. We read and hear very little that is good about business.

Seldom, if ever, is business credited with meeting its basic corporate responsibilities.

I submit that American business is fulfilling vital social responsibilities every day—and with great success. Business does its job when it provides useful jobs at high wages, when it provides useful products at fair prices, when it provides economic growth that produces taxes for government and earnings for stockholders. These are the long-standing social responsibilities of business. Their fulfillment by American business over two centuries has made our America what it is. It is an achievement to be proud of—an achievement to talk about.

Earlier, I said we must be ready to accept change. And business today is expected to respond to the new aspirations of the society it serves. This broad public expectation must be recognized, and these new challenges must be accepted. The costs of many are not prohibitive. For example, the costs of providing greater job opportunities, particularly for minorities, can usually be absorbed in the normal course of business.

The same is true of the cost of supporting community and educational activities—business's traditional citizenship role. And for these, we do get value. However, in other areas—for example, in the control of pollution—costs are usually substantial. To the extent that they cannot be absorbed, they will raise the price of the product and in turn the over-all level of prices in our economy.

As a nation we must be mature enough to face up to the costs involved in meeting our new aspirations. It can mean a weakened competitive position in the world. It can mean higher prices for the consumer and higher taxes for the citizen.

This is no dire forecast; this is already a fact. We are weaker abroad. We have experienced higher prices and higher taxes.

Yet we must not allow this to slow our nation's progress toward the fulfillment of our social aspirations. Our task is to achieve our national social objectives at the least possible cost to our society, to assure full value for the dollars that must be spent, to mount an efficient effort. This is clearly a job where business and businessmen have much to contribute. Society must define its objectives and establish priorities. . . .

Free enterprise has come to a crisis—a crisis in the sense of a time for decision. Tough decisions must be made by all of us, and soon. Society expects much of us. Yet if we are to be effective, we must work together with the other segments of our society.

Instead, at this very time when free enterprise needs support, it finds itself the target of much irresponsible criticism that causes disunity in our society.

Having pitted consumer against producer, some critics are now busy eroding another support of free enterprise—the loyalty of a management team, with its unifying values of co-operative work. Some of the enemies of business now encourage an employee to be disloyal to the enterprise. They want to create suspicion and disharmony, and pry into the proprietary interests of the business. However this is labeled—industrial espionage, whistle blowing or professional responsibility—it is another tactic for spreading disunity and creating conflict.

Stand Up and Be Counted

The dull cloud of pessimism and distrust which some have cast over free enterprise is impairing the ability of business to meet its basic economic responsibilties—not to mention its capacity to take on newer ones. This as much as any other factor makes it urgent that those of us who are in business—who have made business our career, who are justifiably proud of our profession—stand up and be counted.

It is up to us in the business community to reaffirm our belief in free enterprise.

————————

THE CORPORATION AND SOCIETY IN THE 1970'S

Daniel Bell

Private Property or Private Enterprise?

The modern business corporation has lost many of the historic features of traditional capitalism, yet it has, for lack of a new rationale, retained the old ideology—and finds itself trapped by it.

Unhappy is a society that has run out of words to describe what is going on. So Thurman Arnold observed in connection with the language of private property—the myths and folklore of capitalism—which even 30 years ago was hopelessly out of date. *The point is that today ownership is simply a legal fiction.*

A stockholder is an owner because, in theory, he has put up equity capital and taken a risk. But only a minor proportion of corporate capital today is raised through the sale of equity capital. A more significant portion of capital comes through self-financing, by the success of the enterprise itself. In the last decade, more than 60 per cent of the capital investment of the nation's 1,000 largest manufacturing firms was financed internally. Retained capital is the basis of the rise in net assets of large corporations. And the growth of retained capital is the product of managerial skill. (Equally, a large portion of new capital is raised by debentures, which become a fixed charge against earnings, rather than through floating equity or risk stock. Debentures hinge on the stability of the company and the prospect of repayment —again a managerial problem.)

If one were to follow the logic of Friedman's argument, as he does—it is his strength and weakness that he always follows the logic of his argument, to the very end—one would have to outlaw or at least discourage self-financing. Under the "pure" theory of market capitalism, a firm risks a stockholder's capital and then pays back any profits—in the form of dividends—to its legal owners, the stockholders. If it seeks to risk that money again, it should ask those stockholders to reinvest that money, rather than withhold it from them and reinvest it by managerial decision. Friedman argues that it is only the "double taxation" (through corporate and personal income tax) of dividends that prevents such a desirable state of affairs from emerging. But I should say that such a state of affairs is neither desirable nor possible. Given the pattern of stock ownership today—particularly with the growth of mutual funds, pension funds and trust funds—the stockholder is often an "in-and-out" person with little continuing interest in the enterprise. Such an in-and-out procedure may be a useful discipline for management and a measure of economic performance—but then it becomes a form of countervailing power, not ownership. True owners are involved directly and psychologically in the fate of an enterprise; and this description better fits the employees of the corporation, not its stockholders. For these employees, the corporation is a social institution which they inhabit. It is politically and morally unthinkable that ther lives should be at the mercy of a financial speculator.

In other words, the corporation may be a *private enterprise* institution, but it is not really a *private property* institution. (If the assets of the enterprise are primarily the skill of its managerial employees, not machinery or things—and this is preeminently true in the science-based industries, in communications, and in the so-called "knowledge industries"—then property is anyway of lesser importance.) And if ownership is largely a legal fiction, then one ought to adopt a more realistic attitude to it. One can treat stockholders not as "owners" but as legitimate claimants to some fixed share of the profits of a corporation—and to nothing more.

The Meaning of "a Corporation"

What then is a corporation? If one goes back to the original meaning of the term, as a social invention of the late Middle Ages to meet some novel problems, a corporation was an instrument for self-governance for groups carrying on a common activity (artisan guilds, local boroughs, ecclesiastical bodies); it often had common economic assets, and its existence would persist beyond the lives of its individual members. Those who were "members" of the corporation were those directly responsible for its activities, those who were the legatees of the past members, and those chosen to carry on the work.

A business corporation today—like a university today—can be viewed in this original sociological conception of the term. Indeed, if one begins to look on the business corporation more and more on the model of the university, then the fallacy of ownership becomes more apparent. Who "owns" Harvard or the University of Chicago? Legally the "corporation," as composed by the overseers or the trustees. But in any sociological sense this is meaningless. The university is a self-selective ongoing enterprise of its members (administration, faculty, students, and alumni, with differential responsibilities and obligations) who seek to carry out its purposes with due regard to the interests of the particular community which constitutes the university —and also to the larger community that makes the university possible.

As a business institution, the "corporation" is the management and the board of directors, operating as trustees for members of the enterprise as a whole—not just stockholders, but workers and consumers too—and with due regard to the interests of society as a whole. But if this view is accepted, there is a significant logical corollary—that the constituencies which make up the corporation themselves have to be represented within the board of corporate power. Without that, there is no effective countervailing power to that of executive management. More important, without such representation, there would be a serious question about the "legitimacy" of managerial power.

How such constituencies might be represented is a question to be explored. A dozen years ago, Bayless Manning, Jr., until recently the Dean of the Stanford Law School, sought to picture the corporation as if it were in law what it often is in fact, as a kind of "voting trust" wherein the stockholder delegates all his rights, except that of collecting dividends, to the directors. In order to establish some check on the board of directors, he proposed a "second chamber," an "extrinsic body," which would review decisions of the board where conflicts of interest arose—such as compensation of officers, contributions to other enterprises (universities, community efforts, etc.) not directly related to a company's business, clashes with a public interest, etc.

It is beyond the scope of this essay, and the competence of the author, to estimate the viability of these—or other—specific proposals. The problem is there; it is not going to go away; and discussion of possible resolutions is anything but premature.

From Bitterness to Banality

As a debate on these issues continues, one important consideration should be kept in mind—the bitterness of one generation is often the banality of another. Who, today, gives a second thought to Savings Bank Life Insurance? Yet this idea, authored by Louis D. Brandeis in Massachusetts, was fought for five months in passage through the legislature and was marked by one of the bitterest fights ever witnessed on Beacon Hill. (One line of attack was that people would not voluntarily seek insurance, and that they would not take it out at all if the expensive system of soliciting by agents were done away with.) The issue gave Brandeis a national reputation, and eventually brought Brandeis to the Supreme Court. The reputation remained, but the issue itself soon faded.

The lesson, however, was not, and is still not wholly learned—reforms will never be as sweeping in their effects as their proponents hope, and the results will rarely be as damaging and apocalyptic as the opponents fear. Workmen's compensation was an issue that inflamed a generation of radicals and was fought by industry on the ground that it would relieve the workman of "individual responsibility" for his actions; yet who today would deny that industrial safety is a legitimate cost of factory operations?

Such reforms are always an expression of a revision—implicit or explicit—in the American "public philosophy." This kind of "revisionism" is inevitable as men and societies change, and as the dominant values assume a new shape. The private enterprise system has been the primary institution of Western society not because of its coercive power but because its values—economizing and increasing output of material goods—were congruent with the major consumer values of the society. With all its obvious imperfections the system "worked." Today, however, those values are themselves being questioned, not in the way socialists and radicals questioned them a generation ago— that they were achieved at the cost of exploiting the worker—but at the very core, the creation of more private goods at the expense of other social values. I return to a point made earlier that unlike the polity, no one, meeting collectively "voted in" our market economy. But now votes are being taken.

It seems clear to me that, today, we in America are moving away from a society based on a private-enterprise market system toward one in which the most important economic decisions will be made at the political level, in terms of consciously-defined "goals" and "priorities." The dangers inherent in such a shift are familiar enough to anyone acquainted with the liberal tradition. In the past, there was an "unspoken consensus," and the public philosophy did not need to be articulated. And this was a strength, for articulation often invites trials by force when implicit differences are made manifest. Today, however, there is a visible change from market to non-market political decision-making. The market disperses responsibility: the political center is visible, the question of who gains and who loses is clear, and government becomes a cockpit.

But to be hypnotized by such dangers is little less than frivolous. No social or economic order has a writ of immortality, and the consumer-oriented free-enterprise society no longer satifies the citizenry, as once it did. So it will have to change, in order that something we still recognize as a liberal society might survive.

Whether such a change will represent "progress" is a nice metaphysical question that I, for one, do not know how to answer. This was a society "designed" by Locke and Smith and it rested on the premises of individualism and market rationality in which the varied ends desired by individuals would be maximized by free exchange. We now move to a communal ethic, without that community being, as yet, wholly defined. In a sense, the movement away from governance by political economy to governance by political philosophy— for that is the meaning of the shift—is a return to pre-capitalist modes of social thought. But whether this be progress or regress, it clearly makes it incumbent upon us to think more candidly and rigorously about our values, and about the kind of world we wish to live in.

CHAPTER 5

The United States in a Changing World Economy

On August 15, 1971, President Richard M. Nixon, as part of his new plan to combat a deteriorating domestic and international economic situation, suspended international convertibility of the dollar into gold and imposed a temporary 10 percent surcharge on about half of the country's imports. These steps formally acknowledged that American foreign economic policy was in serious trouble and that the arrangements that had underpinned it since World War II were no longer viable. As the world's rich "Uncle" immediately after that war, the United States had assumed the leading role in reconstruction of the world economy. That a situation like that of mid-1971 could develop would have been unthinkable then. How did it come about? Why did it happen? What can be done about it?

No nation is completely self-sufficient; it must engage in economic relationships with others. These relationships, which may involve political, military, and other objectives, as well as economic ones, are measured in two ways. The balance of trade primarily describes the relationship between imports and exports of goods and commodities. The balance of payments describes the total financial relationships between countries, including, in addition to trade items, other items such as tourist expenditures and direct foreign investments. The amount of activity in these two areas in turn is affected by the exchange ratio between domestic and foreign currencies, which defines the price of one in terms of the other. Traditionally, gold has been the ultimate common denominator for expressing these relationships and for settling international accounts. As a developing country in the nineteenth century, the United States exported chiefly raw materials, agricultural products and semi-manufactured goods and imported capital and manufactured products from more developed countries. As the United States became more industrialized, its foreign trade in the first half of this century shifted towards export of manufactured products and imports of raw materials. From the mid-1890's to the early 1970's an overall favorable balance of trade was maintained, with exports exceeding imports, but by 1960 the balance of payments was turning against the United States. As a developing nation prior to World War I, the United States generally owed more abroad than was owed it. That war, however, turned this country into a mature creditor nation. To finance the war, foreign investors liquidated their holdings of American securities, and the Allies turned to the United States for food and munitions. The United States lent the Allies some $10 billion for war and reconstruction, and at the end of the war it claimed repayment. The repayment issue quickly became attached to the Allies' demands that Germany assume full responsibility for the conflict and repay them for its costs. Despite several renegotiations of these issues in the 1920's, the resulting arrangements proved largely unworkable. With the onslaught of world depression, in 1931, the United States declared a moratorium on war debt repayment and for all practical purposes both World War I reparations and war debt payments ended.

Aside from the largely untenable assumption that war finance can be treated like a normal business proposition, the United States had precluded repayment of its loans by refusing to lower its tariff barriers. The idea that the domestic economy should be protected against foreign competition had a strong tradition, and it was stronger than ever in the 1920's. The president had authority to raise or lower tariffs by as much as 50 percent, and out of 37 times that this power was exercised by Presidents Harding and Coolidge, 32 were on the upwards side. High tariffs kept out foreign products that could have been used to reduce the debtor countries' obligations. Meanwhile during the 1920's, Americans, with the encouragement of their government, made extensive loans and investments overseas, in effect, tying German reparations payments and the Allies' war debt installments to the continued export of American capital. But by 1931, a year after the enactment of the highest tariff in United States history, this pyramid, built on circuitous self-deception, collapsed in ruins.

The international economic collapse carried with it the international gold standard, long regarded as a self-regulating mechanism of great strength and importance. Under the gold standard, excesses in international debtor and creditor relationships were supposed to correct themselves. As the balance of payments turned against a country, gold—the international medium of exchange—flowed out of that country to settle its foreign accounts. Prices in the countries to which the gold moved were supposed to rise, automatically making their export prices rise, thus discouraging exports. Conversely, in the country from which the gold flowed, export prices were supposed to fall, making it attractive for other countries to buy more there. But, of course, international economic relationships are complex, and the ingenuity of countries adversely affected by the operation of the gold standard made its hypothetical self-adjusting characteristics subject to many qualifications. Nevertheless, until the early 1930's, international trade and monetary arrangements were based on the gold standard.

Since the common denominator of exchange between currencies was gold, a change in the relationship of a nation's currency to gold could affect its international trade position. "Devaluation" of a country's monetary unit means that prices fall in terms of gold or other currencies. If other countries do not also devalue, the first to do so makes its goods cheaper and, therefore, theoretically more attractive in terms of exchange. But to frustrate this strategy, other countries may also devalue their currencies and/or impose import quotas, raise tariffs, and otherwise control foreign purchases to protect their trade position. Such was the general situation in the 1930's.

Britain, whose pound sterling had been the world's basic trading and reserve unit, was forced off the gold standard in 1931. The United States followed in 1933–1934, outlawing the holding of gold by individuals or the domestic redemption of obligations (including the government's) payable in that metal. At the same time the dollar, which remained tied to gold, was devalued about 40 percent, with the United States buying all gold offered at \$35 per ounce. As the threat of war overtook other countries in the 1930's, gold flowed in an ever-increasing stream to the United States, where most of it was locked up in the vaults of Fort Knox, Kentucky.

While other countries attempted to protect and expand their foreign trade by such devices as import quotas and barter, the United States took a new departure in its tariff policy. Beginning in 1934 with the Reciprocal Trade Agreements Act, favorable trade agreements negotiated with one country were extended to others that did not discriminate against the United States. In return for these concessions, the United States expected favorable terms for such exports as farm products and machinery. The Export-Import Bank was organized in 1934 to finance trade with the Soviet Union, but since then has devoted most of its attention to financing exports by loans or guarantee of loans, many of which have been in connection with Latin American trade. Since 1947, the United States has also been a party to the General Agreement on Tariffs and Trade (GATT), which binds the signatories to follow common trade practices and encourages members to negotiate trade agreements with more than one country at a time.

Over time the reciprocal trade approach has led to a general decline in the level of American import duties, but it has also called for exceptions to protect domestic producers hurt in the process. For specific industries, e.g., sugar, there have also been subsidies and for others, such as petroleum, import quotas.

After a great surge during World War I, exports of American agricultural products shrank rapidly. The resulting surplus of American foodstuffs, particularly grains, contributed to domestic agricultural depression in the 1920's and led to repeated efforts to obtain marketing subsidies that would permit dumping this surplus on the world market. Unfortunately for the farmer, nothing substantial came of these efforts before 1929, and shortly thereafter national and international depression further aggravated the farmer's plight. The resulting efforts to bring domestic agricultural supply and demand into balance worked to price U.S. farm products out of the world market. Despite legislation to promote and subsidize some agricultural exports, the adverse export situation has largely persisted during peacetime.

On the other hand, between 1899 and 1913 the value (in constant dollars) of United States exports of manufactures doubled, and between 1913 and 1929 they more than doubled. Although there was a decline during the 1930's, the value of manufactured exports doubled again between 1937 and 1957. From 1913 to 1959, increases in these exports was more closely related to general expansion of the world market than to either increased shares of individual overseas markets or changing area and commodity patterns of world trade. In fact, the United States was losing ground in terms of actual world market shares during the 1950's.

World War II was a benchmark in economic relations. Untouched physically by the hostilities, the United States literally became the arsenal of democracy. Accumulated agricultural surpluses met the Allies' needs while American industrial plants turned out a vast array of munitions and products destined for overseas. Unlike World War I, however, there was little expectation that such massive assistance could be regarded as a loan to be repaid after the war. Accordingly much of it was offered on the basis of "Lend-Lease," or by outright gift.

By 1944 it was clear that foundations had to be laid for postwar economic relations, and to that end the Allies' representatives to the United Nations gathered at Bretton Woods, New Hampshire. From their deliberations came the institutions, policies, and mechanisms that saw the American dollar replace the British pound as the cornerstone of the world monetary system until the era of American hegemony came to an end on August 15, 1971.

In addition to creation of the International Bank for Reconstruction and Development (World Bank), the Bretton Woods delegates agreed to establish the International Monetary Fund (IMF). Under the resulting articles of agreement, each IMF member country was to establish a par value for its currency in terms of gold or the dollar, and this value was to be maintained through a narrow band of ±1.00 percent on either side of the par value. In effect, this agreement pegged foreign currencies to the dollar.

In this way the American dollar became the world's standard. Since 1945, the United States has annually been the net supplier of private and Government long-term capital and grants to the rest of the world. The movement started with a 1946 loan to Britain and was continued with the massive foreign aid program, first known as the Marshall Plan, adopted in 1948 to aid war-torn countries and to counter a growing Soviet menace. Continued as the Mutual Security and Technical Assistance Program (President Harry Truman's Point Four) and under other names, military and economic foreign aid, was supported by Congress with little question until 1956, when the legislative branch gradually began to pare down President Eisenhower's requests each year. Presidents Kennedy and Johnson encountered even stiffer opposition to their foreign aid programs, with critics charging that it was causing an alarming outflow of gold, that the major recipients had recovered their economic strength, but the United States was still financing their protection with military expenditures overseas.

A major factor in this change of attitude was the formation and success of the European Common Market in 1958, where the major industrial countries of western Europe (with the most notable exception of Great Britain, which did not join until 1972) united to remove trade barriers between them, and to present a united front to the world. Either to take advantage of this development or to avoid clashing with this market, numerous American companies decided to start or expand operations within those countries.

With the benefit of postwar American aid, the European countries, by the late 1950's, were rapidly reaching the position of self-sufficiency. The net result was that American exports to western Europe declined to the point where they did not cover combined American expenditures there of military and economic aid plus private investment. The imbalance was reflected in the steady drain of gold reserves from the United States. Between 1958 and 1962 they fell from $22 billion to $17 billion. To meet this challenge, President Kennedy asked for, and Congress reluctantly granted, presidential authority to raise tariff rates above the 1934 level or lower them beneath the 1962 level by as much as 50 percent over the next five years.

In the first half of the 1960's, the situation was serious; by the second half it was nearing disaster proportions. The requirements of the IMF, plus presidential pressuring, kept foreign countries from demanding payment in gold for their claims on the dollar. Until mid-decade, labor unit costs in the United States fell while those in other countries remained stable. Therefore, the United States was not inundated with imports, despite lowered tariff barriers. But beginning in 1964 the situation changed abruptly.

Domestic inflation, in part caused by the escalating Vietnam War, led to increased labor unit costs and to increased unit value of U.S. manufactured exports relative to those of other industrialized nations. The rate of increase of manufactured exports failed to keep pace with those of imports. Between 1964 and 1968 the volume of manufactured exports rose only 27 percent, compared to 50 percent for West Germany, 38 percent for France, 92 percent for Canada, and 100 percent for Japan. Between 1952 and 1968 the United States' share of manufactured goods exported by the leading industrial countries shrank from 35 to 22 percent.

Meanwhile, as American multinational companies expanded, direct private American investment overseas mounted steadily. It rose from an average of $1.8 billion a year in the first half of the 1960's to $3.3 billion in the second half. In 1970 it reached $4.4 billion. Although income from these investments exceeded the outgo, it did not stem the steady worsening of the nation's balance of payments. The unfavorable balance in terms of goods, services, and remittances (excluding government grants and long- and short-term capital) amounted to $7.6 billion between 1964 and 1971. But in 1971 alone, the balance of payments deficit exceeded this figure. Behind this problem was a surge in merchandise imports, which rose 147 percent between 1964 and 1971, compared to an increase of only 74 percent in merchandise exports.

Because the world's currencies were tied to the dollar, and yet the dollar's value was steadily being eroded by domestic inflation, foreign countries felt that the United States was using the situation to export its inflation, to undermine their production, and to help finance the unpopular Vietnam War. This position was strengthened because foreign treasuries and banks held mounting millions of American dollars that were surplus to their needs, yet could not be collected without serious danger of adverse international consequences. These overvalued dollars in terms of their own currencies, which the IMF required them to maintain at ±1.00 percent of par value in terms of dollars, allowed American companies to acquire foreign businesses at a substantial discount. At the same time, by the failure to call the dollar to account, the United States was able for a time to conduct an escalating war abroad and an expanding domestic economy at home.

The action taken by President Nixon on August 15, 1971, to

suspend convertibility of the dollar into gold or other reserve assets was formal acknowledgement of the serious decline of the dollar's exchange value. Between January and August 1971, the U.S. Treasury had paid out over $3 billion in reserve assets, reflecting an adverse balance of trade and payments. The pressure for conversion mounted steadily while the reserves to meet it shrank below the danger point.

After the suspension, the problem was to find a new relationship of the dollar to other currencies, to expand opportunities for American exports while curbing imports, and to share mutual security expenditures to a far greater extent than had been the case since World War II. In December 1971 the "big ten" industrialized countries agreed that for a time they would expand the IMF parity band from ±1 percent to ±2.25 percent. In return, the United States agreed to devalue its dollar (from $35 per ounce of gold to $38) and to drop the 10 percent surcharge on imports imposed in August 1971. Meanwhile the search continued for arrangements to free the world's monetary systems from gold and dependence on the dollar, neither of which had proved adequate to the changed conditions of international trade.

At the close of 1972 the major industrial countries were still seeking a solution to the exchange problem. Some had let their currencies "float," meaning that their relationship to the dollar was determined by market forces. But this solution was unsatisfactory to foreign countries because it meant that their export prices rose in terms of dollars, adversely affecting their trade.

To promote American exports, the Nixon Administration proposed and Congress approved in 1971, legislation to make domestic exporters more competitive with American firms that conducted manufacturing operations overseas. The latter companies under existing tax law did not have to pay income tax in the United States until their foreign profits were "repatriated" *and* distributed in the country. This provision permitted virtually indefinite postponement of income tax payment on foreign earnings if a company so chose. Companies exporting from the United States, on the other hand, had to pay tax on income from export operations as it was earned. The Revenue Act of 1971 authorized formation of Domestic International Sales Corporations (DISC's) which can defer 50 percent (the Administration had asked for 100 percent) of their income tax indefinitely, subject to the condition that 95 percent of their receipts and assets relate to qualified exports. The availability of the DISC may reduce some of the incentive to establish U.S. manufacturing operations overseas.

Organized labor, pointing to what it feels is the export of American jobs, has asked for reconsideration of tariff provisions that permit exemption from duty on the value of U.S.-made or fabricated components that go into products manufactured abroad and then are imported to this country. Labor spokesmen argue that this tariff provision encourages American firms to use cheap foreign labor because they pay duty only on the value added by this labor to American-made components shipped abroad.

Since August 1971, many steps have been taken to improve the United States' position in the world economy, including expanded authority and leeway for the Export-Import Bank to increase export loans and increased efforts to reduce imports and increase exports. Revaluation of the dollar in 1971 acted to raise the price of products from countries whose currencies moved upwards in terms of the dollar. In addition, specific steps were taken in the fall of 1971 to curb the influx of synthetic fibers and woolen textiles from the Far East, with a resulting adverse impact on some 2.3 million Americans employed in these industries. (Under the GATT, limits were placed on cotton textile imports in 1962.) In early 1971 imports of manmade fibers had risen 80 percent compared to the same period in 1970. Under the terms of voluntary agreements of October 1971 with Japan, the Republic of China, Korea, and Hong Kong, the growth rate of these imports was limited to 5 to 7.5 percent per year. This device worked surprisingly well during its first year, with a projected 7 percent gain in output for the domestic industry.

Agricultural imports and exports have received special attention, as well. For example, dairy prices are supported in the United States. To prevent them from being undermined, many imported products are subject to import quotas, and this list was expanded in 1971. To expand the export market for agricultural as well as other products, the Nixon administration in 1971 lifted the embargo on exports to the People's Republic of China and relaxed the requirement that 50 percent of wheat, flour and other grains destined for Communist East Europe and the Soviet Union be carried in U.S. ships. This action contributed to a major sale of feed grains to the Soviet Union in the fall of 1971 for the first time since 1964, and it was followed by another large sale in the summer of 1972.

By mid-1973 none of these measures had solved the basic imbalance between American exports and imports or between foreign payments and receipts. It was necessary again to devalue the dollar, and the American currency that for nearly two decades after World War II had been the world's standard sank to new lows on international money markets. Although the United States remained the richest and most powerful nation in the world, it was becoming painfully clear that it lacked the resources to simultaneously police the world, improve the standard of living at home, and dominate competitive world markets. For the first time in memory, the country faced peacetime shortages ranging from beef to gasoline. Just as in the case of the domestic economy, Americans in the early 1970's were being forced to reappraise what the costs and benefits of alternative courses of action would be in international economic relationships. As a nation Americans were relearning some of the costly lessons that, as an emerging industrial giant, they had taught other, more mature countries more than seventy years before.

INTRODUCTION:
THE UNITED STATES IN THE
WORLD ECONOMY,
1914–1972

The United States became a mature creditor nation as a result of World War I. What is not often recognized is the extent to which American firms and capital had gone overseas even before World War I. Overall, exports exceeded imports throughout that period until 1971. By the 1960's the balance of payments was beginning to swing against the United States. After a post-World War II dominance of world money markets, the American dollar in the late 1960's began to lose ground rapidly, and by the early 1970's the situation was critical. The following selections trace some of these major developments.

The first selection, from Mira Wilkins' study of multinational companies before World War I, gives an idea of the variety and size of American overseas investment before that world conflict. The next selection is the brief text of Secretary of State George Marshall's 1947 proposal for the United States to come to the economic aid of the countries of Europe that were devastated by World War II. From it emerged a program of foreign economic, and later military, aid that was unprecedented in history. In the following selection the President's Council of Economic Advisers reviews the varied roles of the United States in world trade and money markets six years after Secretary Marshall's epoch-making speech.

As the recipients of American aid regained economic health, they became increasingly stronger competitors of the United States. The next selection, from a distinguished economist's testimony before a congressional committee in 1970, documents the deterioration of the American balance of payments situation. However, Gottfried Haberler remained confident that the dollar—despite its *de facto* incontrovertibility into gold—would remain the world's standard.

But, as the situation continued to worsen, incontrovertibility became a formal position of the American government. The next selection, from the remarks of Arthur Burns, Chairman of the Board of Governors of the Federal Reserve System, in May 1972, addresses the increasingly pressing question of what steps to take towards international monetary reform. He emphasizes the need for improved international communication and cooperation in such matters, a reduced role for gold, and reestablishment of convertibility of the dollar. The final selection, from the April 1973 bulletin of the Chase Manhattan Bank, one of the nation's largest financial institutions, reviews the relationship between adverse foreign trade developments and balance of payments difficulties, reports on different schools of thought about the causes of trade deterioration, and reflects on the possibilities for improvement by the mid-1970's.

THE STATUS OF AMERICAN INTERNATIONAL ENTERPRISE–1914

Mira Wilkins

[My previous writings] . . . leave no doubt that American business-men were involved abroad in the years before 1914—sometimes through international[1] corporations and sometimes through companies that had stakes only in a single country. In fact, practically every prominent industrial tycoon in the late nineteenth and early twentieth centuries was in some manner interested in foreign business. Railroad leaders, such as Collis P. Huntington, E. H. Harriman, Cornelius Vanderbilt, and James J. Hill were likewise concerned. So too was J. P. Morgan, the era's key banker.[2]

Clearly, the alert American entrepreneurs sought opportunities beyond the national boundaries. Both the "push" of conditions at home (the growth of the firm and the economic environment in the United States) and the "pull" of prospects abroad (the possibilities of markets and sources of supplies) contributed to the rising direct foreign investment in the decades before 1914. United States government policies and actions had an impact, but only a small one, on the direct investment pattern; the influence was most pronounced in the Caribbean area.

The Americans who invested abroad before 1914 encountered some of the problems that their successors would meet. They recognized the need to develop strategies to cope with differences abroad: variations in host-country industry structure and host-country governmental attitudes and actions. In the process of expanding abroad, some U.S. companies adapted by joining cartels. Many American firms hired foreign nationals in each nation where they operated, used local directors, and admitted local capital.[3] Many had done so from the origin of their business abroad. The degree to which some companies had become international is evi-

[1] Here I am using the words "international" and "multinational" interchangeably.

[2] I do not refer to portfolio investments or underwriting, but to direct investment.

[3] Charles P. Kindleberger, *American Business Abroad*, New Haven 1969, 180, gives these three items as criteria for multinational corporations.

dent in a 1907 letter from H. B. Thayer, Vice President of Western Electric, to an agent in Bangkok, Thailand:

> You speak of an anti-American attitude on the part of the [Government] Commission. We have offices and factories making our standard apparatus in Great Britain, Belgium, Germany, France, Russia, Austria, Italy, and Japan so that so far as this matter goes we are international rather than American. If there were time we could arrange to have the order go to any one of those countries that might be preferred.[4]

On the other hand, some U.S. companies—especially those that did business in nearby areas and in less developed countries—operated simply "extra-nationally," using methods and procedures adopted at home and merely extending the domestic enterprise.

In Mexico in 1914 American business met intense hostility. Once welcomed, U.S. enterprise now encountered pronounced difficulties. The ambivalence would be a harbinger for the future. In Canada, too, there had been hesitation on the part of the government and the public on how much U.S. capital was desirable, although no actions were taken to impede the flow of U.S. monies to the Dominion. American companies in the Caribbean faced innumerable obstacles in developing their operations. Americans were just beginning to make giant foreign investments in South America, and already they were clashing with some host governments (witness Jersey Standard's tax problems in Peru). In short, in the process of going abroad, American companies met unfamiliar conditions and shaped their strategies accordingly.

Yet how extensive actually was this pre-World War I foreign investment? The skeptic will counter that it is fine to say Americans were interested in foreign investments before the First World War, but that America was nevertheless a debtor in international accounts. Moreover, he argues, in 1914 U.S. foreign stakes were small compared with those of the major creditor nation, Great Britain, and also small in absolute terms. The skeptic will insist that U.S. business abroad was peripheral to most domestic enterprise, and that the companies that could be called "multinational" were few in number.

---

[4] Thayer to C. G. Edward, Edward & Co., Bangkok, Siam, Oct. 9, 1907, Western Electric Archives, New York.

232 THE AMERICAN ECONOMY

TABLE 1.   U.S. and European Foreign Investments in 1914
(BOOK VALUE IN BILLIONS OF DOLLARS)

COUNTRY	TOTAL
United States	$ 3.5[a]
Great Britain	18.3
France	8.7
Germany	5.6
Belgium, Netherlands, Switzerland	5.5

SOURCE: W. S. Woytinsky and E. S. Woytinsky, *World Commerce and Governments*, New York: The Twentieth Century Fund, 1955, p. 191.

[a] Figures on direct and portfolio investments available only for the United States: $2.6 billion direct investment and $9 billion portfolio investment.

It is true that in 1914 America was a debtor—a recipient of more foreign capital than the nation invested abroad. The skeptic is indeed correct that U.S. foreign investments were small compared with those of Britain, and, for that matter, France and Germany (see Table 1). Regrettably, we do not have direct investment figures for the European nations and so have no basis for comparison on this score, but the totals support the skeptic. Mexico, Cuba, and Panama (and perhaps some other Central American countries) were probably the only nations in the world where U.S. foreign (direct or portfolio) investment in 1914 exceeded the British stake.[5]

The skeptic is also right in saying the size of U.S. direct investment in 1914 was small—the estimate is only $2.65 billion. This sum is less than the direct foreign investment *outflow* from the United States in certain individual years in the 1960s. Yet the skeptic is no historian. The historian wants to know how this figure fits into the then contemporary context. The Gross National Product of the United States in 1914 was only $36.4 billion. By simple arithmetic, *U.S. direct foreign investment in 1914 comprised a sum equal to 7 per cent of the U.S. GNP.* In the 1960s we talked about the huge direct investments abroad by U.S. business. In

[5] U.S. Dept. of Comm., Bureau of the Census. *Historical Statistics of the United States,* Washington, D.C. 1960, 565 (international investment position); Herbert Feis, *Europe, the World's Banker, 1870–1914,* New Haven 1930, passim (European investment); W. S. Woytinsky and E. S. Woytinsky, *World Commerce and Governance,* New York 1955, 195 (distribution of British investment).

1966, the GNP of the U.S. was $739.5 billion, while the book value of U.S. direct investment abroad totaled $54.6 billion—or 7 *per cent* of our GNP.[6] Keeping this in mind, let us briefly summarize the U.S. direct investment in 1914 by area and by sector and then consider the last two objections of the skeptic: that foreign business was simply peripheral to domestic business and that the number of "multinational" concerns was negligible.

The evidence makes it clear that before 1914 American enterprise invested in developed, developing, and less developed countries around the world. The stakes differed according to the distance of the host country from the United States and according to the host country's state of economic development. This conclusion —derived from the data presented earlier—becomes explicit as we review in summary and schematically U.S. direct investment in 1914.[7]

The greatest U.S. direct investments in 1914 were in Canada ($618 million), which had just surpassed Mexico, the previous holder of first place. We have seen that U.S. companies investing in the Dominion sought both markets and sources of supply. Canada was nearby, and the per capita income was high enough to provide a market for U.S. goods. In the period before 1914 our evidence indicates that in order to sell in the Dominion, U.S. companies jumped over the tariff barrier and started the development of many Canadian secondary manufacturing industries. This was probably more important than the U.S. stakes "in the direction of perpetuating Canada's traditional status as a staple-producing economy." The Dominion was exceptional in the Western Hemisphere in attracting a large number of U.S. manufactories.[8]

[6] See Table V.2 (1914 figure on U.S. direct investment); *Survey of Current Business* (balance-of-payments data); U.S. Dept. of Comm., *Long Term Economic Growth,* 1860–1965, Washington, D.C. 1966, 167 (Kendrick's National Bureau of Economic Research estimate of GNP—1914); *Survey of Current Business,* September 1967, 40 (1966 direct investment figures); *Economic Report of the President,* Washington, D.C. 1967, 213 (1966 GNP).

[7] All investment figures are from Table V.2 above.

[8] Hugh G. J. Aitken, "The Changing Structure of the Canadian Economy," in Aitken et al., eds., *The American Economic Impact on Canada,* Durham, N.C. 1959, 9. Aitken writes, "At the risk of oversimplification it can be said that the influence of the United States upon the character of Canadian development is in the direction of perpetuating Canada's traditional status as a staple-producing economy." The evidence I have presented earlier would indicate

Mexico ranked second only to Canada in having U.S. direct investment, estimated at $587 million in 1914. A major reason Mexico held this prominent position was its proximity to the United States. The U.S. investments there were dictated by the state of economic development. They predominated in mining and railroads. By 1914 stakes in oil production were rapidly mounting. The traditional pattern of a developed country investing in a less developed country prevailed.

As for the other nearby underdeveloped areas in the Western Hemisphere—the Caribbean islands and Central America (U.S. direct investment estimated at $371 million in 1914)—the main direct investments were in obtaining sources of supply. The stakes were in large part in agriculture. In South America ($323 million in U.S. direct investment in 1914), Americans sought raw materials and the giant investments were made in mining. Underdeveloped areas, with their low per capita income, did not warrant immense direct investments by U.S. companies in distribution and manufacturing to meet the demands in local markets; although the markets were tempting, only small investments were made in these sectors.

By contrast, the substantial U.S. direct investment in Europe ($573 million in 1914) was concentrated in selling, assembling, processing (including oil refining and blending plants), and manufacturing. U.S. manufacturing, petroleum, and insurance[9] companies made such entries. European markets were relatively familiar to Americans, who had emigrated from Europe or whose ancestors had crossed the Atlantic. Europe was "psychologically" nearby. Moreover, Europeans had a relatively high per capita income and could afford American products.

When we turn from the Western Hemisphere and Europe to consider U.S. stakes in more "distant" areas, we look toward regions that have not been treated in detail in this volume. The

---

that this was not true in the years before 1914. See also L. C. A. Knowles, *The Economic Development of the British Overseas Empire*, London 1930, II, 553, for an argument along the same lines as mine. A. E. Safarian, in *Foreign Ownership of Canadian Industry*, Toronto 1966, and Herbert Marshall, Frank A. Southard, Jr., and Kenneth W. Taylor, in *Canadian-American Industry*, New Haven 1936, put emphasis throughout on investments in secondary manufacturing.

[9] Selling only.

reason lies in the limited amount of U.S. direct investment. It is not that American businessmen were not concerned with investment in Asia, Oceania, and Africa; they were. The China trade, as we have seen, was very important to American development; investments in outposts in China were among the early U.S. stakes abroad. In political and business circles in the United States there was in the late nineteenth century enormous attention paid to Asian markets. As we have noted, the acquisition of the Philippines was viewed as a stepping stone to Eastern commerce. The actual investment did no reflect the rhetoric;[10] American direct investment in Asia in 1914 totaled only $120 million. The Orient was far away and relatively unknown to American businessmen; the risks and costs of investment rose with distance. The parts of Asia colonized by European powers were often inaccessible to U.S. enterprise. By 1914 U.S. direct investments in Asia—from the Ottoman Empire to China to the Philippines—were scattered and heterogeneous. By way of brief summary, they included:

1. Outposts of trading and shipping firms (some with long histories). By 1914 roughly 80 American trading and shipping firms had such outlets in China alone.
2. Independent American citizens with a wide range of small businesses (from retailing to manufacturing to sugar centrals). This was especially evident in the Philippines, where the American "colony" (not including the army of occupation) was estimated at from 10,000 to 20,000 individuals in the early 1900s.
3. Traders turned investors in projects (from railroads, to mines, to cotton mills). Before 1914 the American Trading Company had, for example, invested in other than trading enterprises in Korea, Japan, and in China; other American merchants had become investors in the Shanghai Rice Mill Company and the Shanghai Pulp and Paper Corporation.
4. Financial syndicates holding concessions (for railroads, mining, or installing electrical and telephone facilities). Some of those started in China were by 1914 already out of business.[11]

[10] Paul A. Varg, "The Myth of the China Market, 1890–1914," *The American Historical Review,* 73:742–758 (February 1968), has pointed to "the gap between the rhetoric and actualties" of the China trade, 1890–1914. This was true of investment as well as trade.

[11] For example, the American China Development Company, organized in 1895, obtained a concession to build the Hankow–Canton railway in April 1898. In July 1900 it made its first investments. The American shareholders

5. Fourteen Far Eastern branches of the International Banking Corporation.
6. Sales outlets of the larger U.S. insurance companies.
7. Branches and subsidiaries of the giant U.S. manufacturing and petroleum enterprises (mainly for marketing, although a handful of companies were manufacturing in the Far East). Some large corporations were purchasing supplies and had direct outlets for this purpose (International Harvester in the Philippines and American Tobacco in Turkey are examples). To my knowledge, only three international industrial corporations—Standard Oil of New Jersey and U.S. Rubber Company in the Dutch East Indies and Standard Oil of New York in China and Palestine—had investments or definite plans for investments[12] in raw materials. Stakes in Asia—as elsewhere—varied according to a country's state of development or underdevelopment. United States *manufacturing* companies had their key interests in Japan—a relatively developed nation—rather than in Turkey, India, or China. Although there was substantial U.S. direct investment in petroleum distribution in the Orient—"oil for the lamps of China"—the estimated total for *all* of Asia in 1914 was $40 million, which was less than one third of the U.S. direct investment in petroleum distribution in Europe. To repeat, Europe had the larger sum because it had the higher per capita income and thus offered the bigger market.[13]

---

then sold it to a Belgian syndicate—contrary to the provision in their contract, which prohibited the transfer of rights "to other nations." The Chinese demanded the agreement be voided. But in 1905, to restore the original state of affairs, the House of Morgan acquired control of the controversial company. The Chinese still wanted to void the contract and bought the properties for $6,750,000 (Remer, *Foreign Investments in China,* pp. 258–259). There were also the fruitless plans of E. H. Harriman to acquire the South Manchuria Railway and the Chinese Eastern Railway (Eckenrode and Edmunds, *E. H. Harriman,* pp. 98–99).

[12] Standard Oil of New York made its Chinese contract in February 1914. It spent more than $2 million prospecting in 1914 (*China Year Book 1926,* p. 123).

[13] General data on investment in Asia come from company records, interviews in Asia and in the United States, as well as American Exporter, *Export Trade Directories;* James H. Blount, *The American Occupation of the Philippines,* New York 1912; W. Cameron Forbes, *The Phillippine Islands,* 2 vols., Boston 1928; A. V. H. Hartendrof, *History of Industry and Trade of the Philippines,* Manila 1958, 58–59; C. F. Remer, *Foreign Investments in China,* New York 1933; Chi-ming Hou, *Foreign Investment and Economic Development in China, 1840–1937,* Cambridge, Mass. 1965; F. R. Dulles, *Americans in the Pacific,* Boston 1932; Charles Vevier, *United States and China,* New

As for Oceania ($17 million in U.S. direct investment in 1914), the explanation for the very low level of U.S. direct investment lies, I believe, primarily in the matter of distance plus unfamiliarity on the part of Americans. An added reason was that the low population of Australia meant a small sales potential. Yet because of the relatively high standard of living in Australia, as Table 2 will show, aggressive U.S. manufacturing, oil, and insurance companies did make small investments, primarily in marketing.[14] About a handful

---

Brunswick 1955; A. W. Griswold, *Far Eastern Policy of the United States,* New York 1938; Charles S. Campbell, *Special Business Interests and the Open Door Policy,* New Haven 1951; Fred Harrington, *God, Mammon and the Japanese,* New York 1944; Tyler Dennett, *Americans in Eastern Asia,* New York 1941; G. C. Allen and Audrey G. Donnithorne, *Western Enterprise in Far Eastern Economic Development, China and Japan,* 1954; G. C. Allen and Audrey G. Donnithorne, *Western Enterprise in Indonesia and Malaya,* London 1957; John A. DeNovo, *American Interests and Policies in the Middle East 1900–1939,* Minneapolis 1963, 38–42, 169, and Chapter III; *Foreign Relations of the United States;* U.S. Department of State, Bureau of Foreign Commerce, *Commercial Relations of the U.S.* Specific data: Remer, 262 (130 firms; his figure includes not only export-import concerns but all companies; I have reduced the figure to 80); Blount, 440 (size of the American colony in the Philippines); Harrington, 156ff (Korean developments); American Trading Company Records, New York; Remer, 252 (Shanghai companies); "International Banking Corporation," Vanderlip Papers. Special Collections Columbia University; Clyde William Phelps, *Foreign Expansion of American Banks,* New York 1927, 147; Morton Keller, *The Life Insurance Enterprise 1885–1910,* Cambridge, Mass. 1963, 276; U.S. Dept. of Commerce and Labor, *Report on Petroleum Industry,* Washington, D.C. 1909, pt. 3, 589–590; D. M. Fisk, "A Brief History of the First Sixty Years of Texaco," unpubl. paper 1964; U.S. Dept. of Comm. and Labor, Bureau of Corporations, *Report on the Tobacco Industry,* Washington, D.C. 1909; F.T.C., *Report on Cooperation in American Export Trade,* Washington, D.C. 1916, pt. 2, 202, 216–217, 221–222, 236, 242; Toshiba, *History,* Tokyo 1964 (I am indebted to G.E.-Japan's officials for translations of the Japanese text); International Harvester, *Horizons, Foreign Centennial Issue,* n.p. 1951, 29–30; Chapter V above (oil companies); U.S. Rubber, *Annual Report 1910;* Lewis, 588. Figures for Asian and European petroleum distribution are those given on our Table 2. All of the $40 million was in distribution in the east; Miss Lewis was unaware of Standard Oil of New Jersey's investment in the Dutch East Indies. Her European figure ($138 million) includes refineries (for distribution) and also some oil production in Rumania.

[14] The figures in Table 2 give the Oceania investment as $2 million in petroleum (which was all distribution), $5 million in sales organizations (again distribution) and $10 million in manufacturing. My own research indicates that the $2 million in petroleum distribution may be too low a figure, while the $10 million in manufacturing is probably too high. I would suggest that a number of investments that were in distribution were mistaken by Miss Lewis as being in manufacturing.

TABLE 2.　Estimates of U.S. direct foreign investments
for the years 1897, 1908, and 1914 (in million U.S. dollars)

COUNTRY OR REGION	(1) TOTAL[a]			(2) RAILROADS			(3) UTILITIES		
	1897	1908	1914	1897	1908	1914	1897	1908	1914
Mexico	200	416	587	111	57	110	6	22	33
Canada and Newfoundland	160	405	618	13	51	69	2	5	8
Cuba and other W. Indies	49	196	281	2	43	24	—	24	58
Central America	21	38	90	16	9	38	—	1	3
South America	38	104	323	2	1	4	4	5	4
Europe	131	369	573	—	—	—	10	13	11
Asia	23	75	120	—	—	10	—	15	16
Africa	1	5	13	—	—	—	—	—	—
Oceania	2	10	17	—	—	—	—	—	—
Banking	10	20	30	—	—	—	—	—	—
TOTAL	635	1638	2652	144	161	255	22	85	133

SOURCE: Cleona Lewis, *America's Stake in International Investment*, Washington, D.C.: Brookings Institution, 1938, 578ff. Many of these figures are questionable, but they do present the general pattern. The Mexican figures, for example, may be too low for 1908 and too high for 1914. The railroad investment in Central America (1897) is too high since Miss Lewis erroneously included the Panama Railroad. The European 1908 and 1914 totals are substantially larger than the sum of columns 2 through 8. On the other hand, Miss Lewis does not itemize the direct investments of the U.S. insurance companies, which may make up a large part of the difference. The investment in Canadian utilities is probably low. The

went into manufacturing in Australia—for instance, American Tobacco (1894) and National Ammonia (1896). Swift, which opened a meatpacking plant in 1914 in Australia—for export—was an exception.[15]

[15] The best book on U.S. direct investment in Australia is Donald T. Brash, *American Investment in Australian Industry*, Cambridge, Mass. 1966; on U.S. sales and manufacturing investments before World War I, see Brash, 21, 312 (National Ammonia Co.), 292 (International Harvester), 298 (G.E.), 304 (Henry Disston & Sons), 310 (Swift), 316 (Parke, Davis), 317 (Frederick Stearns & Co), 320 (Helena Rubinstein), 325–326 (Kodak). Brash, however, neglects to note that the first U.S. company to manufacture in Australia was American Tobacco. See Bureau of Corporations, *Report on the Tobacco Industry*, pt. I, 69–70, 165. See also on early U.S. stakes in Australia and New Zealand, F.T.C., *Report on Export Trade*, pt. 2, 202, 216–217, 221–222, 236, 242; Commonwealth of Australia, Dept. of Trade, *The Australian Pharmaceutical Products Industry*, Melbourne 1960, 77; Theodore Armstrong, *Our Company*, Dayton, Ohio 1949, 90; Carl Ackerman, *George Eastman*, Boston 1930,

TABLE 2. (Continued)

(4) PETROLEUM[b]			(5) MINING[c]			(6) AGRICULTURE			(7) MANUFAC-TURING			(8) SALES ORGA-NIZATIONS[d]		
1897	1908	1914	1897	1908	1914	1897	1908	1914	1897	1908	1914	1897	1908	1914
1	50	85	68	234	302	12	40	37	—	10	10	2	2	4
6	15	25	55	136	159	18	25	101	55	155	221	10	15	27
2	5	6	3	6	15	34	92	144	3	18	20	4	5	9
—	—	—	2	10	11	4	18	37	—	—	—	—	1	1
5	15	42	6	53	221	9	11	25	—	2	7	10	16	20
55	99	138	—	3	5	—	—	—	35	100	200	25	30	85
14	36	40	—	1	3	—	—	12	—	5	10	6	12	15
1	2	5	—	2	4	—	—	—	—	—	—	—	1	4
1	2	2	—	—	—	—	—	—	1	6	10	—	2	5
85	224	343	134	445	720	77	186	356	94	296	478	57	84	170

il investment in Asia in 1914 excludes Jersey Standard's investment in the Dutch East Indies.

a Total includes sum of columns 2 through 8 *plus* miscellaneous investments.

b Petroleum includes exploration, production, refining, and distribution; the bulk of this s in distribution.

c Mining and smelting.

d Excludes petroleum distribution; includes trading companies and sales branches and subsidiaries of large corporations.

Africa (a bare $13 million U.S. direct investment in 1914) was *terra incognita* for the American investor. Some trading firms, however, maintained outposts. The enterprising Guggenheims and other financial interests had invested in lucrative diamond mining and unprofitable rubber growing in the Belgian Congo. While no large U.S. corporate stakes appear to have existed in gold mining in South Africa, individual Americans in the Transvaal who managed the mines speculated in gold mining stock. As Table 2 will indicate, certain U.S. manufacturing, oil, and insurance companies

179; International Steam Pump Co., *Annual Report 1911;* International Harvester, *Horizons, Foreign Trade Centennial Issue,* n.p. 1951, 29–30; Bureau of Corporations, *Reports on Petroleum Industry,* pt. 3, 589–590; R. Carlyle Buley, *The Equitable Life Assurance Society of the United States 1859–1964,* New York 1967, I, 471–478; F.T.C., *Report on the Meatpacking Industry,* Washington, D.C. 1919, pt. I, 87 (Swift).

established direct distribution outlets in Africa, mainly in South Africa. There, a number of U.S. industrial companies opened sales branches to supply the needs of the gold miners. To this author's knowledge, no U.S. direct investments in manfacturing in Africa existed before World War I. The U.S. oil companies in Africa invested solely in marketing and not, up to 1914, in exploration, production, or refining. Indeed, on the whole, Africa was out of American businessmen's investment orbit. This could be attributed to several factors: to the European political dominance on that continent; to the distance from the United States; to the alternative opportunities for U.S. capital; and, chiefly, to the low per capita income of black Africa, which meant only small markets for American products.[16]

ADDRESS ON EUROPEAN RECOVERY, JUNE 5, 1947

Secretary of State George Marshall

I need hot tell you gentlemen that the world situation is very serious. That must be apparent to all intelligent people. I think one difficulty is that the problem is one of such enormous complexity that the very mass of facts presented to the public by press and radio make it exceedingly difficult for the man in the street to reach a clear appraisement of the situation. Furthermore, the people of this country are distant from the troubled areas of the earth and it is hard for them to comprehend the plight and consequent reactions of the long-suffering peoples, and the effect of those reactions on their governments in connection with our efforts to promote peace in the world.

In considering the requirements for the rehabilitation of Europe,

[16] Bernard M. Baruch, *My Own Story*, New York 1957, 209–211 and Societe Internationale Forestière et Minière du Congo, *Status*, Bruxelles 1950 (details on the concessions in the Congo); interview with Albert van de Maele (a director of *Forminière*), New York, Apr. 19, 1965 (Guggenheims in the Congo); interviews, Johannesburg, 1965; company histories, annual reports, *Mineral Industry 1905*, and S. Herbert Frankel, *Capital Investment in Africa*, London 1938, and interviews throughout the African continent, 1965.

the physical loss of life, the visible destruction of cities, factories, mines, and railroads was correctly estimated, but it has become obvious during recent months that this visible destruction was probably less serious than the dislocation of the entire fabric of European economy. For the past 10 years conditions have been highly abnormal. The feverish preparation for war and the more feverish maintenance of the war effort engulfed all aspects of national economies. Machinery has fallen into disrepair or is entirely obsolete. Under the arbitrary and destructive Nazi rule, virtually every possible enterprise was geared into the German war machine. Long-standing commercial ties, private institutions, banks, insurance companies, and shipping companies disappeared, through loss of capital, absorption through nationalization, or by simple destruction. In many countries, confidence in the local currency has been severely shaken. The breakdown of the business structure of Europe during the war was complete. Recovery has been seriously retarded by the fact that 2 years after the close of hostilities a peace settlement with Germany and Austria has not been agreed upon. But even given a more prompt solution of these difficult problems, the rehabilitation of the economic structure of Europe quite evidently will require a much longer time and greater effort than had been foreseen.

There is a phase of this matter which is both interesting and serious. The farmer has always produced the foodstuffs to exchange with the city dweller for the other necessities of life. This division of labor is the basis of modern civilization. At the present time it is threatened with breakdown. The town and city industries are not producing adequate goods to exchange with the food-producing farmer. Raw materials and fuel are in short supply. Machinery is lacking or worn out. The farmer or the peasant cannot find the goods for sale which he desires to purchase. So the sale of his farm produce for money which he cannot use seems to him an unprofitable transaction. He, therefore, has withdrawn many fields from crop cultivation and is using them for grazing. He feeds more grain to stock and finds for himself and his family an ample supply of food, however short he may be on clothing and the other ordinary gadgets of civilization. Meanwhile people in the cities are short of food and fuel. So the governments are forced to use their foreign money and credits to procure these necessities abroad.

This process exhausts funds which are urgently needed for reconstruction. Thus a very serious situation is rapidly developing which bodes no good for the world. The modern system of the division of labor upon which the exchange of products is based is in danger of breaking down.

The truth of the matter is that Europe's requirements for the next three or four years of foreign food and other essential products —principally from America—are so much greater than her present ability to pay that she must have substantial additional help or face economic, social, and political deterioration of a very grave character.

The remedy lies in breaking the vicious circle and restoring the confidence of the European people in the economic future of their own countries and of Europe as a whole. The manufacturer and the farmer throughout wide areas must be able and willing to exchange their products for currencies the continuing value of which is not open to question.

Aside from the demoralizing effect on the world at large and the possibilities of disturbances arising as a result of the desperation of the people concerned, the consequences to the economy of the United States should be apparent to all. It is logical that the United States should do whatever it is able to do to assist in the return of normal economic health in the world, without which there can be no political stability and no assured peace. Our policy is directed not against any country or doctrine but against hunger, poverty, desperation, and chaos. Its purpose should be the revival of a working economy in the world so as to permit the emergence of political and social conditions in which free institutions can exist. Such assistance, I am convinced, must not be on a piecemeal basis as various crises develop. Any assistance that this Government may render in the future should provide a cure rather than a mere palliative. Any government that is willing to assist in the task of recovery will find full cooperation, I am sure, on the part of the United States Government. Any government which maneuvers to block the recovery of other countries cannot expect help from us. Furthermore, governments, political parties, or groups which seek to perpetuate human misery in order to profit therefrom politically or otherwise will encounter the opposition of the United States.

It is already evident that, before the United States Government can proceed much further in its efforts to alleviate the situation and help start the European world on its way to recovery, there must be some agreement among the countries of Europe as to the requirements of the situation and the part those countries themselves will take in order to give proper effect to whatever action might be undertaken by this Government. It would be neither fitting or efficacious for this Government to undertake to draw up unilaterally a program designed to place Europe on its feet economically. This is the business of the Europeans. The initiative, I think, must come from Europe. The role of this country should consist of friendly aid in the drafting of a European program and of later support of such a program so far as it may be practical for us to do so. The program should be a joint one, agreed to by a number, if not all, European nations.

An essential part of any successful action on the part of the United States is an understanding on the part of the people of America of the character of the problem and the remedies to be applied. Political passion and prejudice should have no part. With foresight, and a willingness on the part of our people to face up to the vast responsibility which history has clearly placed upon our country, the difficulties I have outlined can and will be overcome.

THE UNITED STATES AS WORLD TRADER, INVESTOR, AND BANKER

President's Council of Economic Advisers

The United States is by far the largest producing nation in the world, accounting for more than 40 percent of total industrial production of the free world. Its 188 million inhabitants place it fourth among nations in population, and its unequalled level of per capita income makes it the world's largest domestic market and largest source of savings.

As Trader

The basic purpose of our foreign trade is to exchange goods produced efficiently in the United States for goods which we can produce relatively less efficiently or not at all. International trade lowers costs and raises standards of living both at home and abroad. Foreign trade accounts for a much larger part of transactions of the U.S. economy than is generally appreciated. Even though our merchandise exports are only about 4 percent of total gross national product (GNP), they amount to nearly 9 percent of our total production of movable goods. For some products, overseas demand is exceptionally important; it provides over half the market for such diverse U.S. products as rice, DDT, and tracklaying tractors. Imports by the United States provide materials essential for production and also permit Americans variety and diversity in their consumption. Crucial products like nickel and cobalt come almost entirely from foreign sources.

U.S. exports and imports are a major part of world trade. In the first three quarters of 1962, U.S. merchandise imports were nearly 14 percent of total world imports. For some countries and some commodities, of course, the U.S. market is far more important than this average share implies. For example, U.S. coffee imports are usually over half of total world imports of coffee.

U.S. citizens pay large sums for services provided by foreigners —transportation of goods and persons, food and lodging for American tourists and businessmen traveling abroad, interest, dividends, and profits on the funds of foreigners invested in American enterprise or securities. In addition, the United States spends overseas nearly $3 billion (gross) a year for its own military defense and, indeed, for the defense of the entire free world. This expenditure is made in part directly by the U.S. Government and in part by more than one million U.S. servicemen and their dependents stationed abroad.

The United States is also a major supplier of goods and services, accounting in 1961 for nearly 18 percent of total world exports of merchandise, for nearly one-fourth of world exports of manufactures, and for nearly one-third of world exports of capital goods. It is a principal exporter of many agricultural goods, especially cotton, wheat, tobacco, soybeans, and poultry, and it exports large amounts of military equipment to its allies—some on a grant basis, some for cash payment.

The very size of the United States in the world economy lends to its economic activity and its economic policies special importance and interest abroad. Its rate of unemployment, economic growth, and commercial and financial policies are closely charted and carefully watched throughout the world.

As Saver and Investor

A nation as large and wealthy as the United States is naturally an important source of savings for the entire world, and national savings move abroad both as private investment and as official foreign aid. Its advanced technology invites emulation abroad, and the profitability of duplicating American technology draws American savers and investors beyond domestic borders. Its need for foreign resources to supply American production attracts private U.S. development capital. In addition, the United States has accepted heavy responsibility for the economic development of emerging nations, which require public as well as private capital.

Private long-term investment abroad by U.S. residents has risen markedly in the past decade, from an annual average of $0.9 billion in 1952–55 to $2.5 billion in 1958–61. Much of this increase has gone to Europe.

The U.S. Government provided $3.2 billion to foreign countries and international lending institutions in the first three quarters of 1962—in the form of development loans, Export-Import Bank export credits, sales for local currencies, commodity and cash grants, technical assistance, and contributions to international institutions. This was 12 percent more than in the corresponding period in 1961. U.S. foreign aid to the developing nations has risen markedly since 1954, and under new programs, notably the Alliance for Progress in Latin America, U.S. economic assistance is expected to continue to be high. Total aid expenditures are, however, still below those reached in the late 1940's under the Marshall Plan to assist European recovery.

Both private investment outflows and government aid are appropriate for a high-output, high-saving country such as the United States, and both are expected to yield considerable economic and political returns in the long run. Government and private lending and equity investment add substantial amounts each year to the net foreign assets of the United States, which have risen steadily in the past decade. But in the short run, both also aggravate the U.S. balance of payments deficit. To reduce the impact of the foreign aid program on the balance of payments, a large part of foreign aid expenditure has been tied to the purchase of goods and services in the United States. In the first three quarters of 1962, 76 percent of government grants and capital outflows resulted in no direct dollar outflow, compared with 64 percent two years earlier. Recent changes in the tax treatment of earnings on foreign investments were designed to achieve more equitable tax treatment between U.S. investment at home and abroad. They should reduce the outflow of investment funds to the extent that these funds were attracted by various tax privileges available in several other countries, and should also increase the repatriation of foreign earnings. Thus these changes should improve the U.S. payments position, at least in the short run when improvement is crucially needed.

Though foreign aid and investment absorb only a small part of U.S. savings, the United States is providing a substantial part of the total flow of savings across national boundaries, especially of the flow to the developing nations. The Development Assistance Committee (DAC) of the 20-nation Organization for Economic Cooperation and Development (OECD) estimates that the United States in 1961 supplied 57 percent of official foreign aid and 44 percent of private long-term investment flow from DAC members to the less developed countries.

As Banker

Since the end of World War I, and especially in the past 15 years, the U.S. dollar has emerged as the principal supplement to gold as an international store of value and medium of exchange. The important position of the United States as a market for goods and as a source of goods and savings, its well-developed, extensive, and efficient financial markets, and its long-standing policy of buying gold from, and selling it to, foreign monetary authorities at a fixed price have all made the U.S. dollar an attractive form in which to hold international reserves. Foreign monetary authorities hold more than $12 billion—over one-quarter of their total gold and foreign exchange reserves—in liquid dollar assets, mostly in the form of U.S. Treasury bills and deposits in American banks. In addition, foreign private parties hold $8 billion in dollar assets, and international institutions nearly $6 billion.

These large outstanding claims on the United States indicate the importance attached by the rest of the world to the dollar as an international currency, and the significance of the United States as an international banking center. For a number of years, the deficit in the U.S. balance of payments was financed to a large extent by increases in foreign dollar holdings which enabled foreign governments and nationals to acquire earning assets and at the same time add to their liquid resources. In recent years, about one-fourth to one-half of our over-all deficit has been settled in gold, but the growth in dollar holdings has been an important element in the growth of international liquidity.

But these large balances also make the dollar peculiarly vulnerable. A decline of confidence in the dollar, resulting in widespread conversion of dollars into gold, would create a serious problem for the international payments system and for the economic progress of the free world. Therefore, satisfactory progress in reducing the U.S. payments deficit is essential at this time.

The United States still holds large gold and foreign exchange reserves. Last summer the President reaffirmed U.S. determination to defend the existing parity of the dollar and indicated the country's willingness to use its entire gold stock, if necessary, to do so. In addition to the $16 billion in gold and convertible currencies held by the United States, stand-by arrangements have been entered into with a number of individual countries, and the United States has extensive drawing rights on the International Monetary Fund. The Fund itself was strengthened in October when a special borrowing arrangement, supplementing the Fund's resources by as much as $6 billion, came into force.

THE BALANCE OF PAYMENTS ADJUSTMENT MECHANISM FROM THE AMERICAN STANDPOINT

Gottfried Haberler

It will be recalled that the bad showing of the U.S. balance of payments in the last quarter of 1967 caused a flight from the dollar into gold and some other currencies. The Johnson Administration took fright and imposed severe controls on capital exports and proposed a number of other controls (including an unprecedented tax on U.S. tourists abroad) which fortunately were rejected by Congress. In April 1968 at the height of the crisis the international gold pool through which the leading countries, the U.S. carrying the main burden, had been feeding gold speculation was closed down and the two-tier gold market was established.

Later in 1968 the picture unexpectedly improved. Huge amounts of capital flowed into the United States, attracted by high interest rates and a booming stock market and spurred by the collapse of the French franc as one of the world's strongest currencies and the invasion of Czechoslovakia. Thus in 1968, for the first time in 11 years, the U.S. balance of payments showed a small surplus both on the liquidity and official reserve transaction basis. But the traditional surplus on trade account disappeared and the overall improvement was clearly of a precarious nature. The richest country in the world importing capital on a large scale is obviously an unnatural and probably an unsustainable phenomenon.

The expected deterioration of the balance of payments recurred with a vengeance in 1969. The liquidity deficit for the whole year was at the record level of $7,2 bill and in the first two quarters of 1970 it was not much better, $5,5 bill and $4,8 bill respectively. It is true that until 1970 the balance on the official reserve transactions basis was satisfactory (a surplus of $6,1 bill in 1968 and $2,7 bill in 1969). But it was to be expected that when the inflow of private capital decreased or reversed itself, officially held dollar balances would increase. This happened in 1970 on a very larger scale; In the first quarter 1970 the official transaction deficit reached alltime record of $11,5 bill and in the second quarter $7 bill (annual rates).

The traditional surplus of exports over import (trade balance) almost vanished in 1968 and 1969 but has shown a vigorous improvement in 1970, although it is still much smaller than it was in the good years 1963 and 1964.

The paradoxical thing is that the unprecedented deterioration of the external balance in 1969 has not even caused a ripple in the exchange market as far as the dollar is concerned, while several other major currencies were under the cloud. This is in sharp contrast to the impact of the much smalled deficits in 1967 and early 1968.

What is the explanation? One reason surely is that the inadequacy of the "liquidity definition" of deficit was brought home by the fact that in 1969 official settlement balance was in large surplus ($2,7 bill) while the liquidity deficit rose to a record high. In other words the fact that official dollar holdings abroad fell substantially from $15,60 bill Dec. 1967 to $10, -bill July 1969 has helped to reassure foreign central banks about the position of dollar. This explanation is supported by the fact that the recent sharp rise of official dollar holdings abroad (to $14,8 bill May 1970) has not failed to cause expressions of concern and exhortation addressed to the U.S. Government by foreign central bankers and recently by the IMF chief.

I am convinced however, the deeper and decisive factor that accounts for the strikingly changed situation is a different one. It is, I believe, that the events of the last few years have made it clear to the financial leaders, central bankers, economic journalists etc. that the world is practically on the dollar standard whether they like it or not. In a sense the world has been on the dollar standard ever since the last war (or earlier). But it was not widely accepted and was regarded by many influential experts (from Jacques Rueff Triffin) as an essentially unstable and unsustainable situation. Other countries, it was said, will increasingly become reluctant to hold additional dollar balances and would sooner or later lose confidence in the dollar. There has indeed been a period of increasing mistrust and suspicion of the dollar which reached the point of greatest intensity late in 1967 and early in 1968. But since then the system has regained its stability. What accounts for the change?

The political events of 1968, the students and workers rebellion in France which led to the departure of deGaulle and turned overnight the French Franc from one of the strongest currencies in the world into a weak one—this and the invasion of Czechoslovakia have created a feeling of insecurity in Europe and by contrast revived the confidence in the U.S. and the dollar. True, France has regained a somewhat precarious stability, but this was offset by the continued weakness of the Pound and the political and economic troubles in Italy.

On the technical level the decisive events were the insulation of the American and the world's monetary gold stock from the private gold market and from gold speculation through the introduction of the two-tier gold market. Equally important is the realization that the dollar has become *de facto* inconvertible into gold, at least for large sums. Dollar balances abroad should have become too large for conversions; the point of no return has been passed.

The *de facto* inconvertibility of the dollar into gold for sizable conversions has, of course, never been acknowledged officially and if asked point blank U.S. as well as foreign officials would probably deny it. It is nevertheless a fact, in my opinion, and it would not be difficult to cite numerous statements by responsible officials as well as of knowledgeable economists, financial journalists etc. which show full awareness of the de facto inconvertibility of the dollar. If one of the large dollar holding central banks were to ask for a billion dollars' worth of gold, they would be told that they cannot have it. Because they know it, they don't even ask. Nobody wants to rock the boat.

Implications for Policy of the U.S.

The policy implications for the U.S. of our assessment of the situation are straightforward. American balance of payments policy should be passive. The U.S. cannot change the exchange rate and should avoid direct controls. How about inflation? The U.S. should of course do all it can do to stop inflation. This is the declared policy goal anyway. I feel strongly that inflation must be stopped or at least sharply slowed down for domestic reasons, to put an end to the distortions and inequities that are constantly inflicted on the social economy by inflation. Stopping or slowing inflation will be good also for the balance of payments and the international status of the dollar. At the present time there exists no overt conflict between domestic and external (balance of payments) considerations. On both grounds inflation should be brought to an end as soon as possible. But a conflict between domestic and external objectives may arise in two ways and in a sense may be said already to exist.

First there are limitations on the speed with which inflation is slowed, limitations imposed by the amount of unemployment and loss of output growth which rapid disinflation entails. And the domestically feasible or acceptable rate of disinflation may well be insufficient from the balance of payments point of view. Second the conflict between domestic and external requirements may be sharper: If a country has a weak balance of payments when it suffers from unemployments and slack rather than from inflation, domestic considerations call for monetary expansion while the balance of payments requires monetary contraction. Contrariwise if a surplus country suffers from inflation, internal equilibrium requires tight money (high interest rates) while external equilibrium requires the opposite policy. At present Germany may be said to be in this predicament.

Other countries when confronted with such a dilemma can always escape by changing the exchange rate or, still better by letting their currency float as Canada did again recently. The U.S. cannot do that. What should it do?

My answer is, and many economists share this view, that the U.S. should conduct its monetary policy, or to express it in a somewhat broader fashion, its "demand management policy" in such a way as is best for the achievement of domestic policy objectives (price stability, full employment, growth) rather than as would be indicated by balance of payments desiderata.

To repeat, at the present time, in my opinion there exists no conflict between internal and external requirements. But if a conflict should arise, either with respect to speed and intensity of disinflation or with respect to the direction of monetary policy, domestic policy objectives should take precedence over balance of payments considerations. This implies that we should not create more unemployment or temporary retardation of growth than may be necessary to deal with inflation in view of our domestic objectives and priorities.

SOME ESSENTIALS OF INTERNATIONAL MONETARY REFORM

Arthur F. Burns

On August 15 of last year, in the face of an unsatisfactory economic situation, the President of the United States acted decisively to alter the Nation's economic course. The new policies, especially the decision to suspend convertibility of the dollar into gold or other reserve assets, were bound to have far-reaching consequences for international monetary arrangements. New choices were forced on all countries.

The next 4 months gave all of us a glimpse of one possible evolution of the international economy. Since exchange rates were no longer tied to the old par values, they were able to float—a prescription that many economists had favored. However, last fall's floating rates did not conform to the model usually sketched in academic writings. Most countries were reluctant to allow their exchange rates to move in response to market forces. Instead, restrictions on financial transactions proliferated, special measures with regard to trade emerged here and there, new twists crept into the pattern of exchange rates, serious business uncertainty about governmental policies developed, fears of a recession in world economic activity grew, and signs of political friction among friendly nations multiplied.

Fortunately, this dangerous trend toward competitive and even antagonistic national economic policies was halted by the Smithsonian Agreement. Despite recent developments in Vietnam, which may cause some uneasiness in financial markets for a time, the Smithsonian realignment of currencies is, in my judgment, solidly based. It was worked out with care by practical and well-informed men, and I am confident that the central banks and governments of all the major countries will continue to give it strong support.

Developments in the American economy since last December have been encouraging. Aggregate activity in the United States has begun to show signs of vigorous resurgence. Price increases have moderated, and our rate of inflation has recently been below that of most other industrial countries. Moreover, the budget deficit of the Federal Government will be much smaller this fiscal year than seemed likely 3 or 4 months ago. These developments have strengthened the confidence with which businessmen and consumers assess the economic outlook. International confidence in turn is being bolstered by the passage of the Par Value Modification Act, by the convergence of short-term interest rates in the United States and abroad, and by some promising signs of improvement in the international financial accounts of the United States.

With the Smithsonian Agreement and other indications of progress behind us, it is necessary now to move ahead and plan for the longer future. The Smithsonian meeting was pre-eminently concerned with realigning exchange rates. It did not attempt to deal with structural weaknesses in the old international monetary system. Yet they must eventually be remedied if we are to build a new and stronger international economic order.

We all have to ponder this basic question: Given the constraints of past history, what evolution of the monetary system is desirable and at the same time practically attainable? For my part, I should like to take advantage of this gathering to consider some of the elements that one might reasonably expect to find in a reformed monetary system.

First of all, a reformed system will need to be characterized by a further strengthening of international consultation and cooperation among governments. Our national economies are linked by a complex web of international transactions. Problems and policies in one country inevitably affect other countries. This simple fact of interdependence gives rise to constraints on national policies. In a smoothly functioning system, no country can ignore the implications of its own actions for other countries or fail to cooperate in discussing and resolving problems of mutual concern. The task of statesmanship is to tap the great reservoir of international good will that now exists and to make sure that it remains undiminished in the future.

Sound domestic policies are a second requirement of a better world economic order. A well-constructed international monetary system should, it is true, be capable of absorbing the strains caused by occasional financial mismanagement in this or that country— such as are likely to follow from chronic budget deficits or from abnormally large and persistent additions to the money supply. But I doubt if any international monetary system can long survive if the major industrial countries fail to follow sound financial practices. In view of the huge size of the American economy, I recognize that the economic policies of the United States will remain an especially important influence on the operation of any international monetary system.

Third, in the calculable future any international monetary system will have to respect the need for substantial autonomy of domestic economic policies. A reformed monetary system cannot be one that encourages national authorities to sacrifice either the objective of high employment or the objective of price stability in order to achieve balance of payments equilibrium. More specifically, no country experiencing an external deficit should have to accept sizable increases in unemployment in order to reduce its deficit. Nor should a surplus country have to moderate its surplus by accepting high rates of inflation. Domestic policies of this type are poorly suited to the political mood of our times, and it would serve no good purpose to assume otherwise.

I come now to a fourth element that should characterize a reformed monetary system. If I am right in thinking that the world needs realistic and reasonably stable exchange rates, rather than rigid exchange rates, ways must be found to ensure that payments imbalances will be adjusted more smoothly and promptly than under the old Bretton Woods arrangements.

The issues here are many and complex. There was a consensus at the Smithsonian meeting that wider margins around parities can help to correct payments imbalances, and should prove especially helpful in moderating short-term capital movements—thereby giving monetary authorities somewhat more scope to pursue different interest rate policies. Our experience has not yet been extensive enough to permit a confident appraisal of this innovation. It is clear, however, that no matter how much the present wider margins may contribute to facilitating the adjustment of exchange rates to changing conditions, the wider margins by themselves will prove inadequate for that purpose.

We may all hope that at least the major countries will pursue sound, noninflationary policies in the future. We should nevertheless recognize that national lapses from economic virtue will continue to occur. In such circumstances, changes in parities—however regrettable—may well become a practical necessity. Moreover, even if every nation succeeds in achieving noninflationary growth, structural changes in consumption or production will often lead to shifts in national competitive positions over time. Such shifts will also modify the pattern of exchange rates that is appropriate for maintaining balance of payments equilibrium.

In my judgment, therefore, more prompt adjustments of parities will be needed in a reformed monetary system. Rules of international conduct will have to be devised that, while recognizing rights of sovereignty, establish definite guidelines and consultative machinery for determining when parities need to be changed. This subject is likely to become one of the central issues, and also one of the most difficult, in the forthcoming negotiations.

Let me turn to a fifth element that should characterize a reformed monetary system. A major weakness of the old system was its failure to treat in a symmetrical manner the responsibilities of surplus and deficit countries for balance of payments adjustment. With deficits equated to sin and surpluses to virtue, moral as well as financial pressures were very much greater on deficit countries to reduce their deficits than on surplus countries to reduce surpluses. In actual practice, however, responsibility for payments imbalances can seldom be assigned unambiguously to individual countries. And in any event, the adjustment process will work more efficiently if surplus countries participate actively in it. In my view, all countries have an obligation to eliminate payments imbalances, and the rules of international conduct to which I referred earlier will therefore need to define acceptable behavior and provide for international monitoring of both surplus and deficit countries.

Sixth, granted improvements in the promptness with which payments imbalances are adjusted, reserve assets and official borrowing will still be needed to finance in an orderly manner the imbalances that continue to arise. Looking to the long future, it will therefore be important to develop plans so that world reserves and official credit arrangements exist in an appropriate form and can be adjusted to appropriate levels.

This brings me to the seventh feature of a reformed international monetary system. It is sometimes argued that, as a part of reform, gold should be demonetized. As a practical matter, it seems doubtful to me that there is any broad support for eliminating the monetary role of gold in the near future. To many people, gold remains a great symbol of safety and security, and these attitudes about gold are not likely to change quickly. Nevertheless, I would expect the monetary role of gold to continue to diminish in the years ahead, while the role of Special Drawing Rights increases.

The considerations that motivated the International Monetary Fund to establish the SDR facility in 1969 should remain valid in a reformed system. However, revisions in the detailed arrangements governing the creation, allocation, and use of SDR's will probably be needed. In the future, as the SDR's assume increasing importance, they may ultimately become the major international reserve asset.

Next, as my eighth point, let me comment briefly on the future role of the dollar as a reserve currency. It has often been said that the United States had a privileged position in the old monetary system because it could settle payments deficits by adding to its liabilities instead of drawing down its reserve assets. Many also argue that this asymmetry should be excluded in a reformed system. There this seems to be significant sentiment in favor of diminishing, or even phasing out, the role of the dollar as a reserve currency. One conceivable way of accomplishing this objective would be to place restraints on the further accumulation of dollars in official reserves. If no further accumulation at all were allowed, the United States would be required to finance any deficit in its balance of payments entirely with reserve assets.

I am not persuaded by this line of reasoning, for I see advantages both to the United States and to other countries from the use of the dollar as a reserve currency. But I recognize that there are some burdens or disadvantages as well. And, in any event, this is an important issue on which national views may well diverge in the early stages of the forthcoming negotiations.

I come now to a ninth point concerning a new monetary system, namely, the issue of convertibility of the dollar. It seems unlikely to me that the nations of the world, taken as a whole and over the long run, will accept a system in which convertibility of the dollar into international reserve assets—SDR's and gold—is entirely absent. If we want to build a strengthened monetary system along one-world lines, as I certainly do, this issue will have to be resolved. I therefore anticipate, as part of a total package of long-term reforms, that some form of dollar convertibility can be re-established in the future.

I must note, however, that this issue of convertibility has received excessive emphasis in recent discussions. Convertibility is important, but no more so than the other issues on which I have touched. It is misleading, and my even prove mischievous, to stress one particular aspect of reform to the exclusion of others. Constructive negotiations will be possible only if there is a general disposition to treat the whole range of issues in balanced fashion.

We need to guard against compartmentalizing concern with any one of the issues, if only because the various elements of a new monetary system are bound to be interrelated. There is a particularly important interdependence, for example, between improvements in the exchange-rate regime and restoration of some form of convertibility of the dollar into gold or other reserve assets. Without some assurance that exchange rates of both deficit and surplus countries will be altered over time so as to prevent international transactions from moving into serious imbalance, I would deem it impractical to attempt to restore convertibility of the dollar.

My tenth and last point involves the linkage between monetary and trading arrangements. We cannot afford to overlook the fact that trade practices are a major factor in determining the balance of payments position of individual nations. There is now a strong feeling in the United States that restrictive commercial policies of some countries have affected adversely the markets of American business firms. In my judgment, therefore, the chances of success of the forthcoming monetary conversations will be greatly enhanced if. parallel conversations get under way on trade problems, and if those conversations take realistic account of the current and prospective foreign trade position of the United States.

In the course of my remarks this morning I have touched on some of the more essential conditions and problems of international monetary reform. Let me conclude by restating the elements I would expect to find in a new monetary system that meet the test of both practicality and viability:

1. A significant further strengthening of the processes of international consultation and cooperation
2. Responsible domestic policies in all the major industrial countries
3. A substantial degree of autonomy for domestic policies, so that no country would feel compelled to sacrifice high employment or price stability in order to achieve balance of payments equilibrium
4. More prompt adjustments of payments imbalances, to be facil-

itated by definite guidelines and consultative machinery for determining when parities need to be changed

5. A symmetrical division of responsibilities among surplus and deficit countries for initiating and implementing adjustments of payments imbalances

6. Systematic long-range plans for the evolution of world reserves and official credit arrangements

7. A continued but diminishing role for gold as a reserve asset, with a corresponding increase in the importance of SDR's

8. A better international consensus than exists at present about the proper role of reserve currencies in the new system

9. Re-establishment of some form of dollar convertibility in the future

10. A significant lessening of restrictive trading practices as the result of negotiations complementing the negotiations on monetary reform

I firmly believe that a new and stronger international monetary system can and must be built. Indeed, I feel it is an urgent necessity to start the rebuilding process quite promptly. It is not pleasant to contemplate the kind of world that may evolve if cooperative efforts to rebuild the monetary system are long postponed. We might then find the world economy divided into restrictive and inward-looking blocs, with rules of international conduct concerning exchange rates and monetary reserves altogether absent.

As we learned last fall, a world of financial manipulations, economic restrictions, and political frictions bears no promise for the future. It is the responsibility of financial leaders to make sure that such a world will never come to pass.

PROSPECTS FOR U.S. FOREIGN TRADE

Chase Manhattan Bank, N.A.

The swing in the U.S. foreign trade balance from a sizable surplus to a very large deficit was one of the basic causes of the recent international monetary disturbances. The trade deterioration widened the U.S. balance of payments deficit, thereby further eroding confidence in the U.S. dollar. Loss of confidence, in turn, acted as a catalyst for snowballing disruptive movements of capital particularly to countries whose currencies were considered stronger than the dollar. In this way, a chronic U.S. payments weakness escalated into an international crisis.

The deterioration in the U.S. trade accounts has been substantial. The average annual surplus of $5.4 billion recorded over the 1960–64 period gave way to a deficit of nearly $7 billion in 1972. Imports have consistently grown faster than exports—at compound annual rates of 12% and 8%, respectively, during 1960–72. The charts show that the accelerated trade balance decline of the past two years was virtually across-the-board.

Trade and the Balance of Payments

Trade, per se, is not more or less important than any other component of the balance of payments. International monetary stability requires only that all countries have reasonably balanced positions in their "bottom-line" payments totals. This does not necessarily require a positive trade balance. Obviously, it is impossible for all countries to run trade surpluses simultaneously. A country recording positive offsets in other payments components can live quite comfortably with a chronic trade deficit, and many do.

However, throughout the decade of the sixties, trade was a needed source of strength in the overall U.S. payments picture. It was a major offset to large government and private long-term capital outflows. The recent trade deterioration occurred without compensating gains in other payments accounts. As a result, the overall payments deficit worsened drastically. Looking ahead, the non-trade payments components simply do not appear to have the potential for achieving rapid gains. Thus any realistic hopes for a restoration of U.S. payments equilibrium in the near future must center on a reversal of recent trade trends.

Consequently, the likelihood and timing of a favorable reversal in the U.S. foreign trade position stand as key questions facing the entire world. If the two recent devaluations of the dollar soon produce a strong turn-around—as Eximbank President Henry

Kearns and many academic economists have suggested—then world confidence in the dollar will in some degree be restored. A stronger U.S. performance would reduce the pressures, in both the United States and abroad, toward further measures restricting trade and capital flows. It would also enhance prospects for a successful negotiation of monetary reform. However, if the improvement does not occur, or it is too long delayed, the international economic environment could worsen.

Uncharted Waters

Unfortunately, there is really no accurate method of forecasting U.S. trade patterns over the coming few years. In the past it was possible to obtain estimates of future import and export levels by constructing models relating trade to such factors as domestic and foreign price and output levels. But all the equations used for these forecasts were derived from U.S. experience over periods when most currencies had fixed exchange rates and when price changes tended to occur gradually. Now, two devaluations of the dollar and the floating of various currencies have caused large and sudden shifts in international price relationships. This greatly impairs the usefulness of past experience in forecasting future trends. With the old relationships no longer applying, past U.S. trade performance must be restudied to evaluate the strength of the forces that will affect future developments.

Three Schools of Thought

There are three ways of looking at the causes of the U.S. trade deterioration. One school of thought gives major emphasis to institutional factors—such as the Common Agricultural Policy of the EEC, the Canadian-American automobile pact and foreign export subsidies and import barriers. From this point of view, certain other countries are responsible for the poor U.S. trade performance. Accordingly, the remedy is for the United States to deal firmly with these countries, forcing them to remove barriers to U.S. products. Yet, while it is obviously true that import barriers abroad have dampened U.S. exports, foreign restrictions alone cannot account for the full magnitude or timing of the trade decline.

A second group of trade analysts tends to emphasize relatively short-run factors, focusing on global business cycles and, in particular, on the excess demand generated in the U.S. economy by the mid-sixties "guns and butter" policy. Accordingly, these analysts call for restraints on overall demand until inflationary pressures abate. In theory, such measures should lead to an improvement in trade accounts. The unfortunate reality is that developments did not follow this pattern in 1971. In that year, foreign rates of real economic growth and inflation exceeded those of the United States. Yet the U.S. trade balance deteriorated by a whopping $5 billion, resulting in the first trade deficit recorded in this century.

A third body of thought stresses long-run structural economic shifts that have worked to the detriment of the United States. In this view, the United States emerged from the Second World War as the technological leader in almost all key industries. Technology was, in effect, the factor of production that gave U.S. manufactured goods a strong comparative advantage in world markets through the mid-1960s. But technology has proven to he highly mobile. As Western Europe and Japan acquired U.S. techniques and processes —and increasingly innovated independently—their gains in labor productivity began to surpass those of the United States, and their goods became increasingly competitive in world markets.

Another form of secular deterioration is developing as the U.S. demand for energy increasingly outpaces domestic sources of supply. Petroleum imports, for example, grew more slowly than overall imports over the 1960–70 period, from $1.6 billion to $2.7 billion. But subsequently such imports have risen 60%, reaching $4.3 billion last year. By 1980, some observers feel imports might have to total $25 billion if all potential demands for petroleum are to be met.

Shoring-Up the Trade Balance

Regardless of the exact reasons for past deterioration, the establishment of a realistic value for the dollar will help the trade accounts. Most of this impact should be realized by the middle of 1975.

Between now and 1975, however, unfavorable secular trends will continue to have a negative effect. In fact, they may offset more than half of the potential gains from devaluation. On the other hand, the 1972 trade deficit was swollen by two temporary factors. Possibly one-third of the nearly $7 billion gap was caused by short-term cyclical forces. Roughly another third reflected the fact that devaluations inevitably have an negative initial impact. The unfortunate first effect of a devaluation is to raise the cost of imports. The improvement in exports and dampening of imports comes later. In the absence of these essentially transitory factors, the deficit in 1972 might have been only $2 or $3 billion. If this was the case, and if some $3 or $4 billion of the potential gains from devaluation can actually be realized—a reasonable estimate—then the United States may be able to record a small trade surplus in 1975.

But to the extent that negative structural factors continue to influence developments, it will be difficult to maintain this improvement indefinitely. Some observers argue that other components of the balance of payments—such as income earned on foreign investments—may be strong enough to offset this projected longer-range trade deterioration. However, this possibility is by no means certain. To ensure a reasonable long-run payments outlook, the U.S. must vigorously continue to seek equitable reforms in the rules for global monetary and trading relationships. Efforts to increase U.S. labor productivity in industries that can make an export contribution need to be officially encouraged. And efforts to restrain domestic inflation are vital.

Devaluation is only a short-run cure. The U.S. must demonstrate an awareness of these fundamental forces and show an ability to respond to them if full confidence in the dollar is to be restored.

Suggestions for Additional Reading

For a brief but useful introduction to the period that gave rise to the problems addressed in this book, see:

Weisberger, Bernard A. *The New Industrial Society*. New York, 1969.

For overviews and interpretations of the period since 1900, see:

Allen, Frederick L. *The Big Change*. New York, 1962.

Andreano, Ralph L. *New Views on American Economic Development*. Cambridge, Mass., 1965.

Carson, Robert B. *The American Economy in Conflict*. Lexington, Mass., 1971.

————, Jerry L. Ingles, and Douglas McLaud. *Government in the American Economy*. Lexington, Mass., 1973.

Drucker, Peter F. *The Age of Discontinuity*. New York, 1969.

Fabricant, Solomon. *The Trend of Government Activity in the United States Since 1900*. New York, 1952.

Fine, Sydney. *Laissez-Faire and the General Welfare State*. Ann Arbor, 1956.

Galbraith, John K. *The New Industrial State*. Boston, 1971.

Kolko, Gabriel. *The Triumph of Conservatism*. New York, 1963.

Krooss, Herman E. *American Economic Development*. 2d ed. Englewood Cliffs, N.J., 1966.

Williams, William A. *The Contours of American History*. New York, 1961.

For the spectrum of economists' views, see:

Friedman, Milton. *Capitalism and Freedom*. Chicago, 1962.

Schumpeter, Joseph A. *Capitalism, Socialism, and Democracy*. New York, 1950.

Sweezy, Paul M. *The Theory of Capitalist Development*. New York, 1968.

U.S. Bureau of Economic Analysis. *Long Term Economic Growth, 1820–1970*. Washington, 1973.

On management of the economy, see:

Baruch, Bernard M. *American Industry in the War*. Washington, 1921.

Eccles, Marriner S. *Beckoning Frontiers*. New York, 1951.

Flash, Edward S. *Economic Advice and Presidential Leadership.* New York, 1965.

Hansen, Alvin H. *A Guide to Keynes.* New York, 1955.

———. *Business Cycles and National Income.* New York, 1964.

Heller, Walter. *New Dimensions in Political Economy.* Cambridge, Mass., 1964.

Stein, Herbert. *The Fiscal Revolution in America.* Chicago, 1969.

On poverty and income distribution, see:

Brown, Bonnar and Carol Van Alstyne. *Family Income Patterns, 1947–1968.* Menlo Park, Calif., 1959.

Einsburg, Helen. *Poverty, Economics, and Society.* Boston, 1972.

Humphrey, Hubert H. *War on Poverty.* New York, 1964.

Hunter, Robert. *Poverty.* New York, 1904.

Miller, Herman P. *Rich Man, Poor Man.* New York, 1964.

Romansco, Albert V. *The Poverty of Abundance.* New York, 1968.

Scoville, James G. *Perspectives on Poverty and Income Distribution.* Lexington, Mass., 1971.

On private enterprise in the American economy, see:

Arnold, Thurman. *The Folklore of Capitalism.* New Haven, 1937.

Cochran, Thomas C. *The American Business System.* Cambridge, Mass., 1957.

Galbraith, John K. *American Capitalism.* Boston, 1962.

Hawley, Ellis W. *The New Deal and the Problem of Monopoly.* New York, 1966.

Krooss, Herman E. *Executive Opinion: What Business Leaders Said and Thought, 1920's–1960's.* New York, 1970.

Prothro, James. *The Dollar Decade: Business Ideas in the 1920s.* Baton Rouge, 1954.

Sobel, Robert. *The Age of Giant Corporations: A Micro-economic History of American Business, 1914–1970.* Westport, Conn., 1972.

Weinstein, James. *The Corporate Ideal in the Liberal State, 1900–1918.* Boston, 1968.

Weibe, Robert H. *Businessmen and Reform: A Study of the Progressive Movement.* Cambridge, Mass., 1962.

On the United States in the world economy, see:

Bauer, Raymond A., Ithiel de Sola Pool, and Lewis Anthony Dexter. *American Business and Public Policy: The Politics of Foreign Trade.* Chicago, 1972.

Chalmers, Henry. *World Trade Policies, 1920–1953.* Berkeley, Calif., 1955.

Mikesell, Raymond. *Economics of Foreign Aid.* Chicago, 1968.

Steel, Ronald, *United States Foreign Trade Policy.* New York, 1962.

Vernon, Raymond. *Trade Policy in Crises.* Princeton, 1958.

Weil, Gordon L. *Trade Policy in the 70's.* New York, 1969.

Index

Ackley, Gardner, xiii, 68, 89
Aid for Dependent Children (AFDC), 145, 147
Agriculture, 33–34
  imports and exports, 222, 227–228
Agricultural Adjustment Act, 56
Agricultural Marketing Act of 1929, 54
Alliance for Progress, 245
Antitrust laws, 30, 162, 195, 199
  enforcement, 108, 153, 194
Arnold, Assistant Attorney General Thurman, 162, 198, 213

Bach, G. L., xiii, 67, 79
Balance of payments, 100, 219–220, 221, 224, 226, 228, 229, 246–247, 248–251, 259–260
Balance of trade, 228, 249, 261–262
Bell, Daniel, xiii, 167, 213
Berle, Adolph A., Jr., 154, 157, 158, 186, 187, 188–190, 192
Bretton Woods, 97, 100, 223, 254
Budget, federal, 56, 57, 62, 68–72, 98, 118
  full employment, 60
Burns, Arthur, xiii, 64, 229, 252
Business cycle, 8, 12, 108

Capital, 33, 54, 189
Census, 21, 40
  of 1900, 177, 179–180
  of 1925, 178–179, 180–181
  of 1935, 184
  of 1947, 184
  of 1950, 182

Civil War, 19, 22, 52, 174
Collective bargaining, 30, 33, 108
Commission on Population Growth and the American Future, 14, 41
Community Action Programs, 112, 138, 139–141
Competition, 7, 55, 158, 162, 183, 192, 201
  destructive, 2
  fair, 29
  non-price, 156
  potential, 196
  system, 181, 208
Conglomerate movement, 160–161, 166, 194–198
Coolidge, President Calvin, 201, 202, 220
Corporations, 29, 152–153, 155, 158–159, 167–172, 185, 186, 213
  capital accumulation by, 189
  duty of, 187–195
  meaning of, 214–216
  other-directed, 190–192
  regulation of, 167–172
  responsibilities of, 187
  society and, 213–217
Coughlin, Father Charles, 109
Council of Economic Advisers, President's, 68, 72, 75–77, 229, 243

Dale, Edwin L., Jr., xiii, 68, 97, 101
Davis–Bacon Act, 65, 94
Deficit spending, 57, 58, 59; *see also* Fiscal policy

Social Security, 11, 109, 111
  Act, 70, 120
  Administration, 37
Standard Oil Company, 154, 192, 197, 199
Stein, Herbert, 82, 102–103
Steiner, Gilbert Y., xvi, 115, 120
Surrey, Stanley S., 121

Tariff, 52, 54, 168, 220–221, 224, 227
Taxes, 31, 61, 62
  corporate, 59, 200
  credit, 63
  excise, 52
  gift, 109
  income, 59–60, 108–110, 113, 123, 185
  reform, 9
  see also Fiscal policy, 115
Technology, 28, 32–33, 43, 209, 261
Temporary National Economic Committee, 57–58, 183, 184
Tennessee Valley Authority, 164
Truman, President Harry S., 61, 75, 164, 224

Trusts, 153, 170, 195, 200; *see also* Conglomerate movement; Mergers

Unemployment, 31, 37, 54, 60–62, 64, 66–67, 88, 92–93, 96, 101–102
Unions, 29, 30, 87, 107
U.S. Steel Corporation, 153–154, 157, 160, 164, 198
U.S. Supreme Court, 107, 154, 162

Vietnam War, 9, 11, 63, 97, 101, 224
VISTA, 112, 136, 139

Wages, 63, 65, 93, 106, 119–120
Wage–price controls, 95–96, 102
War on Poverty: *see* Poverty
Wilkins, Mira, xvi, 229, 230
Wilson, President Woodrow, 53
World War I, 7–8, 53, 174, 220, 222, 228
World War II, 7, 13, 59, 62, 115, 223